Imagining the s

Imagining the state

Mark Neocleous

Open University Press
Maidenhead · Philadelphia

Open University Press
McGraw-Hill Education
McGraw-Hill House
Shoppenhangers Road
Maidenhead
Berkshire
England
SL6 2QL

email: enquiries@openup.co.uk
world wide web: www.openup.co.uk

and

325 Chestnut Street
Philadelphia, PA 19106, USA

First published 2003

A catalogue record of this book is available from the British Library

ISBN 0 335 20351 5 (pb)   0 335 20352 3 (hb)

Library of Congress Cataloguing-in-Publication Data
CIP data applied for

Typeset by RefineCatch Limited, Bungay, Suffolk
Printed in Great Britain by Biddles Limited, *www.biddles.co.uk*

Contents

Acknowledgments

Parts of the argument in what follows have been tried out in the following articles: 'The fate of the body politic', *Radical Philosophy*, 108, 2001; 'Privacy, secrecy, idiocy', *Social Research*, Vol. 69, No. 1, 2002; 'Staging power: Marx, Hobbes and the personification of capital', *Law and Critique*, 2003; and 'Off the map: on violence and cartography', *European Journal of Social Theory*, 2003.

Part of the argument in Chapter 1 was presented at the University of Sussex in January 2001 and I am grateful to Andrew Chitty and Darrow Schecter for the invitation. I first presented the argument about secrecy and privacy in Chapter 2 in a paper at a conference jointly organized by the Central European University, Budapest, and the New School for Social Research, New York, held at the CEU in March 2001. I am grateful to the organizers for the invitation and their hospitality, and to G.M. Tamas for his encouragement. An updated version of the paper was given to colleagues at Brunel University in January 2002, who once again smiled and complained in the right places.

Parts of the argument in Chapter 3 were read and commented on (critically) by Magnus Ryner and Matthew Clayton. Robert Fine acted as external reviewer for Open University Press and offered many useful suggestions on the final manuscript. The whole manuscript was also read by David Stevens, whose simultaneous encouragement and 'digging in of liberal heels' allowed me to improve the argument in places; Stuart Elden, who negotiated some of the tensions in our overlapping territories; Nick Moss, who kicked at other doors; and David Murray, who continues to share the pessimism.

Debbie Broadhurst provided love and support, Poli provided crucial help around the computer, and KK once more provided the difference.

Introduction

There is a famous image associated with Thomas Hobbes' *Leviathan* (1651), which first appeared on the book's frontispiece. On the bottom half of the page the book's title is surrounded by various symbols of power – a castle, a cannon, a crown. In the foreground is a city, beyond which the ground rises into a small hill. Behind the hill appears the top half of a male figure: the mighty Leviathan. The figure is formidable and imposing. He stands way above both the hill and the city. In his hands are the symbols of justice and sovereignty – a sword and sceptre – while on his head there rests a crown. His body is protected by what at first glance appears to be chain-mail, but on closer inspection turns out to be a mass of human figures. These persons not only appear to constitute the body of the figure, but also face up at him. The only face we see is that of the Leviathan, who stares directly at us. At the top of the page is a quote from the *Book of Job*: *non est potestas super terram quae comparetur ei* – 'upon earth there is nothing to compare with his power'.

The image of power that the frontispiece encourages has haunted generations of thinkers ever since. It suggests the embodiment of power in an individual figure, with a body incorporating the whole of the people, eyes which survey the terrain, a bounded territory under his control and, by implication at least, a mind with which everything else may be known. As an image it has played a central role in what I will call the 'statist political imaginary'.

I take the idea of the political imaginary from Susan Buck-Morss' work with Russian philosophers Valerii Podoroga and Elena Petrovskaia. The term is not to be confused with contemporary uses of the term 'imaginary' as it is currently widely employed within social and political theory – for example in Laclau and Mouffe's 'Jacobin imaginary', Castoriadis' 'social imaginary' and the 'imaginary' of Lacanian theory. In such accounts 'the imaginary' involves little more than the logic of discourse. In the Russian, in contrast, the concept implies a representational concreteness lacking in these other accounts. The Russian *politicheskoe voobrazhaemoe* contains the notion of *obraz*, which signifies 'shape' or 'form' as a graphic representation, and is used to mean 'icon'. As

Buck-Morss explains, '*politicheskoe voobrazhaemoe* is thus a topographical concept in the strict sense, not a political *logic* but a political *landscape*, a concrete, visual field in which political actors are positioned'.[1]

In social and political theory the visual field and political landscape have been dominated by the image of the state. This is perhaps unsurprising since a central axiom which has guided most research into questions of power in modernity is that 'real' societies develop under the protective shadow of the state. This axiom, which constitutes the core feature of the statist political imaginary, has become so predominant a part of modernity that much of how we think is shaped by it. Every historian and theorist of the state has for some time now emphasized that over the last five centuries the state is *the* major political reality that humanity has constructed. Despite the fact that thought of the state is beset by intellectual contradiction – it is seen as the cause of war and yet the agent of peace, the cause of injustice and yet the ground of justice, the instigator of ecological disaster and yet the saviour of the environment – it has so determined the way we think that the idea of a society without a state is seen as either wildly perverse – do those Marxists and anarchists never give up? – or as primitivism. As Pierre Clastres has shown, the idea of the 'primitive' is allied to ideas about the state. 'Primitive' societies are imagined as suffering a fundamental *lack*, they are *incomplete*, they *fail* as *real* societies, they are without history and outside history: they are without a state.[2] Such ideas about the primitive of course lend weight to the dismissal of Marxism and anarchism: in talking about the possibility of a stateless society they themselves must be 'primitive' political movements.

Michael Walzer once commented that in one sense 'the state is invisible'. As such, 'it must be personified before it can be seen, symbolized before it can be loved, imagined before it can be conceived'.[3] This book aims to explore some of the contours of this imagination. Since the 1980s there has been a large amount of work on the role of the imagination in political formation. Whether taking its cue from Stuart Hall's work on the reasons why the Conservative Party under Thatcher kept winning even though most voters identified with the policies of the Labour Party, or from Benedict Anderson's argument that the nation is an imagined community, or from the aforementioned discourse analysis, many came to argue that, as Hall put it, we need to consider the way 'people make identifications symbolically: through social imagery [and] in their political imaginations'.[4] What went unnoticed in virtually all that was said thereafter was that the *political* dimension of imagination had been fully appreciated well before the 1980s and 1990s. If we look back over some of the major debates from 200 years before, for example, we find that Edmund Burke's attack on the French revolutionaries is shot through with assumptions about the importance of the 'moral imagination' which covers 'the defects of our naked shivering nature', the way 'acts of rapacious despotism present themselves to [our] imagination'.[5] And responses to Burke play on this theme. Structuring her response to Burke around his 'lively imagination' and the extent to which his 'reason may have often been the dupe of [his] imagination', Mary Wollstonecraft comments that had Burke been French he would have been a 'violent revolutionist': 'your imagination would have taken fire'. To Burke's defence of property she comments that the 'imagination revolts' against the distress of poverty, and to his attack on the remodelling of the French constitution she claims that if the constitution had been modelled by the 'lovers of elegance and beauty' it 'is natural to suppose that the imagination would have erected a fragile temporary building'.[6] Thomas Paine similarly describes hereditary monarchy as 'a thing in imagination', a 'thing as various as imagination can paint'; likewise, 'monarchy, aristocracy, and democracy, are but creatures of the imagination'.[7]

That Burke, Wollstonecraft, Paine and the myriad other protagonists in the pamphlet wars of the 1790s in part structured their arguments around the possibilities, limits and in some cases horrors of the political imagination should not surprise us, since the words 'imagination' and 'imaginary' once formed part of the common vocabulary of political discussion.[8] It was once held that it is treason 'when a man doth compass or imagine the death of our lord the king'. Its usage in this context (the *Statute of Treasons* of 1351, 25 Edward III) tells us that part of the original (and political) meaning of 'imagine' had a very real purposive sense of 'design', 'devise' and 'intend': imagining was thus part and parcel of political struggle. In thinking through the issues involved in imagining the state, then, I will be touching on the very themes which those involved in the pamphlet wars of the early 1790s realized were at the heart of any political imaginary (that is, at the heart of any political struggle): power and property, identity and subjectivity, violence and order.

At the very least, this will distinguish this book from any of what have by now become the standard approaches to the state. Such approaches tend to be organized around either ideological positions (liberalism and the state, socialism and the state and so on), thinkers (Rousseau and the General Will, Locke and private property and so on), themes (sovereignty, legitimacy and so on), or historical periods (the absolutist state, the totalitarian state and so on). But for a start, there are more than enough books on the state organized in these ways, and there surely cannot be any need for another one, especially given that these approaches tend to take for granted the central axiom identified above. More important, however, is the fact that one of the intentions in this book is to tease out some of the ways in which ideologically diverse writers and politically distinct movements end up sharing what turns out to be a common ground: the ground of the state. In other words, part of my argument here will be that the statist political imaginary is to varying degrees shared by writers with very different positions and politics.

To spell out how and why this situation came about I aim to take seriously the ways in which the state has been imagined as having a particular 'shape' or 'form'. In English, the word used to capture the notions of both shape and form is 'figure'. This latter term is also useful in the sense that it has connotations of representation and imagery on the one hand, and, on the other, embodiment in general and of the human form in particular. One of the ways in which this complex of meanings come together is as 'an embodied (human) form', 'a person considered with regard to visible form', and 'an artificial representation of the human form' (*Oxford English Dictionary*). Likewise, the earliest meaning of 'image' in English was a physical figure.[9] Thus I aim to 'figure out' the state by exploring the ways in which it has been imagined as an artificial representation of the human. It is well known that in order to comprehend the nature of the state as it emerged from the collapse of feudalism, an extensive vocabulary had to be invented.[10] Much of this vocabulary (contract, legitimacy etc.) is now the stuff of political thought. But as a theoretical provocation I shall argue that one trend within this vocabulary has gone unnoticed, and that this trend took its cue from categories associated with human subjectivity. In other words, I shall be aiming to show that the state has figured in the political imagination in terms traditionally associated with the human. If we avoid the question of what the state is and instead ask how has it been spoken of, we discover that it has been spoken of in terms associated with human subjectivity. In 'figuring out' the state I therefore aim to excavate the combination of the political, psychic and cultural constitution of the state as a subject imagined as possessing a will of its own: a body, mind, personality and home.

Each of the four chapters is thus structured around one of these four thematics of subjectivity. In Chapter 1 I first explore the reasons why the idea of the body proved so important to the statist imaginary, teasing out its role in the imagining of order. The chapter then aims to refute a widely held view that the theme of 'the body politic' disappeared from the political imagination with the bourgeois democratic revolutions and only resurfaced with the resurgence of fascism in the twentieth century. In contrast, I argue that the image of the body politic was transformed in ways consistent with bourgeois democratic thought and which were used to legitimize the exercise of state power, often in the most violent of ways. In Chapter 2 I focus on a set of rhetorical tropes centred on the idea of mind, such as 'reason' and 'intelligence', in order to identify the ways in which the statist tendency in political thought has imagined the state as a necessary mechanism for human knowledge and, moreover, a knowing subject in itself. This process, I argue, has facilitated the state in shaping civil society according to its own imperative of knowledge. In Chapter 3 I isolate and analyse the idea that some forms of collective power can be imagined in terms of personality. The chapter shows that the political issue of the personality of the state, first fully identified by Hobbes, has fed into the political imagination and supported the way other forms of power, such as capital, have been constituted. Through a critique of company law and a discussion of the pluralist account of group life, the chapter comes to suggest that capital and the state share an important and politically telling affinity. Finally, Chapter 4 explores the way the statist political imaginary is essentially and necessarily territorial, and the way that this territorial imperative is imagined and legitimated through the rhetorical trope of 'home'. In this chapter the theme of violence raised in previous chapters comes to the fore: territory and terror are shown to be mutually implicated in the project of state power.

Taken together the four thematics associated with human subjectivity around which this book is structured will allow me to generate a set of related claims about the three icons of the political imaginary: the political collective, the common enemy and the sovereign agency. To show how the thematics have been central to state power in the West and have shaped the three icons in question the argument will work on a number of levels, each of which feeds into the chapters to varying degrees.

First, I aim to show how the categories of body, mind, personality and home have helped configure the state as the repository of sovereignty and *the* most fundamental political collective. Second, I examine the way such ideas have been used by the state in its continual attempts to fashion and (re)order civil society. I build here on my arguments in *Administering Civil Society* (1996) and *The Fabrication of Social Order* (2000), in which I sought to show how the state emerged as a project for the constitution and fashioning of a social order ('civil society') founded on wage-labour. The argument here is that imagining the state as a subject in its own right helps sustain the practices through which the state administers civil society and fabricates social order.

Third, I argue that in sustaining the idea of the state as an ordered unity the four thematics help legitimize the domination that takes place under the name of the state. I hope to show, for example, that images such as the body politic and tropes such as the 'homeland' are not simply decorative metaphors or convenient conceptual arrangements, but ways of making us think about and orient ourselves to the state and the kind of order it is engaged in producing, a process which critical theory understands as the 'transformation of ideas into domination'.[11] This legitimization of domination rests on the generation of the figure of the enemy.

Fourth, I explore the way that such ideas have often lent weight to fascism. I again build here on an earlier argument, in *Fascism* (1997), in which one of my aims was to show the extent to which fascism is an ideology and movement generated by modern industrial capitalism which features as the negative potential – that is, the potential for human destruction – implicit in the nature of bourgeois modernity. Part of the excavation of the statist political imaginary in what follows indicates, albeit for the most part in a relatively elliptical way, the extent to which fascism shares the four thematics of subjectivity. This will be the extreme end of my theoretical provocation, for I will be suggesting that fascism is not aberrant to the statist imaginary but is rather its limit case.[12] This last argument is neither fully-fledged nor an attempt to ignore the important differences between the liberal and fascist understanding of modernity. Rather, it is a series of hints and provocations as to some of the links between fascism, the political constitution of sovereignty in bourgeois society and ways of violently dealing with questions of order.

The last point should indicate to the reader that this is a polemical book about a polemical topic. As such, I should be clear about my intentions. If a hidden agenda seems nasty, then an exposed one looks downright impudent.[13] Writers these days increasingly like to stand aside from the affray. This is nowhere more obvious than in books in which affray is a central issue – namely books on issues such as the state, power and capital. On the one hand, this is no doubt due to the fate of the academy in contemporary capitalism – academic research assessment exercises which seem to have knocked the political stuffing out of seemingly political writers (best not write anything *too* political about this political topic, in case it damages one's promotion prospects). On the other hand, it is also clearly connected to the demise of any coherence the Left once had. Writers on the Left appear to be happier to retreat into ever more exegetical work on text after text, with little sense as to the purpose of reading political writers in the first place. Or, worse, they have bought into the stunningly naive socio-political claim that we have moved into a world in which there is politics without enemies.[14] (And if there are no enemies, then there is no ground for any fundamental disagreement and thus no real need to say anything interesting at all.) Too many intellectuals on the Left have thus developed an instrumental inability to think beyond the instructions and parameters provided for them by the state and one of its key ideological apparatuses – the university. So let me say that this book is written from outside the statist political imaginary (or at least as much as one can be outside it), and also against it. To write against the statist imaginary is thus intended as an act of resistance – though admittedly not the bravest act of resistance one might imagine, since the state aims to dominate the thought of even those who oppose it (indeed, one might say *especially* those who oppose it). Pierre Bourdieu has argued that 'to endeavour to think the state is to risk either taking over, or being taken over by, the thought of the state',[15] and as I argue in Chapter 2, as part of its administration of civil society the state aims to structure the way we view the world by generating the categories through which citizens come to imagine collective identity and thus their own political subjectivity. One of the implications of this is that the statist political imaginary has assisted the state in setting limits on the theoretical imagination, acting as a block on the possibility of conceiving of a society beyond the state.

This is a book that tries to think the state without either taking over or being taken over by the thought of the state. It therefore rests on a different political imaginary, one which I mention here and return to only briefly at the very end of the book, which arises out of the tradition of the oppressed which teaches us that the 'state of exception' in which we live is not the exception but the rule. As Walter Benjamin recognized, to write against the state of exception in this way is to aim to bring about a real state of emergency which imagines the end of the state, and thus an end to the possibility of fascism.[16]

1 The body of the state

'The story begins with the closeup of a bottom.' This is how Ronald Reagan opens his first biography, written in 1965 to help his campaign for the governorship of California. The statement was indicative of the extent to which his body was, to him, his supporters and, sadly, his detractors, a permanent feature of the debates surrounding his political career. During his presidency Reagan and reporters repeatedly drew attention to a structural homology between his body and the nation: 'Reagan's Nose Could Change the Whole Face of the World'; 'Reagan Appeals to Congress for His Economic Plan, Saying He is Recovered but the US Isn't'; 'Reagan Lashes Out: "There is Bitter Bile in My Throat" '.[1] The assassination attempt got him one of the highest ratings in the polls he ever achieved, and his dodgy prostate gland and polyp-besieged rectum were the talk of many a dinner table. Even after his presidential reign his greatest publicity came about through the body: after hand surgery (January 1989), falling off a horse (July 1989) and having water drained from his brain (September 1989).

The reason for this obsession with the body of the leader lies in the identification between Reagan's body and the body of the nation, the American people. His body, he believed and others encouraged, was one with his family and both were one with the country. His body, in other words, was identified with the body politic.

One doesn't hear too much about the body politic these days. This is more than a little odd since social, political and cultural theorists have in recent years become saturated with discussions of the body. A certain loss of confidence in previously established categories combined with a desperate attempt to consign politically charged concepts to yesteryear has provoked a widespread focus on the body as the basis of attempts to develop the understanding of society and politics. The consequence of this has been that one can hardly move for new works on the body; as Terry Eagleton once commented, there will soon be more bodies in contemporary criticism than on the fields of Waterloo.[2] But for this new somatic it is the *individual* human body that is the issue – how it is shaped by power, how it resists power, how it is reworked in the search for identity. Little is ever said about the body which once dominated discussions of politics and society: the body politic.

At first glance it may appear that one reason the idea of the body politic barely gets a look in is because it has largely lost its appeal for social and political discourse. A recent work from within the new somatic tells us that 'under the twin suspicions of theoretical insufficiency and political perniciousness' the metaphor of the body politic has lost its appeal.[3] Others have made similar points, claiming that 'the imagery of the body politic no longer delights and instructs', or simply that the metaphor had lost much of its point by the mid-seventeenth century and suffered further decline thereafter.[4] Either the suspicion of theoretical insufficiency (the analogy appears essentially premodern and thus either redundant or irrelevant for the liberal democratic age) or the worry of political perniciousness (the analogy's association with fascist regimes, which I discuss below, has rendered it politically suspect) have meant that where theorizing explicitly about the body politic once occupied a central place in intellectual debate, it now appears to have dropped out of favour.

Part of the intention in this chapter is to brush against the grain of these assumptions by arguing that the idea of the body politic has been a central theme within the statist political imaginary. If there is any substance to the claim that in post-Restoration Europe the phrase 'body politic' became a synonym for 'state',[5] as I think there is, then it is clear that to understand the idea of the state we must grapple with the idea of the body politic. After first exploring the reasons for the long use of the idea of the body politic, I shall argue that the image of the body has been a central way of imagining order and, as a consequence, has played an important role in legitimizing the exercise of state power. To sustain this argument I shall show that the original polemical force contained in the idea has been retained but been re-employed in different guises. As we shall see, some have argued that the emergence of bourgeois democracy led to an abandonment of the idea of the body politic. In contrast, I shall argue that the emergence of a more liberal democratic mode of ruling *transformed* the idea rather than abandoned it. And while the political perniciousness of the 'body of the state' or the 'body politic' that has arisen from its association with fascist regimes may have rendered it politically suspect, this merely serves to tell us something important about the nature of the liberal democratic state. The purpose of the chapter is not to argue that the state either *is* a body or *should* be thought of as a body, nor to revive the idea of the body politic as a mechanism for the critique of power – for reasons that will become clear, I remain unconvinced by those who have sought to use the idea of the body politic for dissent and critique – but to highlight the ways in which bodily tropes surround the ideology of state power, serving to legitimize the state and the exercise of the most extreme forms of violence. To understand the long historical transformations of power and sovereignty one must therefore interrogate the ways in which ideas based on the body have been used and refined throughout the centuries of state development. To understand state power, in other words, one must explore the ways in which the metaphor of the body is employed and manipulated in different ways by different political forces.

Absolute bodies

The analogy of the body politic was one of the most basic and commonplace analogies of early modern thought and political practice. In his *Policraticus* (1159) for example, John of Salisbury defines a republic as 'a sort of body':

> The position of the head in the republic is occupied . . . by a prince subject only to God and to those who act in His place on earth, inasmuch as in the human body the head is stimulated and ruled by the soul. The place of the heart is occupied by the senate, from which proceeds the beginning of good and bad works. The duties of the ears, eyes and mouth are claimed by the judges and governors of provinces. The hands coincide with officials and soldiers. Those who always assist the prince are comparable to the flanks. Treasurers and record keepers . . . resemble the shape of the stomach and intestines . . . Furthermore, the feet coincide with peasants perpetually bound to the soil.[6]

Heavily influenced by John of Salisbury, Christine de Pizan claims that the three types of estate – princes, knights and nobles, and the universal people – 'ought to be one polity like a living body', for the polity is like 'a body having life':

> There the prince and princes hold the place of the head in as much as they are or should be sovereign and from them ought to come particular institutions just as from the mind of a person springs forth the external deeds that the limbs achieve. The knights and nobles take the place of the hands and arms. Just as a person's arms have to be strong in order to endure labor, so they have the burden of defending the law of the prince and the polity. They are also the hands because, just as the hands push aside harmful things, so they ought push all harmful and useless things aside. The other kinds of people are like the belly, the feet, and the legs.[7]

Similar points are made by writers across Europe through the centuries of early modern political thought. For example, Marsilius du Padua compares the well-ordered state to an appropriately formed animal:

> For if an animal's body had its individual members directly joined to its head, who would not regard it as monstrous and useless for the perfomance of its proper functions. For if the finger or the hand were joined directly to the head, it would not have its proper position, and hence it would not have its proper power, movement and action. But this does not happen when the finger is joined to the hand, the hand to the arm, the arm to the shoulder, the shoulder to the neck, and the neck to the head, all by proper joints. For then the body is given its appropriate form, and the head can give to the other members, one through the other, their proper individual powers in accordance with their nature and order, and thus they can perform their proper functions.

And he adds that this must be heeded in civil regimes.[8] In the fifteenth century, Sir John Fortescue argued that:

> just as the physical body grows out of the embryo, regulated by one head, so the kingdom issues from the people, and exists as a body mystical, governed by one man as head . . . [I]n the body politic the intention of the people is the first living thing, having in it the blood . . . The law, by which a group of men is made into a people, resembles the sinews of the physical body.[9]

What might be the source of such a way of thinking about political communities? One answer may lie in the fact that such analogies had a long tradition, going back to classical political thought: the argument in Plato's *Republic*, for example, hinges on the shift Socrates makes from the individual body to the state and back again; and for Aristotle the state is comparable to a 'whole body' produced by nature. But while such a tradition allowed early modern writers to lean heavily on the crutches of antiquity, to really understand why the idea of the body politic became central to the modern state the starting point must be medieval Christianity rather than ancient Greece, for the political powder keg which ignited the explosion of interest in the analogy was the struggle between the Pope and political leaders from the thirteenth century onwards, and the partial resolution of these struggles in the Reformation.[10]

Historically, Christianity lay claim to some kind of universal community, founded and governed by God, in which mankind constituted a single and internally connected people: one 'mystical body'. This gave rise to the doctrine of the sovereignty of the spiritual power, the idea that all political arrangements should be regarded as part and parcel of the ecclesiastical organization. Since mankind is one mystical whole, so there must be only one sovereign body, and that body must be the Church. In 1302 Pope Boniface

VIII declared that 'Urged by faith we are bound to believe in one holy Church, Catholic and also Apostolic . . . which represents one mystical body, the head of which is Christ, and the head of Christ is God'.[11] Such ideas are traceable to St Paul's claim in *Corinthians* (1.12) that 'just as the body is one and has many members, and all the members of the body, though many, are one body, so it is with Christ. For by Spirit we are all baptized into one body . . . You are the body of Christ and individually members of it'. While Boniface's use of the term *corpus mysticum* (mystical body) had no biblical tradition, it nonetheless possessed political and social connotations not present in the idea of *corpus Christi*. Boniface's definition of the Church as a mystical body treated the Church as a body politic and thus on a level with secular 'political bodies'. As Otto Gierke argues:

> Throughout the whole Middle Age there reigned, almost without condition or qualification, the notion that the Oneness and Universality of the Church must manifest itself in a unity of law, constitution and supreme government, and also the notion that by rights the whole of Mankind belongs to the Ecclesiastical Society that is thus constituted. Therefore it is quite common to see the Church conceived as a 'State'.[12]

Boniface's argument betrays the effort by the spiritual power to answer and overcome the nascent self-sufficiency of secular political bodies. Bent on putting the nascent political entities in their proper place, the Pope argued that any political bodies had a functional character only within the world community of the Church. Since the head of the Church is Christ and its earthly head is the Pope, the latter is both priest and king – a temporal as well as a spiritual monarch. The logic of this argument was that to acquire the divine sanction – 'acquire' on the grounds that political organizations of some sort or another clearly existed before the Church and outside the Church – the state needed to be hallowed by the authority of the Church. On this basis, it was from the Church that temporal powers received their true being, and from the Church that princes and kings received their right to rule. For this reason the temporal powers were subject to and expected to obey the one spiritual power; the offices of both prince and king were, in effect, ecclesiastical ones.[13] Mankind as a whole constituted a mystical body, while the various bodies within it, such as the Universal Church and Empire, particular Churches and particular states, as well as every other human group, were compared to a natural body.

In its early formulations the idea of the body politic often involved little more than a minimal refinement of Paul's description of the Church as a body. Attempts by writers such as John of Salisbury and Christine de Pizan to identify the precise relationship between the various parts of the body – the prince as head, the soldiers as hands, and so on – rested squarely on Paul's presentation of the various parts of the universal body of Christ as necessarily existing in mutual dependence, and on his presentation of the Church as containing various functional roles – apostles, prophets, teachers, miracle workers, helpers, administrators. But such attempts came to be of crucial importance in identifying the nature of the new political bodies that were then emerging as historical actors. For as the idea of the *corpus mysticum* gradually came to describe the body politic (*corpus iuridicum*) of the Church, so by transference *corpus mysticum* came to be applicable to any body politic, either religious or secular. Indeed, once the idea of a political community endowed with a 'mystical' character had been articulated by the Church, the secular state was almost forced to follow the lead and ape the language of corporeal unity upon which theological universalism appeared to rely. The concept of the *corpus mysticum* became increasingly politicized, lost much of its transcendental meaning, and thus fell prey to the world of statesmen, jurists and political thinkers developing new ideologies for the nascent territorial and secular states. The new state quarried the wealth of ecclesiastical notions, as Ernst Kantorowicz puts it, searching for ideas with which to justify and legitimate its own powers. The theological and canon law doctrine that the Church, and Christian society in general, was a *corpus mysticum* with Christ as its head was transferred from the theological sphere to that of the state with the king as its head. The state, as it emerged from this encounter, had a whiff of incense about it.[14] In other words, although the idea of the body politic can be traced back to antiquity, the early modern jurists and political theorists transferred to the prince and state the most important social, organic and corporational elements normally serving to explain the relationship between Christ and the Church. The concept of the *corpus mysticum* became applicable to any *corpus politic*, and the possibility emerged of comparing the state as a *corpus politicum* with the *corpus mysticum* of the Church.

This can be seen in the way political leaders came to use the body metaphor in their struggles with Rome. In his skirmish and subsequent break with Rome, for example, Henry VIII appropriated the idea of a body politic (to the extent that, according to one writer, it became Henry's favourite analogy),[15] using it to figure an emergent Protestant notion of nation and state. 'This realm of England is an empire . . . governed by one Supreme Head and King . . . unto whom a body politic, compact of all sorts and degrees of people', which was distinguished from the body politic of the Church.[16] And those around Henry VIII, such as his chaplain, Thomas Starkey, carried this through in their writings. In *A Dialogue Between Reginald Pole and Thomas Lupset* (c.1535–8),[17] Starkey has Pole utilize the idea of England as a body politic to argue against the 'ignorant', 'vicious', 'idle' and 'unprofitable' lives of the bishops, prelates, priests, monks, friars and canons. Of these Church figures 'we have over-many, which altogidder make our politic body unwieldy'. The solution is a reform of the monasteries, a change in religious practices such as the language in which service is given, and a removal of privileges allowed to religious figures.[18] But a further implication of such an argument is that if political bodies could be compared to the Church, they could also be compared to each other. This gives rise to the possibility of conflict between various body politics. Starkey thus compares the English body politic with that of other emergent European powers. In other words, another transformation was effected: from the idea of one body with one head – the universal Church and Pope – to a variety of competing bodies (English, French, Spanish, Italian, German and so on) beginning to take shape as independent states, each with its own head.[19]

One reason why many found in the body metaphor a useful way of imagining power and sovereignty lies in the fact that a community imagined in terms of the body appeals because it connotes unity and integration, identity and concord, wholeness and indivisibility. In other words, *order*. (The same can be said about the associated concepts 'person', 'corporate' and 'incorporation', which will be explored in Chapter 3.) The image of the body provided a way of inscribing the political community within a fairly coherent epistemic framework that made it possible to explain the origin and historical trajectory of the communities in question in the same terms as those used to account for the history of living beings – that is, in terms of their organization, unity and structural coherence.[20] In terms of order internal to the body politic, this means that sovereignty is against division and disintegration, incompleteness and division. Significantly, partisan politics, and thus 'party' politics, stems from the concern for order within the body politic. In this period 'party' was thought to divide the body politic created by God, and thus be a crime against the lord in Whitehall. Partisanship is about division and thus inimical to the political body.[21]

But there is more to the story than just order. This period, in which personal forms of sovereignty were replaced by the impersonal state, was also the period which saw the growth and consolidation of new forms of division and disorder generated by a new and increasingly dominant form of property. Feudal property had been part of the body of the monarch, but the new forms of property that were emerging rested on claims of personal ownership, to the exclusion of all others – a system of private property, in other words. The passage from the body of the monarch to the body of the state thus coincides with the early development and expansion of capital. This development created a sense of crisis, revolving around the relations between the new groups – 'classes' – that were then emerging. The problem of protecting the new property released from the body of the monarch was deeply connected to the question of the nature and condition of the newly emergent class of wage-labour. In conceptual terms, these independent individuals were imagined as a 'dissolute condition of masterlesse men'. Outside the traditional feudal forms of power and law, such masterless men were 'without subjection to Lawes, and a coercive Power to tye their hands'.[22] As masterless men their social, economic and political condition appeared to undermine social order. Historically, the state emerged to impose order amidst this new society of increasingly independent 'individuals' free of their historic submission to the authority of the lord. More pertinently, this is the period in which the processes of primitive accumulation that created the preconditions for a mercantile mode of production involved the violent reorganization of society and labour that foreground the interests of those who stood to profit from the dispossession and displacement of the feudal producing classes.

As a consequence, while earlier uses of the idea of the body politic had played heavily on the idea of the body as a unity in which all parts work together towards the same goal, the metaphor increasingly shifted such that part of its core ideological claim came to concern the conflicts *internal* to the body politic. For example, in his *Dialogue*, Starkey highlights the joint problem of a redundant nobility and idle multitude. The 'old world' of the nobility is 'brought up . . . in all vain pleasure, pastime and vanity' while the lower orders have not yet learned that they are 'born to labour and travail'. In both cases, the problem is *idleness*. A 'great part of these people which we have here in our country is either idle or ill-occupied . . . by the reason whereof this body is replenished and over-fulfilled with many ill humours, which I call idle and unprofitable persons'.[23] The range of illnesses which affect the body politic are for the most part brought about by such idleness and its negative effect on profit. Dropsy occurs when the state is full of 'idle and unprofitable' people, while the 'moving and shaking of palsy is at the cost of profit and pleasure', a 'moving and stirring' which 'bringeth neither profit nor true pleasure to the politic body'. The idle gluttony associated with gout is a disease of the lower orders who are 'negligent and slow to the exercise thereof which pertaineth to their office and duty', which has a deleterious effect on profit: 'Like as in gout the hands and feet lie unprofitable to the body'.[24]

It is clear that writers committed to safeguarding the interests of the ruling classes found in the organic model a metaphor which still enabled them to reassert an ethic of order and unity in an increasingly divided society – or to at least *imagine* such an order. The general appeal of a bounded, cohesive and hierarchical community articulated in corporeal terms had particular resonances in a situation in which the political order was becoming increasingly multifarious and an ascendant class of private property owners, whose property had been freed from the body of the monarch, was beginning to clash with a new class of 'free' wage-labourers. In this sense, the sovereign 'body' of the state emerges as an attempt to resolve or defer what turns out to be *the fundamental crisis of modernity*. Concomitantly, the image of the body of the state emerges as a way of *imagining order* amidst this crisis.

The theme of order present in the idea of the body politic goes hand in hand with a related theme concerning the perpetual nature of sovereign power. To explain this we need to accept Kantorowicz's argument that the idea of the body politic must also be associated with the doctrine of the king's two bodies. This doctrine runs as follows:

> The King has in him two Bodies, *viz.*, a Body natural, and a Body politic. His Body natural (if it be considered in itself) is a Body mortal, subject to all Infirmities that come by Nature or Accident, to the Imbecility of Infancy or old Age, and to the like Defects that happen to the natural Bodies of other People. But his Body politic is a Body that cannot be seen or handled, consisting of Policy and Government, and constituted for the Direction of the People, and the Management of the public weal, and this Body is utterly void of Infancy, and old Age, and other natural Defects and Imbecilities, which the Body natural is subject to.[25]

In this doctrine Kantorowicz claims to find the solution to one of the most interesting features of sovereign power: its ability to be passed from one sovereign to another. This can be seen in the iconography, rituals, legal mechanisms and political ideas around which the king's two bodies are organized. For example, French royal funeral ceremonies inherited the English practice of using a wax effigy of the king during the king's funeral ceremony. In time, the status of the effigy came to eclipse that of the body of the king. Since 'the importance of the king's effigy in the funerary rites of the sixteenth century soon matched or even eclipsed that of the dead body itself', the effigy came to play 'an independent role of its own, apart from the king's dead body'.[26] Thus the king's own mortal body came to be buried either naked or in a winding sheet, while the effigy came to be clothed in the royal regalia. The regalia came to be reserved for the effigy, the true bearer of the royal glory. Why? Because whereas the actual body of the king was plainly dead, the effigy was the symbol of a power which never dies. The effigy came to represent something supposedly *immortal*: the sovereign power. Metaphysical or even metaphysiological nonsense as this may be,[27] such formal rituals and legal mechanisms around which the king's two bodies were organized tell us something important about the way sovereignty and thus state power was imagined as *perpetual*. Thinkers in this period were faced with the long-standing philosophical problem of time. Since time means change and change means decay there was the presumption that any order must come to an end in time.[28] Politically, this posed a question of fundamental importance concerning sovereignty: its survival. The 'problem of order' (i.e. the problem of stability) was thus tantamount to finding the proper means of escaping the 'problem of time' (i.e. the inherent corrosiveness of temporal change). Lawyers and political thinkers were at this stage formulating the idea of the state as a perpetual corporation, but were either unable or unwilling to separate state and monarch. Embodied

problem of time

in the king, the perpetual nature of sovereignty had to allow the royal *dignitas* to survive the physical person of its bearer; it is this that the doctrine of the king's two bodies allows for, and which is captured in the phrases 'the king never dies' and 'the king is dead, long live the king'. Thus despite its incorporation in the body of the king, the body politic could be imagined as something ontologically separate from the existence of the ruler within it, as something transcending the life of the ruler. This not only solved the problem of time and decay, but also gave rise to a crucial part of the conception of sovereignty: its perpetual nature. (As Jeremy Bentham was to put it much later: 'By *bodies-politic*, we generally understand privileged bodies, which have, under this name, an existence more or less permanent; they are often perpetual, and of a limited number'.)[29] It therefore encouraged thinkers to imagine the *perpetual nature* of *any entity* in which sovereignty was 'embodied'.

Moreover, the formula 'the king never dies' expresses the sovereign power's *continuity* to the extent that it expresses the *absolute* nature of that power.[30] This is unsurprising, since the perpetual and absolute nature of sovereignty are hardly far apart. As Jean Bodin puts it, 'sovereignty is that absolute and perpetual power vested in a commonwealth': it is perpetual because it is absolute and it is absolute partly because it is perpetual.[31]

Once monarchy came to be undermined, any 'body' which came to replace it would inherit these characteristics. The body that did so was the newly emergent form of rule known as the state, which by the end of the sixteenth century was being imagined in its recognizably modern sense as not only an impersonal power, as Quentin Skinner has shown at length,[32] but also as permanent and absolute. The developing political and juridical formulations concerning the omnipotence of the state, a secularization of the theological formula concerning the omnipotence of God,[33] were captured in the idea of sovereignty (hence Hobbes' 'mortal God' and Rousseau's 'tutelary God'). As Gierke explains, in the early modern period:

> The word 'sovereignty' becomes something in the nature of a magic wand, which can conjure up the whole sense and content of the State's general power. The original negative conception – the conception of a power which is not externally subject to any *Superior* – is made to assume a positive form by being as it were turned 'outside in', and used to denote the relation of the State to everything which is within itself. From the quality of being the 'supreme' earthly authority, there is deduced the whole of that absolute omnipotence which the modern state demands for itself. The champions of popular sovereignty vie with the defenders of monarchism in exalting its claims.[34]

Equally important here is the fact that although conceived of as a form of impersonal rule, this new institutional ensemble was none the less also conceived as a 'body'. The body politic was decreasingly founded in the physical presence of the human sovereign and increasingly rooted in the new state form.

Michel Foucault once commented that 'we need to cut off the King's head: in political theory that has still to be done'. This was his way of signalling an attempt, taken up with a vengeance by his followers, to move the debate about power beyond the question of sovereignty.[35] What such a beheading fails to recognize, however, is the possibility that the sovereign *body* remains alive and kicking. The evidence suggests that the long process which saw the gradual secularization and depersonalization of sovereign power – the process, in other words, of state formation – involved a shift from the sacred body of the king to the abstract body of the state. Where the prince once stepped into the shoes of the Pope, the state now stepped into the shoes of the prince.[36] The modern concept of state thus inherited the 'body' of the monarchic state and reinvented it in a new form. And as it became possible to separate state from monarchy, so it became possible to see the state as possessing the characteristics of the king: the state became a perpetual corporation. Whereas the doctrine of the king's two bodies was a *legal* fiction intended to account for the fact that kings died but the king survived, so there emerged what we might call a *political* fiction: that whatever may happen to its particular form, the state survives. Can we imagine the death of the state? is an interesting question to ask.[37] On the one hand, the state does change; on the other hand, the state is always there. It is a body but not mortal, and no mortal body personifies it sufficiently to symbolize its downfall. Despite its corporeality, the state is here imagined as something that cannot – will not – die: the sovereign world is thus a world in which the limit of death is done away with.[38] Thus with the birth of the state what appears to be a permanent centre for the accumulation of power was created, a centre around which all other power – such as the power of social classes – would come to operate.

Given that 'body politic' and 'mystical body' are used without great discrimination in this period, this political fiction might best be understood as a form of *political mysticism* – the mysticism that surrounds the sovereign state. I will develop the argument concerning the mysticism of state into the question of state secrecy in Chapter 2. For the moment, I wish to illustrate the ways in which the mystery of the omnipotent power of the body of the state unfolds in Hobbes' *Leviathan* (1651).

Here is how Hobbes introduces the Leviathan:

> Nature (the Art whereby God hath made and governes the World) is by the *Art* of man, as in many other things, so in this also imitated, that it can make an Artificial Animal. For seeing life is but a motion of Limbs, the begining whereof is in some principall part within; why may we not say, that all *Automata* (Engines that move themselves by

springs and wheeles as doth a watch) have an artificiall life? For what is the *Heart*, but a *Spring*, and the *Nerves*, but so many *Strings*, and the *Joynts*, but so many *Wheeles*, giving motion to the whole Body, such as was intended by the Artificer? *Art* goes yet further, imitating that Rationall and most excellent work of Nature, *Man*. For by Art is created that great LEVIATHAN called a COMMON-WEALTH, or STATE, (in latine CIVITAS) which is but an Artificiall Man; though of greater stature and strength than the Naturall, for whose protection and defence it was intended; and in which, the *Soveraignty* is an Artificiall *Soul*, as giving life and motion to the whole body; The *Magistrates*, and other *Officers* of Judicature and Execution, artificiall *Joynts*; *Reward* and *Punishment* . . . are the *Nerves*, that do the same in the Body Naturall; The *Wealth* and *Riches* of all the particular members, are the *Strength* . . . *Counsellors*, by whom all things needfull for it to know, are suggested unto it, are the *Memory*; *Equity* and *Lawes*, an artificiall *Reason* and *Will*; *Concord*, *Health*; *Sedition*, *Sicknesse*; and *Civill war*, *Death*. Lastly, the *Pacts* and *Covenants*, by which the parts of this Body Politique were at first made, set together, and united, resemble that *Fiat*, or the *Let us make man*, pronounced by God in the Creation.[39]

This passage marks a central contribution to the theory of the state. Earlier writers had understood the body metaphor in terms of an ontological similarity between two natural entities. For Aristotle, the 'body' of the *polis* is given by nature, and the individual political animals constitute the 'parts' of the body:

the state is by nature clearly prior to the family and to the individual, since the whole is of necessity prior to the part; for example, if the whole body be destroyed, there will be no foot or hand, except homonymously, as we might speak of a stone hand; for when destroyed the hand will be no better than that . . . The proof that the state is a creation of nature and prior to the individual is that the individual, when isolated, is not self-sufficing; and therefore he is like a part in relation to the whole.[40]

Here the state is a creation of nature, and while Aristotle does not call the *polis* a body, he treats the *polis* as similar to a body. The fact that the *polis* can be described in such a way reveals a fundamental ontological similarity between the body politic and the body of the individual animal, a similarity which legitimizes the *polis* as a naturally given totality. In contrast, Hobbes understands the metaphor in terms of a similarity between two modes of creation: the state is the result of an activity which simulates the process of divine creation. The state, in other words, is a product of the work of art of man. And yet despite this 'artificiality', the state is not merely *like* a body, but *is* a body.

Since in 'the *Universe*, being the Aggregate of all Bodies, there is no reall part thereof that is not also *Body*', the state has to have bodily form. 'The World (. . . the Universe, that is, the whole masse of all things that are) is Corporeall, that is to say, Body . . . [E]very part of the Universe, is Body'.[41] That which is not body does not exist. As Hobbes puts it elsewhere when defining the main aims of philosophy: 'The principal parts of philosophy are two. For two chief kinds of bodies, and very different from one another, offer themselves as search after their generation and properties; one whereof being the work of nature, is called a *natural body*, the other is called a *commonwealth*, and is made by the wills and agreement of men.'[42] The Leviathan is a *body politic* designed to exert authority over individual *bodies in motion*. The state is a body, then, but made by humans rather than nature.

But then what kind of body is the Leviathan? Hobbes takes the image from Chapter 41 of the *Book of Job*, in which the Leviathan is depicted as a huge, powerful and uncontrollable sea-monster. Some have therefore compared the Leviathan to a fierce and, in the liberal interpretation, uncontrollable animal. Locke's claim that men are not 'so foolish that they take care to avoid what Mischiefs may be done them by *Pole-Cats*, or *Foxes*, but are content, nay think it Safety, to be devoured by *Lions*' is a fairly clear hint at the untameable animal he thinks Hobbes has created in the Leviathan, while playing on the original Biblical meaning.[43] But this is to miss some crucial yet intriguing points about Hobbes' creation.

The Leviathan makes four appearances in Hobbes' text. The first is in the passage from the Introduction cited above, in which it is understood as a huge artificial man, a huge artificial animal, and a huge machine. In Chapter 17 the Leviathan is described as a 'Mortall God', while in Chapter 28 the Leviathan is refered to in the discussion of the chapter in *Job* in which the monster appears. The fourth occurrence is as an image on the frontispiece, which shows a huge person. Now, in none of these appearances is the Leviathan a monster. Rather, its key feature is its *power*. The passage from *Job* at the top of the image makes this clear: 'upon earth there is nothing to compare with his power'. This is a point repeated by Hobbes at the end of Chapter 28 in which he reiterates the claim that there can be nothing greater than the Leviathan. And of the many points made about the Leviathan in the Introduction, one is that this creation turns out to be far superior – 'of greater stature and strength' – to any natural body. In other words, the point of the Leviathan is not to appear as a monster, or even a fierce animal such as a lion, but as power – more pertinently, omnipotence; nothing less than a mortal God. Indeed, in some ways the Leviathan's earthly omnipotence is more significant than heavenly power – it is in the sovereign powers of the state to decide what qualifies as a miracle, for example.[44]

Moreover, however much the Leviathan is a body, and however much it is described in terms which support an interpretation of it as 'natural' – a person or animal, for example – it is always presented as a human artefact. As a person (an idea which I take up in Chapter 3) it is different from other, 'human', persons; it is an 'Artificiall man'. It is worth recalling here that as well as being thoroughly materialist, Hobbes was one of the three most important 'mechanical philosophers' of the mid-seventeenth century. Heavily influenced by Descartes, Hobbes transfers Descartes' rational-mechanical model of the animal body onto the sovereign power, grafting Descartes' account of the mechanical body (man as a machine) onto the traditional metaphor of the body politic.[45] Because the body in question can possess only *artificial* life, the state is created as a form of being that is brought to 'life' and yet is a man-made rather than 'natural' object. Indeed, the artificiality of the created state is highlighted in comparison with the natural state from which it emerges. The body politic created in the contract exists in opposition to the natural state in which humans would find themselves.

In its suggestion of an omnipotent mechanized person, the image of the Leviathan attains the highest level of mythical force.[46] The culmination of the intrinsic logic of the artificial product 'state' in Hobbes' *Leviathan* is not a human person but a man-made political machine; not an omnipotent monster, but an omnipotent technology of power. And this omnipotent entity appears 'natural' by figuring in its subjects' minds as a *corpus*. The 'huge artificial man' refered to in the Introduction is reiterated by the frontispiece in which the Leviathan has the form of a huge human body made up of the individual bodies of its subjects: 'For man is not just a *natural body*, but also a part of the state, or (as I put it) of the *body politic*'.[47]

In other words, this state-machine is the most mystical body known to man. As a machine the concept of sovereignty is truly depersonalized, while as a body it retains some of the 'human' features characteristic of an age of personal power. In his own historical period, Hobbes' theory of sovereignty was functional to the development of monarchic absolutism, but its general schema is applicable to the state in the most abstract sense of the term. It expresses theoretically the historical dynamic in which machines of power – states – were emerging as the integral political centre of European modernity.[48] The modern concept of the state thus inherited the patrimonial body of ancient monarchy and reinvented it in a new form: the body of the king had become an omnipotent political body-machine, an inhuman person with a force and will of its own.

Social bodies

It is clear then that in the centuries in which the state was being formed, the body provided one of the central categories through which it was imagined. As I noted earlier, many writers have suggested that the idea of the body politic is an essentially pre-modern notion which disappears with the slow advance of liberal democracy following the bourgeois democratic revolutions of the late eighteenth century. Scholars have described the cultural and ideological transition that took place in the eighteenth century as a shift from an iconic system centred on the body politic, and especially the body of the king, to a logocentric universe that enshrined the word of law, in which law became king and in which an impersonal bureaucratic sovereign state came to replace a form of sovereignty based on the personal body of the monarch. Generally speaking, this has been presented as the culmination of three related processes.

First, the rise of liberalism and, in particular, the liberal contribution to contract theory. For example, although John Locke describes men 'agreeing together mutually to enter into one Community, and make one Body Politick', 'united together into one Body' and consenting to make a community 'one Body, with a Power to Act as one Body',[49] he never views the state as a natural or living creature. Locke resists granting the body a status or rationale of its own, for the key task of the *Two Treatises* is to preserve the individual bodies and property of citizens. By emphasizing the bodies and rights of individuals, Locke automatically downplays any idea of the collective body, preferring instead to view the state as an option chosen by individuals, equivalent in form to the business contract. In this sense the individual is rendered superior to the collective, and the metaphor traditionally used to stress the subordination of parts to the whole is substantially weakened. One could also point here to Adam Smith's use of the phrase only in the context of discussing writers with whom he is disagreeing, a point to which I shall shortly turn.

The second process said to be important in this shift is the ongoing rationalization of society, signalling a wider 'modernization' of society. It is a commonplace of intellectual history that the French Revolution played an important and symptomatic role in this process, and it is equally a commonplace that the defining revolutionary gesture of the period was the beheading of the king. Given the centrality of the body of the king to the body politic and the extent to which French kings liked to portray themselves as the embodiment of state power – '*l'État, c'est moi*' – the French revolutionaries focused on the weaknesses of the actual body of the sovereign king. (For example, the impotence of Louis XVI, especially set against the supposed sexual superpowers of Marie Antoinette, was used to undermine the body politic of the *ancien-régime*.) In terms of the wider historical process of rationalization, beheading is taken to be a significant modernizing gesture, for in formally beheading the body of the king the revolutionaries are said to have depersonalized sovereign power, obliterated the question of charisma from the political agenda and thus removed the mystery of sovereignty in one fell swoop.[50]

The third process is said to be the replacement of organicist accounts of society and the state with mechanistic accounts. As Jonathan Gil Harris writes, 'the standard narrative about the notion of the body politic . . . is that the analogy was delivered its death-blow by the new empirical medicine and natural science of the seventeenth century, which viewed the body less as the template of cosmic or political order, than as a self-contained machine'. On this account, the view of 'society as an organism' came to be replaced with the view of 'society as a mechanism'.[51]

An argument developed by Claude Lefort, Phillipe Lacoue-Labarthe and Jean-Luc Nancy, and appropriated by many others, connects this supposed demise of the metaphor of the body politic to the rise of bourgeois democracy from the late eighteenth century. They claim that a democratic political discourse has little intellectual time for an essentially pre-modern metaphor such as that of the body politic, and that the democratic regime is one in which any notion of the organic unity of the polity is dissolved. Lefort, for example, claims that 'the democratic revolution . . . burst out when the body of the king was destroyed, when the body politic was decapitated and when, at the same time, the corporeality of the social was dissolved. There then occurred . . . a "disincorporation" of individuals'.[52] Reiterating Lefort's point, Simon Critchley adds:

> with the advent of democracy in the French revolution, the place of power becomes an empty space. In democracy, those who govern cannot incarnate power . . . In democracy power is not occupied by a king, a party leader, an egocrat or a *Führer*, rather it is ultimately empty; no one holds the place of power. Democracy entails a disincorporation of the body politic, which begins with a literal or metaphorical act of decapitation.[53]

Democracy, in this view, involves what Lacoue-Labarthe and Nancy describe as 'the desubstantialization of the body politic'.[54] The general argument being made by these writers is that the *rationalization* and *modernization* associated with the rise of democracy entails a *disincorporation* of politics and thus an end, at least temporarily, to the metaphor of the body. I say 'temporarily' because what is at stake in the account of these discussions of the fate of the body politic is not just our understanding of democracy, but of fascism too. Lefort's work on the revolutions of the late eighteenth century, for example, is in fact a pretext for his analysis of 'totalitarian' regimes, and Lacoue-Labarthe and Nancy's aim is to show that fascism constitutes the frenzied resubstantialization of the social body as a form of reincorporation, or reincarnation, or reorganization of the body politic. The same is true of Critchley's intentions, and Slavoj Žižek, Ernesto Laclau and Chantal Mouffe, and John Keane all make similar points.[55] And it is worth noting that Kantorowicz's highly influential research on the king's two bodies can in fact be read as an attempt to grasp the implications of the political theology of fascism, especially that developed by Carl Schmitt.[56]

In the rest of this chapter I shall take issue with this reading of the fate of the body politic. I shall argue that far from signalling the decline of the body as a central trope of political thought, it is in fact only with the *advent* of liberal democracy that the body image comes into its own. This is because the trope of the body remains a core feature of bourgeois ideology and thus the statist political imaginary. I shall argue that far from there being a disincorporation of individuals, what took place from the late eighteenth century was *incorporation in a new form*, a form appropriate to the bourgeois states that were to emerge from the democratic and intellectual revolutions set in motion in the late eighteenth century. This new form was the *body of the people*, or the *social body*. In other words, the apparent turn away from the body politic was in fact a turn towards a new imagination of the political *corpus*, centred on the people.

This is not just an exercise in the history of ideas, however, for the political implications of this were and are enormous. First, this reconsideration of the fate of the body politic will allow us to rethink some of the connections between bourgeois democracy and fascism – connections founded on the corporeal register. I shall be arguing, in effect, that fascism's use of the corporeal metaphor is less a revival of a pre-modern idea, as Lefort *et al.* suggest, and more a radicalization of the notion of the social body; in other words, I shall be arguing that this dimension of fascist thought is deeply rooted in the statist political imaginary and its role in bourgeois ideology. Second, I shall also be arguing that the political imagination centred on the body *intensified the exercise of state power over the social body*, facilitating and encouraging an image of society centred on *violent practices* thought necessary to defend the body politic. The suggestion at the end of the chapter will be that the prevalence of the corporeal register in the language of both bourgeois democracy and fascism is a symptom of the centrality of order and sovereignty in the statist political imagination.

At the start of the eighteenth century 'society' referred either to the leading 'social' circles in courtly or sophisticated life, or to a legally recognized association, a relatively small organized grouping of people. Otherwise, it was a barely used concept. The same can be said for the term 'social'. During the eighteenth century and the rise of the Enlightenment, both 'society' and 'social' came to play far more important roles in intellectual argument.[57] Significant here is Rousseau's contribution to the theory of the state. While it is true that Hobbes and Locke both talk about the importance of contracts in creating a sovereign power, their main concern is with either the might of the Leviathan or the limits of government. With Rousseau one gets the first sustained reflection on the contract as a *social* phenomenon. Rousseau was one of the first writers to use 'society' as a key concept and 'social' as an adjective in a systematic way – as witnessed by his consideration of 'social order', the 'social system', the 'social bond' and the 'social spirit', as well as the title of his major work (*The Social Contract*).[58] It was during this period that the term 'society' gradually expanded to include all social units, and the term 'social' came to designate forms of relations which were somehow more fundamental than political or legal relations. One of the outcomes of this sort of theorizing was that 'society' in general and 'social' as an adjective came to occupy a central place in the political imagination. In the case of France, it has been argued that 'after the publication of *Du contrat social* there was a definite increase in the use of the adjective "social" ' and that 'thinking in terms of social relations represented a significant new trend'.[59] The same point could be made for Britain following the Scottish Enlightenment thinkers' reference to 'social intercourse', 'social war', 'social pleasure', 'social duties', 'social virtues', 'social good humour' and so on.[60]

However, this new 'society' and set of 'social' relations were still imagined in terms of the language of the body. Rousseau's main argument is for an 'act of association creat[ing] a corporate and collective body, composed of as many members as the assembly contains voters, and receiving from this act its unity, its common identity, its life, and its will', and he adds that 'this public person, so formed by the union of all other persons, formerly took the name of *city*, and now takes that of *Republic* or *body politic*; it is called by its members *State* when passive, *Sovereign* when active, and *Power* when compared with others like itself'.[61] Because the body politic is identified with the sovereign,[62] however, and because sovereignty lies with 'the people', Rousseau is pushed into identifying the body politic with the people. 'The people' is thus understood as a body (*corps du peuple*) in its own right:[63] '*Car la volonté est générale, ou elle ne l'est pas; elle est celle du corps du peuple, ou seulement d'une partie*' ('Will either is general, or it is not; it is the will of the body of the people, or only of part of it').[64] But because Rousseau's work is equally saturated with the language of the social, the body of the people is conceived of as nothing more or less than the *social body* (a fact sometimes obscured by poor translations of *corps social*). Thus he criticizes political theorists for engaging in conjuring tricks in which '*après avoir démembré le corps social par un prestige digne de la foire, ils rassemblent les pieces on ne sait comment*' ('after first dismembering the social body by an illusion worthy of a fair, they reassemble the pieces together we know not how').[65]

When Rousseau discusses the social body elsewhere it is, unsurprisingly, in terms identical to his comments on sovereignty and thus the body politic more generally. He comments, for example, on the undertakings which bind us to the social body, the will of the social body, the inalienability of right within the social body: '*Les engagemens qui nous lient au corps social ne sont obligatoires que parce qu'ils sont mutuels*' ('the undertakings which bind us to the social body are obligatory only because they are mutual'); '*Lumieres publique résulte l'union de l'entendement et de la volonté dans le corps social*' ('public enlightenment leads to the union of understanding and will in the social body').[66] And in *Emile*, published the same year as *The Social Contract*, he comments that the value of the citizen '*est dans son rapport avec l'entier, qui est le corps social*' ('depends upon the whole, that is, on the social body').[67]

A similar development from 'body politic' to 'social body' via 'the people' can be found in Adam Smith's *Wealth of Nations*. Smith uses the term 'body politic' in either the context of regimes and forms of governing which he opposes, such as monopoly and mercantilism, or in discussing the works of writers he is critical of, such as Quesnai: 'Mr. Quesnai, who was himself a physician, and a very speculative physician, seems to have entertained a notion . . . concerning the political body, and to have imagined that it would thrive and prosper only under a certain precise regimen'. Quesnai 'seems not to have considered that in the political body, the natural effort which every man is continually making to better his own condition, is a principle of preservation capable of preventing and correcting, in many respects, the bad effects of a political oeconomy, in some degree, both partial and oppressive'.[68] Otherwise, the terms 'body politic' and 'political body' make no appearance in the *Wealth of Nations*. Instead, another image takes centre stage: the 'great body of the people'. This 'great body' is not identical to the old body politic. Most of Smith's uses of the phrase leave its meaning undefined, but it would appear that the 'great body of the people' is the labouring sub-group of the 'whole body of the people'. After outlining the misery brought about by the division of labour – it makes men stupid, renders them incapable of taking part in rational conversation and leaves them lacking in 'generous, noble, or tender sentiment' – Smith comments that 'in every improved and civilized society this is the state into which the labouring poor, that is, the great body of the people, must necessarily fall'. The sub-group is thus what would otherwise be known as the working class. The 'whole body of the people', in contrast, refers to 'society' in general.[69]

The 'social body' and the 'body of the people' are also central to the two great revolutions of the period. In Section 39 of *The Federalist Papers* Madison defines a republic as:

> a government which derives all its powers directly or indirectly from the great body of the people, and is administered by persons holding their offices during pleasure for a limited period, or during good behaviour. It is *essential* to such a government that it be derived from the great body of the society, not from an inconsiderable proportion or a favored class of it.[70]

Similarly, in France leading revolutionaries framed their arguments concerning society and the people in terms taken from the register of corporeal discourse. The Abbé Sieyès's famous description of the Third Estate as that group which had until now been nothing but which must become everything is developed on the basis of the new language of the social body of the citizenry. 'A political society cannot be anything but the whole body of the associates', he claims, in which the body is nothing less than 'the great body of the people', or 'the whole body of the citizens'. And this Third Estate, or rather the nation, 'demands nothing less than to make the totality of citizens a *single social body*'.[71] This logic of incorporation is pushed to its limit in Sieyès' account of representation, for which he is most widely known. For Sieyès, the Third Estate is the whole nation, an indivisible body. The process which unites the great citizen body and the body of the National Assembly is representation: 'The deputy is member of the body of the Assembly and member of the body of the Nation for which he legislates'. As Antoine de Baecque points out, Sieyès here defines a corporeal doubling that recalls the double sovereign body of monarchy: symbolic body/physical body of the king.[72] Representation is thus a projection of a symbolic social body onto a real institutional body, of the eternal sovereign body of the people onto an active assembled body in which representation organically links the real body of the National Assembly to the symbolic body of the nation. The double corporeal perpetuity reminds us not only that national sovereignty is modelled on royal sovereignty, but that the National Assembly is a body that has become perpetually political, in rivalry with the body of the king. In tandem with arguments such as these, the *Declaration of the Rights of Man and Citizen* (1789) was presented as a document to be placed 'constantly before all the members of the Social body', while Section 39 of the 1793 version of the *Declaration* made it clear that the social body was the new entity to be defended: 'There is oppression of the social body whenever a single one of its members is oppressed. There is oppression of each member whenever the social body is oppressed'.[73] By representing themselves as a political community united in one single body, the revolutionaries did not *reject* the image of the state-body, but *rethought* it to help facilitate the shift from one regime to another: they moved from the 'body of the king' to the 'body of citizens' – that is, to the 'social body'. It is perhaps this, more than anything else, that is the 'social' aspect of the French Revolution. Thus although historically the French Revolution has been thought of more as the defeat of the form of sovereignty embodied in the king than the elaboration of a fresh corporeal metaphor, metaphors of the body in fact saturate the revolutionary imagination, a fact that has been lost amidst the widespread assumption that the metaphor is characteristic of the monarchical representation of state power.

An important dimension to this development was the changing nature of 'the people'. for this new *corpus* was a term which properly covered not just the citizens but also the 'lower orders' for the first time. 'The people' was beginning to be thought of as properly consisting of all the human members of a society: the social was thought to contain the poverty-stricken multitude.[74] This in part explains why Smith's definition of the 'great body of the people' and Sieyès's definition of the Third Estate are economic ones based on their

conception of the importance of labour and industry. As 'society' was discovered it had to find a place for the labouring mass – that is, the working class
– and to conceptualize it as consisting of active members of the social body
rather than as objects of pity at the bottom of the heap. In effect, the image of
the social body helped turn the multitude into a people. Why did this have to
happen? Having cut off the king's head (either literally or symbolically), the
ruling class worried whether the embrace of 'popular' sovereignty (though at
this stage it could hardly be described as 'popular' at all) could create social
order. To this end it retained the ancient and feudal idea of the body politic but
rethought it in the context of an increasingly hegemonic bourgeois form of
rule. The concept of the social body thus comes to carry traces of the 'body
politic', in which it has its origins, and the increasingly important domain of
'economic' life, to which Smith's and Sieyès's account of productive labour
refers. While on the one hand it appears to act as a mediating mechanism
between state and economy, referring to a set of institutions which are neither
political nor economic, so on the other hand it appears to apply to society in
general, and thus becomes the thing to be protected.

The significance of imagining a new social body in this way should not be
underestimated. It may appear that 'to say that the people had to be integrated
into the body politic was an opinion requiring no more sophistication about
organicism than had been present in the work of John of Salisbury in the
twelfth century',[75] but this is to miss the significance of the emergence of this
new body on the political landscape. Rousseau, Smith and the republicans
were in their different ways expressing the fact that what was occuring was a
transition from the body of the king to the body of the people and, as a consequence, a dissolution of sovereignty into the larger body of society. As such,
they were crucial in completing a transition from the theology of the *corpus
mysticum* to the socio-biology of the nineteenth and twentieth centuries.
Where sovereignty had once moved from the body of the monarch to the body
of the state, so it now moved to the body of the people. Where the notion of
the *corpus mysticum* had once been politicized, giving rise to the *corpus politicum*, it now became socialized: the *corpus* in question became society itself.[76] It
was now the citizenry which embodied sovereignty. Playing on the doctrine of
the king's two bodies, one might say that what took place in the late eighteenth century was not the death of the metaphor of the body politic, but its
demise. The metaphor lives on, in another form: the sovereign body is dead,
long live the sovereign body.

Dirty bodies

If the argument in the preceding section has any substance, questions must be
raised about the widespread claims concerning the disappearance of the meta-

phor of the body politic from the political imagination. Moreover, questions must also be raised about any reading of fascism which assumes that it is purely a revival of 'pre-modern' and 'pre-democratic' ideas concerning the body metaphor. In this section I shall first spell out the importance of the idea of the body to the fascist political imagination – this will then allow me to tease out the more general dangers in the idea.

In opposing 'mechanical' conceptions of society, defining modernity as the loss of organic community and following through the logic of defining the state as a living organism, fascism adopts wholesale the idea of the body politic. For example, Filippo Marinetti describes the Italian people as an 'excellent wrestler'. Robert Brasillach compares the unity of the French nation with the unity of a sports team, Alfred Baeumler thinks of the collective body of the German *Volk* as a political team and Oswald Mosley describes the fascist system as 'a state organised like a human body'.[77] From this vision fascism aims to realize the policy of 'corporatism' and thus 'incorporation' – a doctrine, that is, of bodily containment – as a means for constructing a new order out of the body of the people. Fascism aims at the defence and rejuvenation of the nation through its virilization, putting the 'life' back into the social body through the overcoming of the degenerate illnesses supposedly brought about by the 'mechanistic' doctrines of liberalism and communism. On the one hand, this appears to be a return to key features of pre-modern ideas concerning the body politic, such as the revival of the obsession with the body of the leader. The leader as the new embodiment of sovereign power appears to offer the chance to incorporate and personify the previously 'faceless' entity of the liberal state. It is in this context that the health and virility of the leadership is of crucial importance (regardless of the fact that most fascist leaders fail to conform to their own ideological stereotype of the virile body). On the other hand, and more pertinent to the argument here, is the fact that fascist campaigns of terror reveal an image of the body politic in which the enemy of the people is regarded as a parasite or a waste product to be eliminated.

The idea that the body politic may contain diseases which require elimination has of course long roots; it is found in the work of both Starkey and Hobbes, for example,[78] while Sieyès's account of the social body of the citizens utilizes the organic analogy to attack privilege, transforming the themes of disease and degeneration into a bourgeois revolutionary trope – the privileged class is like a 'horrible disease eating the living flesh on the body of some unfortunate man', 'a malignant tumour in the body of a sick man'.[79] In biologizing all the ills that may occur in the body of the state, such arguments assume correspondences exist between political and natural bodies in the realm of pathology. The body politic comes to be imagined less as a complete body – individual, whole and balanced – and more as a problematic and even diseased body. Fascism utilized such ideas, employing medical and biological terminology to describe problematic and opposition elements. Jews were portrayed by the Nazis as 'parasites in the body of other peoples', while enemies such as communists and gypsies as well as Jews were variously described as malignant, tuberculosis, a form of syphilis, a cancer, a tumour, a plague, or a growth.[80] Communism, in the words of Goebbels, was a '*Krebsgeschwür*' that '*muss ausgebrannt werden*' – 'a tumour that must be burnt out'. The result was the medicalization of Nazism's enemies, formalized with the Nuremberg laws of 1935 which put German racial legislation on a biological basis. Thus the Nazis justified the establishment of a separate section for Germans on the streetcars of Warsaw on the grounds that this 'is not merely a question of principle; it is also, at least as far as Warsaw is concerned, a hygienic necessity'. The establishment of a Jewish ghetto at Lodz was justified as a measure necessary to protect against the dangers of epidemic disease. The idea that the Jews were a 'diseased race' and 'disease incarnate' within the body of the German nation meant oscillating so wildly between political and medical discourse that one can barely tell them apart – hence the term 'racial hygiene'. Thus the Nazi 'war on cancer' not only targeted the disease itself, but also facilitated subtle and not-so-subtle changes in the language and uses of cancer research. As one Nazi medical text of 1941 put it: 'The idea of the social parasite, as exemplified in the Jew amongst our people, can also be seen, symbolically, in the human body in many cases. The alien germ living in the body whose prosperity depends upon a conflict with a particular organ, a disharmony in the body, a disease – is this not the same role played by the Jew in the body of the people?' Conversely, while medical imagery was used to dehumanize racial and political undesirables, so cancer cells were sometimes described as Bolshevists, anarchists, spongers, rebellious and breeders of chaos, while nascent tumours in actual bodies were described as a 'new race of cells, distinct from the other cell races of the body'.[81]

In Italy Marinetti described communism as 'the exasperation of the bureaucratic cancer that has always wasted humanity', a cancer defended by Bolshevik 'social doctors who are changing themselves into masters of a sick people'. The fascist project aims at 'defending every part of [the fatherland's] body'. This means 'amputating all the ideologies'.[82] Mussolini increasingly came to describe the art of government as a 'medical' art designed to rid the state of 'parasitic encrustations', while public security measures were openly presented as 'social hygiene' and 'national prophylaxis': 'We remove [dangerous] individuals just as a doctor removes a contagious person from circulation'.[83] Such comments enable us to rethink some of the non-lethal but standard fascist practices such as the force-feeding of castor oil to anyone remotely disorderly or resistant. After recounting some of the 'castor oil experiences' of ordinary civilians, including sometimes the force-feeding of whole villages, Luisa Passerini notes that:

> The ritual of castor oil drew on the parallel between the social and physical body. If the human body particularly lent itself to symbolis-

ing the social system (so that control over it could be taken as an expression of social control), this was possible because the symbolic codes relating to the two bodies had a significant bearing on each other. By exploiting a forbidden bodily function, Fascist violence revitalised an age-old ritual, namely, inciting disorder to constitute new order, leaving a deep impression through the physical association of the social body with the individual human body.[84]

And as I argued in *Fascism*, the concept of syphilis plays a crucial role in fascist ideology because it expresses the danger of collective as well as individual physical degeneration, brought about through sexual contact with enemy persons. Syphilis is not something one *has*, but is either a condition deliberately *given* or a function of enemy intelligence. This medico-political terminology has remained central to fascist discourse.

The historical outcome of such ideas is genocide in the guise of social hygiene: the body politic assuring itself of its own identity by expelling its waste matter and averting the threat of any further intrusion by alien elements. The image of the body constituted for fascism the foundation of the well-known violent state practices to 'cure', 'purge' and 'invigorate' a disorderly society. It is this corporeal theme within the political imagination which supplies the grounds for what Lacoue-Labarthe and Nancy describe as the frenzied resubstantialization of the social body and what Lefort describes as the 'feverish' aspect to totalitarian societies. 'The enemy of the people is regarded as a parasite or a waste product to be eliminated . . . The pursuit of the enemies of the people is carried out in the name of an ideal of social prophylaxis . . . What is at stake is always the integrity of the body. It is as if the body had to assure itself of its own identity by expelling its waste matter.[85]

But while there is clearly a lot of mileage in such a reading of fascism (and other contemporary authoritarian groups, all of which tend to mobilize the notion of the body to this end),[86] to present it as a revival of a political metaphor supposedly abandoned by bourgeois democracy is to assume too categorical a difference between bourgeois democratic and fascist ways of thinking. It assumes that fascism has merely *revived* yet another *pre-modern* idea. Yet rethinking the emergence of bourgeois democracy as a *new form* of sovereign body rather than an abandonment of it, as I have above, enables us to note what turns out to be a remarkable consistency between the fascist and non-fascist political imaginations concerning the social body, its 'diseases' and 'waste products', a consistency rooted in the dialectic of modernity out of which fascism develops and in the statist political imaginary which it ultimately shares with certain strands of non-fascist ideology. Thus we find that with the final triumph of the bourgeois class, medico-political discourse has been most obviously used against political enemies of another kind, shared by both bourgeois democracy and fascism: communism and, concomitantly, the

agency of communist transformation, the working class. The political practices which this dialectic generated were and remain part of the foundation of
the exercise of state power.

In their account of English state formation, Corrigan and Sayer comment
on the three great 'ideas' which energized the system of national improvement that was state formation in this period – the 'statistical idea', the 'edu-
cational idea', and what they see as the much more subordinated 'sanitary
idea'.[87] In terms of the argument here, the last of these was crucial, for it
helped consolidate the idea that the social body was something that needed to
be administered by the state. An example can be found in the notions of
contagion, miasma and dirt, which became the obligatory reference points for
observing and understanding the myriad problems of the social order of
industrial society. Biological terms such as 'contagion' are never merely biological, and apparently innocuous terms such as 'dirt' are never as innocuous
as first appears. The category 'contagion', for example, was fashioned in the
1830s and 1840s as a political as much as a medical category, for it was shot
through with the 'social question' – the political problem of poverty.[88] Significantly, this was the period in which poverty became linked with contagion
and the poor were seen as spreading dirt and disease throughout the social
body. As I have argued elsewhere, the period of the emergence of the social
question was also the period in which the metaphors of pollution and moral
contagion became the standard form of expression in social commentary and
in which the sanitary condition of the social body was at the forefront of
commentators' minds. The residuum was considered dangerous in part
because, by its very existence, it served to contaminate the classes immediately above it.[89] John Stuart Mill, for example, thought that the working class
was actually fond of dirt, having failed to acquire the cultivated love of cleanliness, and dirt was a central theme of Chadwick's *Report on the Sanitary Condition of the Labouring Population of Great Britain* (1842). Chadwick's principal
concern was with the open cesspools, garbage and excrement in the streets,
the filth and scum floating in the river and in particular the 'miasma' emanat-
ing from them, while for many writers it was the effluvia exhaled by the lower
orders – 'human miasms' Chadwick dubs them – that was more poisonous
than the miasma created by decomposing matter. 'It is my decided opinion',
Chadwick approvingly cites one reformer as saying, 'that the vitiation of the
atmosphere by the living is much more injurious to the constitution than its
impregnation with the effluvia from dead organic matter'.[90] Given the
imagined correspondence between the 'sanitary condition' and the condition
of the working class, words such as 'residuum', 'refuse' and 'offal' were used to
denote both the excrement and sewage waste that constituted the sanitary
problem and the 'human waste' that constituted the social problem. In other
words, the miasma theory pointed to human agents of infection concentrated
in the class of poverty. The logic was that the task of cleaning (human) dirt

and filth from the street was the task of cleaning dirt from the social body; the physical cleanliness of the social body was taken to be a sign of its moral and social cleanliness. Just as the sewer (the 'bowels of Leviathan' as Victor Hugo called it)[91] appeared to speak to the nineteenth century about its dangerous moral and material condition (the ever-present possibility of contagion and contamination), so to sewage or refuse and the working class could be seen as simultaneously the source of disease and the subversion of all order. The purge thus becomes a fundamental political phenomenon. In the English language 'purge' originally referred to the act of physical cleansing, but also had religious connotations through its links with purgatory. In the nineteenth century, however, the word increasingly came to refer to the act of *political* cleansing, while in France '*épuration*' was first used in 1832 in connection with cholera and then in 1835 to mean 'elimination by a society of members deemed undesirable'.[92]

By imagining society as a body, the ruling class could automatically use the idea of disease to frame the social question as one of hygiene and cleanliness. Moreover, turning the problem of order into a question of the health of the social body ('public health') helped depoliticize the working class in the name of national hygiene and well-being, turning the question of 'reform' into the question of 'sanitary improvement' and thereby pre-empting any real working-class incursion into the arenas of political and social power. The historical outcome of associating medical categories with specific social groups in this way was the introduction of a comprehensive system of surveillance and administration of the social body, and in particular the parts supposedly most susceptible to contagious diseases. In other words, the introduction of a set of monitoring operations over the social groups regarded as dangerous. The only remedy for the social body's illnesses and diseases, both actual and potential, was thought to lie in the police powers of the state. Nineteenth-century movements for sanitary reform should therefore be seen as part of the political imagination of a disorderly state, the consequence of which was a concerted attempt to impose order on the social body by the state, embodying a faith in the reordering capacities of the state over the population.

With the development of international communism in the twentieth century the political imagination which considered the working class as a diseased and dangerous force (dangerous because diseased) was refocused onto the international communist movement. Thus one finds medico-political discourse to be one of the central tropes through which the bourgeois democratic state has imagined the communist movement in the twentieth century. Churchill referred to communism as 'a pestilence more destructive of life than the Black Death or the Spotted Typhus':

> Bolshevism is not a policy; it is a disease. It is not a creed; it is a pestilence. It presents all the characteristics of a pestilence. It breaks

out with great suddenness; it is violently contagious; it throws people into a frenzy of excitement; it spreads with extraordinary rapidity; the mortality is terrible; so that after a while, like other pestilences, the disease tends to wear itself out.[93]

In America, Truman's attorney general, J. Howard McGrath, claimed that each communist 'carries with him the germs of death for society', while Hubert Humphrey, senator and vice-president, described Chinese communism as 'a plague – an epidemic'. For Reagan, communism was like measles.[94] J. Edgar Hoover's obsession with what he called the 'slimy wastes of communism' was connected to his wider obsession with the dirty body. Joel Kovel sums up Hoover's position:

> What is American is clean and innocent; what is alien, or Communist, is the introduction of 'slimy wastes' into the body politic. This preoccupation extended from 'filthy impulses' to a direct focus on 'dirt' itself, and its passage inside and outside the body. The director [of the FBI] became a man obsessed with defending both his own body and the body social from the intrusion of 'slimy wastes'. All of Hoover's ideological preoccupations – with keeping the innocents safe, with protecting America from aliens, with the 'lechery' and 'pollution' of Communism, with unwashed and promiscuous student radicals, and perhaps with that great American menace, the Black Stud – may be read as defences of the collective body against contamination.[95]

Influential figures behind US cold-war policy, such as George Kennan, articulated the same sort of idea. Kennan's 'Long Telegram' of 1946 and 'X' article, 'The Sources of Soviet Conduct' of a year later, two of the most influential documents of the cold war, declare the Soviet Union to be an 'impotent' and 'sterile' nation, 'bearing within itself germs of creeping disease' and 'the seeds of its own decay'. Outside the Soviet Union 'world communism is like a malignant parasite, which feeds only on diseased tissue', the strongest antidote to which is the 'health and vigor of our own society'; 'We must study it [the Soviet Union] with the same courage, detachment [and] objectivity . . . with which a doctor studies unruly and unreasonable individuals'.[96] This medicalizes the view of world communism just as much as fascism does, and suggests that political posturing has been replaced with the cool detachment of scientific judgement followed by action with the precision of a surgeon. And of course when surgeons cut, they do so minimally and clinically. The vision of the surgeon's knife evokes not the brutal image of a knife slashing a communist throat but the more civilized image of a surgeon's scalpel cutting out abnormality from an unhealthy body.[97]

The historical outcome of arguments such as Kennan's was the policy of 'containment', and it is worth pausing to reflect on what this means in relation to the discussion here. Because the body is a model which can stand for any bounded system, its boundaries tend to represent spaces which are threatened or precarious. Bodily orifices thereby come to represent points of entry or exit for social units. The general interest in the body's apertures is replicated in the preoccupation with social exits and entrances, which easily come to be seen as escape routes and invasions.[98] Imagined as a body, then, the state approximates more to the 'grotesque' body described by Mikhail Bakhtin than to a cleanly closed-off entity. In contrast to 'an entirely finished, completed, strictly limited body' in which 'all the orifices of the body are closed', the grotesque body 'is not a closed, completed unit; it is unfinished, outgrows itself, transgresses its own limits. The stress is laid on those parts of the body that are open to the outside world, that is, the parts through which the world enters the body or emerges from it, or through which the body itself goes out to meet the world'.[99]

This grotesqueness has meant that diseases which have been regarded as threats to the health of the body politic have historically been seen as originating from outside. When syphilis began its epidemic sweep through Europe towards the end of the fifteenth century, for example, it was understood as essentially 'foreign'. The English, Italians and Germans referred to it as the French sickness ('French pox'), the French as the *morbus Germanicus*, the Poles as the German sickness, the Muscovites as the Polish sickness, the Flemish, Dutch and north-west Africans as the Spanish sickness. The Portuguese called it the 'Castillian sickness', the Florentines thought it came from Naples, the Japanese understood it as either the Chinese or Portuguese disease, while the people of the East Indies also thought it hailed from Portugal. A 1524 tract listed over 200 names for the disease, each identifying it as originating in a specific foreign location.[100] A similar process occurred with the plague, as the opening paragraph of Daniel Defoe's *A Journal of the Plague Year* (1722) suggests:

> It was about the beginning of September, 1664, that I, among the rest of my neighbours, heard in ordinary discourse that the plague was returned again in Holland; for it had been very violent there, and particularly at Amsterdam and Rotterdam, in the year 1663, whither, they say, it was bought, some said from Italy, others from the Levant, among some goods which were brought home by their Turkey fleet; others said it was brought from Candia; others from Cyprus.[101]

More recently, the onslaught of AIDS played the same function in the political imaginary: public-health officials in the USA first thought of it as a disease originating from Haiti and/or Africa, Europeans imagined it as coming from Africa (though the French also sometimes saw it as an American disease), Africans described its roots in Europe, Mexican migrant labour in North America believed it to be an exclusively North American disease, the Greek media blamed Albanian migrants while public health officials in Albania attributed the proliferation of new viruses there to movement in the opposite direction, and so on.[102]

Susan Sontag has argued that fears formulated in medical terms are usually animated by political concerns;[103] they are imagined in terms of their effects on the body politic and thus on social order. It has been said that 'because the body is the most potent metaphor of society, it is not surprising that disease is the most salient metaphor of structural crisis. All disease is disorder – metaphorically, literally, socially and politically'.[104] Conversely, we might add that disorder also tends to be seen as disease, from the period in early modern thought when the idea of the state was being formed -- from 'pestilence' (bubonic plague) came 'pestilent', whose figurative meaning is 'injurious to religion, morals, or public peace' (1513), and 'pestilential', meaning 'morally baneful or pernicious' (1531) – right through to twentieth-century analytical liberals such as John Rawls.[105] Imagining disorder as disease encourages a view of statecraft as a therapeutic art: its main aim is to render the social body 'immune' to whatever bio-political enemy that may threaten it. ('Immune' is one of those terms which oscillates between the medical and political registers: a medical term deriving from the Latin root *in-munus* but referring originally to an exemption from Roman state prescription which compromised life prospects, such as gladiatorial service).[106] Thus although the image of the body appeals because it connotes order in the form of unity and integration, identity and concord, wholeness and indivisibility, as we have seen, because such an image necessarily assumes grotesqueness the order is always imagined as an order under threat. It is partly for this reason that the policing of borders and 'others' – those 'foreign' or 'alien' to the territory – is so important to state power, and these are issues I take up in Chapter 4. The point here is that it is because territory is imagined in corporeal terms that the state seeks to secure its borders – its orifices and entry-points – from infiltration and penetration. As Derrida argues, the body politic reconstitutes its unity and secures its inner order by aiming to exclude from its territory external threats or aggression using whatever violence may be necessary.[107]

But this is a task that can never be fully successful since it is part of the grotesqueness that the body politic has to be open to some degree to the 'outside'. It is the nature of bodies – political, social, natural – that the distinction between inside and outside is never clear. Thus although the perceived threats and aggression towards the body appear to come from *outside*, they are also frequently confused with threats *inside*. This is the problem of the boundary. Madison, for example, claims that the state of Maryland 'persisted for several years . . . although the enemy remained the whole period at our gates, or rather in the very bowels of our country'.[108] The enemy here is constructed as occupying a place both at the gates and inside the territory: outside or at the border and yet also within the social body.

This is what was (is?) at stake in the US policy of containment. There are two different meanings of containment, as Andrew Ross points out: 'one which speaks to a threat *outside* of the social body, a threat which therefore has to be isolated, in quarantine, and kept at bay from the domestic body; and a second meaning of containment, which speaks to the domestic *contents* of the social body, a threat internal to the host which must then be neutralized by being contained or "domesticated"'.[109] It is for reasons such as these that the metaphor of the social body has lent itself to the authoritarian trope of 'national security', which in both theory and practice oscillates between the 'foreign' and 'domestic' spheres.

The implication of what I have been arguing here is that the incorporation of medical ideas into politics via the notion of the social body is far from being an entirely fascist trope. Rather, it follows (logically and politically) from the corporeal model of social order and a political imagination which reads the state through the idea of the body. The concepts of disease, purge, pestilence and so on are never innocent. Talk of the diseases of the social body is at best an oversimplification of what is complex; at worst it is an invitation to slaughter. The conjunction of bodily and military metaphors – 'war on cancer', 'immunological defences', 'alien organisms', 'defence' and 'invasion', 'immunity' and 'vulnerability' – indicates the intimate connection between bodily tropes and the exercise of violence. To describe a social or political phenomenon as a 'cancer' or 'plague' is an incitement to violence, for the point is not just to recognize the disease but to *expel it from the body politic*. Genocide, in this reading, can be thought of as another attempt to render the body politic orderly, to reinstate a particular form of order within the body of the state by carrying the logic of the vision of society as a body to its natural conclusion. The horrors achieved through such an exercise of state power are really an expression of the power of the body of the state to violently crush the bodies of human subjects; the image of the body politic here reveals nothing less than the essence of the state: its absolute power and violence. If we are to oppose the fascist political imagination because of its embodied notion of the social, then (as Lefort *et al*. wish us to) we should also oppose the bourgeois political imagination on the same grounds.

Bourgeois ideology and fascism are brought together in this way because they share a common political imagination centred on the state, the fundamental concerns of which are 'order' and the location of sovereignty. These concerns arise in a politically charged way with the breakdown of feudalism and thus a new 'disorderly' (bourgeois) society on the one hand, and the emergence of an abstract state entity on the other. (Dis)order thus becomes an essentially bourgeois concern and the need to ascertain what is required to fabricate and maintain order becomes the core feature of virtually every writer within the classical liberal and conservative traditions (and one which, sadly, many socialists have aped); necessarily so, since it is a core feature of ruling class strategy. It is this that connects bourgeois thought with fascism, in a whole range of ways: the understanding of the need for order in a society dominated by the everlasting uncertainty generated by capital accumulation; the understanding of the working class as an inherently disorderly one that needs to be brought to order; the presentation of any threats to the regime of capital as disorderly ('anarchy', 'chaos' etc.); and the link drawn between legality and order (the 'law and order' syndrome). And for these political traditions one of the major solutions to disorder is the correct location of sovereignty. Whether derived from theological origins or from a fictitious social contract, whether it lies with he who decides on the exception (Schmitt) or oscillates between 'sovereign individuals' and their representative body (liberalism), sovereignty is expected to fabricate and maintain order at any cost and, concomitantly, absorb all challenges to its authority.[110]

Thus, far from being a universal metaphor which permeates all cultures and all types of social and political thought, as anthropologists and some social and political theorists like to insist, the corporal metaphor is an ideological tool aimed at achieving good order and locating sovereignty. It is for this reason that Marx, in forgoing the obsession with order and sovereignty, was able to forgo the corporeal model. More pertinently, it is for this reason that the corporeal model is a dead end for any critical politics of radical transformation, and why those writers who have sought to use the idea of the body politic for dissent and critique have presented arguments which are highly unconvincing.[111] Far from being the basis of any kind of dissent or critique, the corporeal idea has the tendency to undermine dissent and critique before it has got off the ground. The fate of the 'body politic' in the twentieth century should make it anathema to anyone who wishes to move beyond the bourgeois and authoritarian assumptions inherent in the statist imaginary.

2 The mind of the state

If the state can be imagined in terms of the body, can it also be imagined in terms of the mind? Some writers have certainly thought as much. Towards the end of the nineteenth and at the beginning of the twentieth century some of the writers in what has been known as the 'New Liberalism' came to think of society in this way. John Hobson, for example, argues that the 'organic treatment of Society is, of course, still more essential, if we consider society not merely as a number of men and women with social instincts and social aspects of their individual lives, but as a group-life with a collective body, a collective consciousness and will'. In this view society is an organism in the sense that it has a 'common psychic life'. Since 'we have no experience of the existence or the action of any sort of mind without the body', so Hobson thought it reasonable to postulate 'the existence of a social body corresponding with and related to the social mind'.[1] The roots of this idea lie in earlier British readings of Hegel. Bernard Bosanquet, for example, argues in *The Philosophical Theory of the State* (1899) that 'the outward organisation of society is really as it were a body which at every point and in every movement expresses the characteristics of a mind'.[2]

One might dismiss such claims as too idiosyncratic to be taken seriously, evidence of the negative effect of transporting Hegel's argument concerning the state as 'Mind' objectified;[3] nothing more than Hegel translated into poor English. But to do so might be a little rash – maybe writers such as Hobson and Bosanquet were on to something. Did we not find that the image of the body politic turned out to have rather a lot of mileage in it after all? In this chapter I explore the extent to which the statist political imaginary posits the state as (in some sense) a form of mind. I shall do this by suggesting that it is an idea rooted in the fact that the state emerges from the sixteenth century onwards as an institution autonomous of civil society (at least, relatively so), with interests of its own. Part of these interests lies in the constitution and fabrication of civil society, and part of this constitutive-fabricatory function is the attempt to *know* civil society in the fullest sense possible. On this basis the exercise of state power can be said to be rooted in a set of claims made by the state and for the state concerning knowledge, intelligence and rationality, which in turn depend on and reinforce a set of political technologies for the ordering of civil society. As Foucault once noted, the idea of a 'political anatomy' which arises from the idea of a body politic can go in different directions: it might involve the study of the state in terms of a 'body', as we have seen in the previous chapter, but it might also be concerned with the 'body politic' as a set of material elements and techniques that support power-knowledge relations. This latter approach would examine the way that power-knowledge relations invest human bodies and subjugate them by *turning them into objects of knowledge*.[4] The argument I wish to make here is that this generates the idea and practice of the state as the knowing subject.

Raison d'État: a rationality of expedience

In January 2002 in the midst of the US 'war against terrorism' and the public outcry (in non-US states at least) concerning the treatment of Afghan prisoners being held at Guantanamo, the US Secretary of Defence Donald Rumsfeld appeared on television to deal with the concerns. He claimed that while he accepted part of the liberal concern over the treatment of prisoners, he could not see why the Geneva Conventions applied to them since they were not bona fide combatants. At the same time, however, he also 'made it clear that *raison d'État* would determine the US government's approach to this question'.[5] Regardless of the Geneva Conventions and liberal hand-wringing, US policy would be decided on the basis of a political doctrine first formulated in the sixteenth century: reason of state. Put simply, reason of state 'tells the statesman what he must do to preserve the health and strength of the State'. For each state at each particular moment there exists one ideal course of action, one ideal reason of state (*ratio status, ragion di stato, raison d'État, razón de Estado*). The statesman's role is to discern this course. As such, *raison d'État* is 'the fundamental principle of national conduct, the State's first law of motion'.[6]

The first clear statement of the principle is found in the work of Francesco Guicciardini. For Guicciardini, 'political power cannot be wielded according to the dictates of good conscience'.[7] Because all states are founded on violence and, as such, are 'illegitimate', Guicciardini argues that one should not expect to engage in politics on the basis of ethical principles – and especially not Christian ethical principles – concerning good conduct and morality: 'You see the position to which someone who wanted to govern states strictly according to conscience would be reduced. Therefore when I talked of murdering or keeping the Pisans imprisoned, I didn't perhaps talk as a Christian: I talked according to the reason and practice of states'.[8]

This principle's first appearance in Guicciardini's text and subsequent prominence in political discourse marks a dramatic transformation in the language of politics, as Maurizio Viroli has shown.[9] Two and a half centuries after politics had been defined as the ruling of a city according to reason, Guicciardini and those that follow him took the position that besides moral reason there is another reason – the reason of state. The rise of the state saw the rise of claims for the independence of sovereignty from traditional values. The century in which the impersonal form of rule came to the fore was also the century which saw the rise to prominence of the concept which, more than any other, came to act as the most important justification for state power. Statesmen, political thinkers and jurists became conscious of the idea of the good of the state as a major objective; that the state, as a form of rule, had interests of its own to be pursued. 'Interest of state' and the 'good of the state' thus became the core principles of reason of state.

In one sense, and unsurprisingly, the monarchic principle initially lay behind the doctrine: the idea of a divine right of sovereignty in which the will of the ruler was to be exercised above the limitations of civil law and according to the needs of the state had been central to monarchical rule. When the state stepped into the shoes of the prince, however, reason of state could appear in a non-monarchical form. Reason of state could then appear as the science of government that the sovereign power might use for the general good. In another sense, however, the wider historical context is important here. Reason of state arguments elaborated an account of interest in which the state emerged as an entity which appeared to be separate or autonomous from civil society. This separation occurred simultaneously with the emergence of an new form of social order increasingly splintered by competing interests, both economic and political, which would later become known as 'civil society' and/or '*bourgeois* society'. As Marx argues, this establishment of the political state and the dissolution of civil society into independent individuals is part of the same historical process – the process of abstraction: 'the abstraction of the *state as such* belongs only to modern times, because the abstraction of private life belongs only to modern times. The abstraction of the *political state* is a modern product'.[10] This abstraction is a process through which 'the state has become a separate entity' and which 'set[s] free the political spirit'.[11] It is clear from these and related phrases – 'the political constitution *as such*', 'the state *as such*' – that Marx is identifying the crucial moment in which a doctrine of reason of state becomes possible. Thus although some semblance of the idea may have been present in political thought for centuries – in Thrasymachus' view that justice is whatever is in the interests of the stronger party, for example – it could only be fully understood as reason of state when politics had been abstracted out of social relations. Reason of state is thus an idiom beyond the political discourse of feudalism, since the structural specificity underlying the doctrine of reason of state lies in the 'abstraction' of the state from civil society, an abstraction which is constitutive of the private sphere of the market and hence inseparable from capitalist relations of production.[12] Only as a 'separate' entity in a society dominated by competing interests can it become possible for the state to declare itself as possessing interests of its own. The state is thus dependent on (class) forces outside itself, but appears none the less as an *active subject* with *interests of its own to pursue*. Reason of state is here connected to the theory that the state is a corporate entity, a juristic person in its own right, and I shall turn to the specific legal issues concerning this in the following chapter. The point here is that the logic of defining the state as an entity with interests of its own encouraged the view that the state could act as a *subject* with reasons for its own actions. Moreover, the agent which defined the state's interests and determined which actions were appropriate to defend them was none other than the state itself, albeit through its chief spokespersons.

Writers have identified two important and interrelated aspects to the doctrine of reason of state. First, there is the general question of the relationship between politics and morals, and whether they can ever be reconciled. The simplest answer to the problem of politics and morality was to deny the relevance of the latter to the former. This is generally said to have its classic formulation in Machiavelli's account of *necessità*, in which the prince 'cannot practice all those things for which men are considered good, being often forced, in order to keep his position, to act contrary to truth, contrary to charity, contrary to humanity, contrary to religion'.[13] Courses of action that would be condemned as immoral if conducted by individuals could be sanctioned when they were undertaken by the sovereign power. Guicciardini's defence of the murder of Pisans is replicated in Machiavelli's comments on the murder of Remus by Romulus in the founding of Rome: 'though the deed accuses him, the result should excuse him . . . Romulus . . . deserved excuse for the death of his brother and his companion [for] what he did was done for the common good'.[14] There is then the possibility that certain political actions require the sovereign to be *autonomous* from morality. The state could break traditional and conventional moral codes and be above the law because it was thought to have interests of its own to pursue, interests bound up in its own identity as a state.[15]

In asserting the superiority of politics over morality the doctrine appeared to undermine the very foundations of Christian values. Trajano Bocalini, for example, defines reason of state as 'a law useful for Commonwealths, but absolutely contrary to the laws of both God and Man', and we have seen that Gucciardini believed that when he was talking of the reasons of states he was not talking as a Christian.[16] Historically, it appeared as though the 'forces of evil' which had hitherto been subdued by the Christian ethic had won a partial but fundamental victory – the devil had forced his way into the kingdom of God – and the doctrine was thus easily assimilated to atheism.[17] On the other hand, once the doctrine found a firm footing it quickly came to be defined in more morally neutral ways, and Christian thinkers were gradually convinced by the force of the doctrine to the extent that that they themselves came to argue that it could be entirely consistent with morality. Initial Christian outrage at reason of state was little more than a 'holy pretence', as George Mosse calls it, as the Church and Christian thinkers were easily reconciled to the idea.[18] Botero, for example, sought to justify the doctrine within the context of Christian morality, and as a body politic the Catholic Church had long held a view close to 'reason of Church'. It was therefore not difficult to move from the idea that the state was divinely ordained to the view that its actions could be morally legitimated regardless of how 'evil' they may appear. Moreover, as *raison d'État* gradually lost its negative connotations it could be defined in more neutral ways. Botero opens *The Reason of State* (1589) with the following definition: 'State is a stable rule over a people and Reason of State is the knowledge of the means by which such a dominion may be founded'.[19] In being defined in neutral terms and reconciled with morality, reason of state became at worst an innocuous doctrine and, at best, a doctrine entirely in accordance with the principles of 'justice'. Thus by the early seventeenth century the doctrine was widely accepted as part and parcel of political dialogue – 'to reason of state and the preservation of state is most fit in this place', it was stated in the British House of Commons in 1621.[20]

The second aspect of the doctrine concerns the question of law and the legal limits on state power. The assumption inherent in the doctrine was that the state should be autonomous from law as well as morality or, if not autonomous, then operate according to a higher legal principle founded on a higher form of reason. Hence Bocalini's definition stated above and Machiavelli's comment that the prudent intellect will never 'censure anyone for any unlawful action used in organizing a kingdom or setting up a republic'.[21] The view is captured in the traditional maxim *salus rei publicae suprema lex* – the security of the state is the supreme law. In this sense reason of state was never clearly defined beyond the general 'what is needed to preserve the state', nor could it be. 'Reason' in this context refers not to Ciceronian reason, understood as a search for universal principles of justice, but is closer to what we would now call instrumental reason – the idea that the means must be appropriate ('rational') to the end and that the means which are the best ('most rational') are the ones most likely to succeed (to preserve the state). The doctrine thus superimposes the appearance of reason onto the ordinary and extraordinary practices of state power. It is a rationality of expedience, as Carl Friedrich puts it.[22] Scipione Ammirato, for example, in his *Discorsi sopra Coernelio Tacito* (1594), claims that reason of state is a 'contravention of ordinary reason in favour of greater or more universal reason' concerning the preservation of the state.[23] The concept refers less to a specific legal entity and more to the capacity of those in power to judge what is good for the nation at large.

For obvious reasons, then, the doctrine easily lent its weight to the absolutist trope of an omnipotent sovereign state. But the horrors of absolutism are nothing to write home about. The case gets more interesting when we consider that the doctrine was historically given credence by writers who, working within a liberal tradition, allowed it in via crucial concessions to the necessity of state action 'above the law', despite the fact that it clearly contradicts the rule of law and the idea of constitutional limits on state power. John Locke, for example, concedes that 'the good of the Society' requires that some things be left to the discretion of the executive as events may occur where 'strict and rigid observation of the laws may do harm'.[24] The reason for this lies in the way Locke obliterates any distinction between external and internal affairs of state. Internal affairs ('the Society *within* itself') are the province of the executive power; external affairs ('the *security and interest of the publick without*') are the province of the federative power. Yet Locke comments that these two powers 'are hardly to be separated' and 'are always almost united'.[25] This unity of the two powers allows the society to be governed internally according to the same principle as that through which society is governed in its external affairs. Because ultimately external affairs have to be governed according to the public good and protected from the designs of foreigners, this unity of powers 'is much less capable to be directed by antecedent, standing, positive Laws . . . and so must necessarily be left to the Prudence and Wisdom of those whose hands it is in'.[26] The prerogative which is used by the federative power to govern external relations is thus transposed onto the executive power; and 'prerogative' is defined by Locke as the 'Power to act according to discretion, for the publick good, without the prescription of the Law, and sometimes even against it'.[27] What Locke achieves in these moves is to import into his argument a space for the exercise of prompt and flexible action outside the legal and constitutional limits placed on the state: the magistrate may 'restrain or compel', 'command or forbid' particular actions for no other reason than 'the necessity of state and the welfare of the people called for them'.[28] As we have seen, this is the central feature of reason of state arguments. While Sheldon Wolin may not be quite right in claiming that the *pivotal* figure in the expansion of reason of state arguments proved to be the liberal Locke rather than the absolutist Hobbes, he is nonetheless surely correct in pointing to arguments such as Locke's in the democratization and legitimization of what only a century before had been widely regarded as an abhorrent doctrine.[29] A century later Adam Smith would argue against reason of state on explicit liberal grounds: 'to hinder . . . the farmer from sending his goods at all times to the best market, is evidently to sacrifice the ordinary laws of justice . . . to a sort of reasons of state'. Yet he immediately comments that such a sacrifice *is* acceptable 'in cases of the most urgent necessity' – precisely the cases when it had been exercised anyway.[30] Thus despite being superficially opposed to a doctrine originally founded on supposedly anti-liberal assumptions, liberalism, like Christianity, in fact helped consolidate the doctrine's centrality to political thought and action. What we find, then, is that the overlap between security, interests and necessity of state animates the search for absolute sovereignty outlined in the previous chapter, a search supported and legitimized rather than challenged by the liberal position. Historically this meant that the doctrine of reason of state was never confined to monarchical absolutism. Rather, 'the doctrine filtered into a tradition of enhanced royalty, but it gained just as much ground in countries with a parliamentary – that is, republican – constitution'.[31]

In being able to legitimate state power in all its guises the influence of the doctrine of reason of state has been enormous. It quickly became a weapon which the modern state could brandish while asserting its power *vis-à-vis* other states, and some 400 years after being first formulated by Guicciardini it remained the key ideological mechanism of superpower confrontation, being the only common language between the Soviet Union and the West, feeding into the political discourse of non-superpower states, and remaining in place well after the end of the cold war.[32] It also contributed enormously to the political doctrine of fascism, for example in Carl Schmitt's argument that the political sphere has its own criterion of evaluation and that the sovereign is one who decides when the violation of all other principles and the suspension of all law is permitted.

More pertinent to the argument here, however, is the fact that reason of state has also been a doctrine with which states seek to preserve and strengthen their power *vis-à-vis* their own subjects, for the doctrine was (and remains) concerned with *domestic* as much as foreign politics, as Locke's manoeuvring over internal and external powers suggests. The doctrine has merged into its sister concepts 'interest of state', 'security of state' and, in the twentieth century, 'national security', all of which are political technologies for dealing with concrete problems of foreign policy on the one hand and questions of internal (dis)order on the other. Like national security, reason of state postulates the interrelatedness of so many different *internal* political, economic and social factors that virtually nothing is beyond its concern; the rationality of expedience means that the state may concern itself with any and every area it so wishes: it is fundamental to the police project whereby the state fabricates social order and fashions civil society according to the shifting forms of class rule.[33] 'Security policy' and 'interest of state' concern not just external threats, but are the grounds for the dissolution of democracy and legitimacy into *realpolitik* and *raison d'État*. In other words, for reasons of state – for 'security reasons' – the state can legitimately do whatever it feels right. Reason of state is therefore concerned with the *penetration of civil society by the state*, as becomes apparent in appeals to national security, the immunization of state officials from ordinary procedures of law[34] and the classification of state documents as 'secret' (to which I return below). As Max Weber points out, 'in the final analysis, in spite of all "social welfare policies", the whole course of the state's inner political functions, of justice and administration, is repeatedly and unavoidably regulated by the objective pragmatism of "reasons of state" '.[35] Reason of state has thus remained the mechanism by which the state continually defines the purpose of its actions and refines its modes of oppression.

It is both *because* of this penetration and *part* of this penetration that the state seeks to *know* civil society, and what follows in the rest of this chapter is in part an attempt to spell out the importance of the question of knowledge to the project of fabricating social order. The argument is that what was and remains central to reason of state arguments is the question of political knowledge. The aim is to show that state power was consolidated and the idea of the state legitimated via a political imagination which sees the state as producer and defender of 'knowledge'. In this sense, we are dealing with the state as an epistemological project. The state not only constitutes the social body, fabricates order and controls a territory, it also occupies an epistemological space. It is in this sense that the statist political imaginary encourages us to think of the *mind of the state*. The idea that the state *knows* and can *reason* is used by the state to legitimize its power over civil society and circumvent attempts to impose limits on its power *vis-à-vis* its own subjects.

Character angelicus: the intelligent state

Botero's definition of reason of state as the knowledge of the means by which such a dominion may be founded points to the new process which was to be central to the rise and consolidation of the state: it was a possessor of knowledge. Foucault notes that knowledge was historically integral to reason of state:

> Government is possible only when the strength of the state is known: It is by this knowledge that it can be sustained. The state's capacity and the means to enlarge it must be known. The strength and capacity of other states, rivals of my own state, must also be known . . . A government, therefore, entails more than just implementing general principles of reason, wisdom, and prudence. A certain specific knowledge is necessary: concrete, precise, and measured knowledge.[36]

Thus virtually all the texts on reason of state from the late sixteenth century held that in order to win and maintain its territory the state had to develop a system of knowledge of its subjects and of other states. Here the doctrine picks up on and feeds off a wider connection concerning order, sovereignty and knowledge.

Hobbes, for example, replaces the idea of 'conscience' with a concept without any religious significance: opinion. In *Elements of Law* he defines 'conscience' as 'nothing else but a man's settled judgement and opinion', while in *Leviathan* he claims that 'private Consciences . . . are but private opinions'.[37] Thus conscience turns into private morality. But the state is a structure in which private moralities and mentalities are deprived of their political effect – 'The Law is the publique Conscience'.[38] Hence Hobbes' view that 'a man must submit his opinions, in matters of controversy, to the authority of the commonwealth' – 'Private Reason must submit to the Publique, that is to say, to God's Lieutenant'.[39] A state can exist only if the plurality of individuals and parties which constitute it succumbs to a morality which accepts the absolute political sovereignty of the ruler as a moral necessity. Richard Tuck has suggested that although Hobbes does not make use of the term 'reason of state', the extent of writings on reason of state in the Bodleian library in which he worked through the 1630s would imply that the culture of reason of state was clearly what the young Hobbes was most at home in.[40] While this may be the case, it is just as likely that what manifests itself in Hobbes' work is the conjunction of absolutism and rationalist philosophy. We saw in the previous chapter that the Leviathan superimposes Descartes' model of the mechanical body onto the traditional metaphor of the body politic. Hobbes also adapts Descartes' mind-body dualism. In the *Discourse on Method* (1637) and *Meditations* (1641) Descartes provided the first statement of the philosophical position which treats the mind and body as separate entities – 'the mind, by which I am what I am, is wholly distinct from the body'. This view, and all other knowledge claims, is arrived at through reason – 'we ought never to allow ourselves to be persuaded of the truth of anything unless on the evidence of our reason'.[41] Hobbes' conception of the body politic adopts and adapts Descartes' narrative concerning the mind-body problem and its rationalist foundations. For Hobbes, the sovereign body is essentially rational and, moreover, consists of and protects the bodies of its subjects by disassociating body and mind. As bodies, individual subjects are political. As minds, however, they are relegated to a politically powerless private realm – the realm of private opinion. This separation is an effect of the rationality of the sovereign body: the rational (sovereign) mind controls the body politic. In other words, as Koselleck points out, Hobbes circumvents the question of ethics and politics which had been a central feature of debates about *raison d'État*; to the question of the relationship between traditional moral doctrines and politics Hobbes opposes the doctrine of political reason. In doing so he recasts Descartes' philosophical problem as a question of political exigency, an effect of political order whose constitutive authority Descartes fails to recognize. The rationality of the body politic thus disassociates each individual body from its mind. What follows from this is the idea that the decisive moral commandment is the duty to obey and, more crucially, the idea that what is being obeyed is nothing less than the *rationality* of the sovereign state. The rationality of the Hobbesian state thus lies not in the minds of its individual subjects but in the form and structure of the collective body politic as it is governed by absolute sovereignty.[42] The fact that, as minds, individuals are merely private beings reinforces an assumption that the practice of reason and the claim to knowledge are part and parcel of the sovereign body's claim to authority. As Cornelia Navari explains, *Leviathan* approaches the problem of knowledge through a procedural device which runs something like 'we the citizens cannot know, so we must let the sovereign decide'.[43] The formula presupposes awareness that the sovereign must decide because the citizens not only cannot know, but also know that they cannot know.

At the same time, however, Hobbes' 'natural state' is one in which life is not merely 'solitary, poore, nasty, brutish and short' but in which 'no Knowledge' is possible.[44] Hobbes' position, then, is that without the state knowledge is simply not possible: disorder in politics is identical to a disorder of knowledge.[45] Knowledge is an attribute of political order: power is knowledge and questions of epistemology are questions of political power. The Leviathan's power lies, in part, in its role as the producer and regulator of knowledge.

While Hobbes' contribution to the understanding of the knowledge-power nexus is heavily determined by the absolutist tropes in his work, these do not in themselves explain his account of the nexus. For Hobbes was making a major contribution to what became a central theme in the statist imaginary: the idea that the state is so central to human life that knowledge is impossible without it. Although modern academic disciplines have separated questions of knowledge from questions of power – epistemology and political science have gone their separate ways[46] – in the statist political imaginary the assumption is always that the state and knowledge are, ultimately, integrally related. Oversimplifying somewhat, one might point to three important strands in these accounts.

First, there is the idea that in knowledge lies the key to the subordination of nature and culture, and thus the key to man's mastery of his conditions of existence, a view found most clearly in Francis Bacon's observation that 'the sovereignty of man lieth hid in knowledge'.[47] Here lies the basis of Adorno and Horkheimer's account of enlightenment as a form of domination: 'Knowledge, which is power, knows no obstacles: neither in the enslavement of men nor in compliance with the world's rulers'.[48] A second strand rests on the assumption that some forms of power act as a constraint upon knowledge, excluding and regulating it according to 'illegitimate' (for which read 'illiberal') political demands. This has fed into the liberal political tradition. As Thomas Richards writes:

> The thread uniting the thought of Bentham and Mill with the thought of Russell and Keynes and C.P. Snow was the idea that knowledge is inconceivable without the state: that the question of the

state is a question of knowledge, especially scientific knowledge; that the classing of knowledge must be underwritten and directed by the state in its various capacities; that all epistemology became and must remain state epistemology in an economy of controlled information.[49]

Finally, there is the philosophical tradition which identifies reason with the rational organization of a society by the state. Realized reason comes to be identified with the state itself; the state is treated as the becoming of reason, to the extent that in some cases it becomes mind objectified. The most sophisticated philosophical version of this is Hegel's *Philosophy of Right*, but the particular features of Hegel's argument concerning the state as the embodiment of reason should not obscure its longer and diverse philosophical heritage. As Gilles Deleuze and Félix Guattari explain:

> Ever since philosophy assigned itself the role of ground it has been giving the established powers its blessing, and tracing its doctrine of faculties onto the organs of State power. Common sense, the unity of all the faculties at the centre constituted by the Cogito, is the State consensus raised to the absolute. This was most notably the great operation of the Kantian 'critique', renewed and developed by Hegelianism.[50]

The general point is that from the birth of the modern state there developed a whole line of reflection on the relation of the state to reason – as rational-technical and/or as reasonable-human – which in all cases imagined the state as the guarantor of knowledge. To write about the state is thus to write about the way that sovereignty asserts itself in the sphere of knowledge:[51] first, through the way *state has been imagined as an institution of and for knowledge* and, second, through the way this *power-knowledge nexus has legitimized state practices over and through civil society*.

Let me develop this argument by considering the idea of the state as an intelligence-gathering machine. The common-sense understanding of 'intelligence' when applied to the state tends to focus on the so-called 'intelligence community'. In and of itself this constitutes a vast network of institutions: in Britain it would include the Secret Intelligence Service (SIS, better known as MI6), MI5, Government Communication Headquarters (GCHQ), the Defence Intelligence Staff (DIS), the Joint Intelligence Committee (JIC), the Overseas Economic Intelligence Committee (OEIC), the Coordinator of Intelligence and Security (CIS, based in the Cabinet Office), the Official Committee on Security (OCS), the London Signal Intelligence Board (LSIB), the Permanent Secretaries Committee on Intelligence (PSIS), the Security Commission, the *ad hoc* Ministerial Group on Security, the Security and Policy Methods Committee, the

Personnel Security Committee and the Electronic Security Committee. (Note how 'intelligence' and 'security' slide into one another when discussing such organizations.) These institutions have facilitated the rise of a cult of intelligence, whose holy men are the professionals of such 'intelligence services', whose patrons and protectors are the highest officials in the elected parts of the state, whose membership extends into the centres of social as well as political power, and whose sympathizers include individuals and groups from influential spheres such as the mass media and the academic world. The cult is the semi-secret fraternity of the ruling class.[52] There is a twofold danger, however, in focusing our attention on this 'community' when thinking about intelligence and the state. First, it encourages us to think of the state's search for intelligence as concerned solely with knowledge of *foreign* powers, when in point of fact the 'intelligence' is as much about obtaining knowledge of its own civil society. The myth pandered by liberal democratic states is that it is only 'in the lesser democratic nations [that] leaders frequently use intelligence as a weapon against their own people and domestic rivals to maintain their control of power',[53] as though such practices were not equally commonplace in liberal democracies. But states have mutual spying machines – indeed, in some sense *are* mutual spying machines. Civil society, however, lacks this sense of equality or reciprocity with the state and has no 'spying machine' to speak of. The best it can hope for is some kind of Left opposition keeping tabs on the state, but this will always be at a serious technical and organizational disadvantage. (And in recent years more and more of its members have retreated into their private universes, a point to which I shall return in this chapter.)

Second, such a focus distracts from the other institutions of state intelligence, the far more mundane institutions of political administration which police civil society. Such policing relies heavily on the gathering of intelligence (in the guise of 'information') about the social body. We therefore need an *expanded* concept of state intelligence, one that reaches beyond the more narrowly defined 'intelligence community' to include the various institutions and processes through which civil society is administered by the state – intelligence as 'the soul of all public business', as Daniel Defoe puts it, or 'policy as the intelligence of the personified state' in the words of Clausewitz.[54] 'Intelligence' could then be understood as the term to describe all the necessary information, both overt and secret, which states need for fashioning their policies and doing their work. From this perspective, the 'intelligence community' consists of all agents of the state, whose remit is, to all intents and purposes, unlimited.[55]

Historically, 'intelligence' was associated with not only the faculty of understanding but also with the obtaining of knowledge and information on behalf of the state. The specific association of 'intelligence' with the information needed for war and peace, an association absent in the Latin *intellego*, enters the French and English languages in the sixteenth century, after which political and social meanings connected to such usage come to dominate the word.[56] Johnson's *Dictionary* suggests that actual usage situated the word in political and social rather than in a more narrowly defined philosophic discourse. Johnson relegates the philosophic meaning of 'intelligence' to fourth place in his list of definitions, after intelligence as 'commerce of information; notice; mutual communication; account of things distant or secret' and 'commerce of acquaintance, terms on which men live with one another'. He cites Bacon: 'It is . . . in the order of nature for him to govern that is the more intelligent'. The sovereign therefore needs to be properly 'intelligenced' and needs skilful 'intelligencers'.[57] Just as reason was drawn into the ambit of state power through the idea of reason of state, so intelligence was associated with the question of power in the guise of 'political intelligence'.

One tradition in the political theology of the Middle Ages ascribes a *character angelicus* to the sovereign, an attempt to recapture the Platonic unity of political power with perfect intelligence.[58] In this tradition the philosopher-king had the character of an angel: not quite properly divine but endowed with intellectual powers unattainable by other mortals. If fully realized, such powers would combine absolute knowledge with political power. But because the sovereign was always liable to fall short of this absolute knowledge – just as the king possessed a corporeal and thus faulty body, so his intelligence was also faulty – sovereignty was imagined as permanently precarious. The historical consequence has been the necessity to employ 'spials and intelligencers':[59] to govern through diplomacy, spying, surveillance and intelligence-gathering, devices designed to obtain information about the sovereign's territory, subjects and enemies. Intelligence, then, has its origins in the discourse of diplomacy and culture of spying in court society from the fifteenth century onwards, as both Norbert Elias and Walter Benjamin have noted.[60] Political intelligence was the result of the mutual observation and social competition of court society, overseen by the royal sovereign. The modern state, in so far as it inherited this necessity and commitment from monarchical rule, is animated by the strategic relationship between knowledge and power in the search for perfect intelligence about all that it surveys or which comes into its orbit; the dream of state power is the will to know – nothing less than to know just who is related to who and in what degree of intimacy. Leviathan 'seeth everything below him' (*Job*, 41.9; or as Joseph Goebbels liked to claim: 'He who knows everything fears nothing'). The outcome has been the search for information about all that the state administers.

This search for information on everything permeates the workings of state officials at all levels, from the absolutist monarch – Louis XIV saw in the search for intelligence the need to be 'informed of everything'[61] – to the everyday meetings of intelligence officers (one member of the British wartime Ministry of Information, when asked what intelligence officers talked about when they met, replied 'Everything, just about everything').[62] As Warren Hastings put it in 1784 in discussing the relation of knowledge to power in the colonial context, 'every accumulation of knowledge and especially such as is obtained by social communication with people over whom we exercise dominion founded on the right of conquest, is useful to the state'.[63] More recently, in 1997 General Fogelman, Chief of Staff of the US Air Force told the House of Representatives that 'in the first three months of the twenty-first century we shall be capable of finding, tracking and targeting virtually in real time any significant element moving on the surface of the earth'.[64] At a more mundane level the whole system of what I elsewhere describe as social police and am here rethinking as an expanded intelligence community (social workers, social security officers, and the police themselves) is geared towards the gathering of information (one police officer reports that 'we were taught that no informa-tion is really useless'),[65] while the mechanisms by which the state administers the population, such as the passport, the driver's licence, the identity card, as well as the more underhand means of information-gathering such as phone-tapping, bugging and letter-opening, are all at one level intelligence-gathering tools.

Now, my comments here may appear to merely replicate the widespread claim that we have moved into an 'information society'. But the problem with the notion of an 'information society' is that even when articulated with a Marxisant gloss or through a critical lens[66] it buys into the idea of fragmenta-tion – that we are bombarded by fragmented information from all directions. This is the culmination of a trend which began in the late nineteenth century, when many people stopped using the word 'knowledge' and started using the word 'information' instead. 'Information' had, and has, overtones of scattered, disjunct fragments of fact. This way of using 'information' shifts the focus away from the question of knowledge, which has a sense of a prospective unity. In the nineteenth century the problem of the disorganization and dis-unity of knowledge – the problem of information – came to replace the prob-lem of the organization and unity of knowledge. Richards notes that our idea of information still has something about it of the frustration the Victorians felt.[67] Information is knowledge fractured into bits and pieces that appear to be flexible and malleable but never really assembled successfully into an inte-grated whole. Information is the name given to 'knowledges' that come from everywhere and end nowhere, seemingly vast but not total, extensive but not complete. The problem with 'information' as a category of social analysis, then, is that it appears to connote knowledge without a central structuring agency or a totalizing and stable structure. In other words, it shifts the focus away from the question of which agent may seek to unify this knowledge. The aim here is to deal with the state not just as the accumulator of information or part of a nebulous 'information society', but as the possessor of knowledge, capable of unifying and totalizing knowledge in its attempt to properly know the social body. Of course, the state has never been able to achieve a totally unified knowledge, but such unity is part of the state's never quite fulfilled desire. (Note, however, the degree to which such scenarios have been central to fictional dystopias.)

To achieve this knowledge the state has engaged in an immense labour of organization, standardization, recording and reordering. I want to focus here on two mechanisms of this labour, for they illustrate the point well enough: statistics and the census. Statistical knowledge has become central to the way we imagine the modern condition and the 'information society'. As Ian Hacking puts it:

> Statistics crowd in upon us. The statistics of our pleasures and our vices are relentlessly tabulated. Sports, sex, drink, drugs, travel, sleep, friends – nothing escapes. There are more explicit statements of prob-abilities presented on American prime time television than explicit acts of violence (I'm counting the ads). Our public fears are endlessly debated in terms of probabilities: chances of meltdowns, cancers, muggings, earthquakes, nuclear winters, AIDS, global greenhouses, what next? There is nothing to fear (it may seem) but the probabilities themselves.[68]

Although statistics gradually became synonymous with the gathering of figures and analysis of numerical information, to the extent that it now appears to have no necessary connection to the state, the fetishism for 'facts and figures' and obsession with the statistical chances of pleasures and vices descends directly from the development and consolidation of state power in the West and the doctrine of reason of state.[69] The method of statistics presup-poses a universe of equivalent individuals – that is, individuals who can be compared, contrasted, added and subtracted from each other as abstract per-sons; its immediate basis was the trade in commodities which stimulated the development of specialized bookkeeping and accounting from the sixteenth century onwards. Such a process was impossible in the feudal period, in which the key category of measurement was the fiscal unit rather than the individual. What this means, in effect, is that statistics only becomes fully possible with the emergence of the calculating rationality of the bourgeois class. On the one side, then, statistics presupposes the bourgeois category of population, within which the abstract individual is situated; on the other side it presupposes the universal object to which they are related – the state.[70] In its origins, statistics was thus a synthesis of bourgeois and bureaucratic rationality.

First publicly employed in 1672, statistics (*Staatenkunde*) became a subject of study in German-speaking areas through the eighteenth century. The first national statistical bureau, the 'Department of Tables' (*Tabellverket*), came into existence in Sweden in 1749, while Norway and Denmark set up their own bureaus in 1797; the term entered the English language in 1770 in the translation of J.F. Bielfeld's *Elements of Universal Education*, and had its first systematic exposition in John Sinclair's multi-volume *Statistical Account of Scotland* (1791–8). The sense of the word 'statistics' that prevailed through the eighteenth century was less a collection of numerical data or a branch of mathematics and more a statement or view of the civil condition of a people. The term was derived from new Latin and understood as a science dealing with facts of a state, including details on intangibles such as national character and the satisfaction of the citizenry. Unsurprisingly it was part and parcel of the cameralist tradition of *Polizeiwissenschaft*. Early members of the Statistical Society of London, founded in 1834, called themselves 'statists' in view of the connection. 'Statist' and 'statistician' were terms used interchangeably in other European countries, and American 'statists' were understood to be both 'statesmen' and familiar with statistics.[71] That 'statistics' comes from the same root as 'state' testifies to an important point, made by Raymond Williams: 'without the combination of statistical theory . . . and arrangements for collection of statistical data, symbolized by the foundation of the Manchester Statistical Society, the society that was emerging out of the industrial revolution was *literally unknowable*'.[72] Statistics, then, became a key political technology for knowing the social body. Moreover, the resulting 'avalanche of numbers' was in part generated by an obsession with *analyse morale* in general and the condition of the working class in particular, as the statistical analyses were centred on social groups regarded as problematic, the class of poverty and the sub-groups said to be spawned by that class – the vagrant, criminal, prostitute and drunk (*les misérables* was a standard topic in the world statistical congresses).[73] Those groups, in other words, imagined as a threat to the bourgeois order.

Statistics thus emerged as one of the most important techniques in the exercise of state power, becoming not just a mechanism for the 'taming of chance', transforming a qualitatively complex world into a mass of supposedly decipherable information, but also insinuating itself into the practices of power by becoming a form of intelligence-gathering of the most general kind since, as with information-gathering, there is by definition nothing beyond its scope: *nothing may escape their gaze* is how one nineteenth-century statistician described their task.[74] Moreover, because statistical 'facts' are derived from enumerative practices they have the appearance of being objective. State 'knowledge' thus appears to be free from any taint of subjectivism; free, that is, from any suggestion that the 'knowledge' in question is anything other than 'real' knowledge.[75]

The outcome was the simultaneous claim on the part of the state to the right to act on the basis of knowledge held, and the rendering of the social world more amenable to control. This is true of all state forms. What we might therefore call the 'statistical imagination' has been central to state-building of both the liberal[76] and fascist kind: 'I do not exaggerate when I say that at this moment statistics are the order of the day throughout the world', Mussolini informed the first High Council of the Central Institute of Statistics (ISTAT) in 1926, adding that 'of the many institutional creations of the fascist regime, that of the Central Institute of Statistics is the most important'. Meanwhile, one member of the General Directorship of Statistics (DIRSTAT) described statistics as a sort of anatomy and physiology of the social body.[77] In Nazi Germany, the leader of IBM Germany ('Dehomag', as it was known), commented in a speech to a crowd of Nazi officials in 1934 that the statisticians at Dehomag 'are very much like the physician, in that we dissect, cell by cell, the German cultural body. We report every individual characteristic . . . on a little card . . . We are proud that we may assist in such a task, a task that provides our nation's physician [Adolf Hitler] with the material he needs for his examinations'. Similarly the *Allgemeines Statistisches Archiv*, the official journal of the German Statistical Society, ran articles throughout the 1930s commenting on the importance of statistics to the regime: 'The government of our *Führer* and Reichschancellor Adolf Hitler is statistics-friendly' (1939); 'several important problems are being tackled currently, problems of an ideological nature. One of those problems is race politics, and this problem must be viewed in a statistical light' (1934); 'in using statistics, the government now has the road map to switch from knowledge to deeds' (1939); 'statistics is identical in character with the National Socialist idea' (1934).[78]

Central to the statistical foundation of political knowledge is the census, and under the fascist regimes the census was crucial. Using the most up-to-date technology such as the punch cards provided by IBM (slogan in Germany in 1934: 'see everything with Hollerith punchcards'), the Nazis found in the census the ideal method for knowing just who was related to who, and just who constituted an enemy of the state. 'The only way to eliminate any mistakes is the registration of the *entire* population', wrote Karl Keller in the *Allgemeines Statistisches Archiv* in 1934. In his work on the role of IBM in helping the Nazis register and administer the Jews, Edwin Black comments that 'whenever Jewish persecution was reported, the media invariably reported the incessant registrations and censuses as Nazidom's initial step'. As the Italian statistical institute explained in 1931, 'if this work [the census] is characteristic of the modern State, it is so to an even greater extent in the fascist State'.[79] The use of the census in the transformation of human subjects into objects of political administration has remained a key feature in the genocidal process: reports from the genocide in Rwanda suggest that the identity cards classifying people into 'tribes' issued by the political authorities (and devised originally as a tool of colonial administration) were a vital source of information on which their slaughter was based.[80]

The 'uniqueness' of genocidal events such as the Holocaust is now often taken as read, but the census and the history of statistics are yet more evidence to show that many of the bureaucratic methods and administrative procedures used in carrying out the Holocaust have their roots in a long tradition of attempts by the state to count and statistically analyse the population and its various sub-groups. Now understood as merely a counting procedure, the census was historically important in the period of the state's search for knowledge. Sweden produced a census in 1749, Norway and Denmark in 1769, central German states such as Mecklenburg, Hesse-Darmstadt and Bavaria in 1776 and 1777, Austria and Spain in 1787, while the USA became the first nation to inaugurate a periodic census in 1790. In 1791, a colonel of militia mobilized the clergy of Scotland to send him inventories of their parishes, while in France the revolutionaries encouraged greater counting of the population; Britain took its first census in 1801. Far from a mere counting procedure, the census is a model of the encyclopaedic quest for total knowledge.

But as well as being a political technology for *knowing* the population, the census is also a mechanism for *ordering* the population according to the classificatory schema by which political administration operates. There is an etymological link between *census* and *censor* in the Latin *cēnsēre*. The *censor* was the Roman officer who both drew up a register of citizens and who supervised public morality. The two ideas were so inextricably linked that in debates about the first modern censuses some preferred to talk of 'numberings' of the people to avoid the explicit connotations of moral control and political observation by the 'censorial eye' as Burke called it.[81] Censuses taken by ecclesiastical authorities combined this double meaning of censing and censoring more explicitly: inscribing people's names on the official list of communicants was a way to remind them of their religious obligations. Politically, however, the point was made by Jean Bodin, who recognized that a modern idea about the census was emerging – 'the word *census* means simply an assessment of each individual's belongings' – but who also saw the value in using such knowledge in 'disciplining and reprimanding the subject'. For Bodin, 'the first advantage to be derived from taking a census relates to the ordering of persons':

> One can find out the standing and the calling of each individual, and how he earns his living. This makes it possible to get rid of those parasites which prey upon the commonwealth, to banish idlers and vagabonds, the robbers and ruffians of all sorts that live among good citizens like wolves among the sheep. One can find them out, and track them down wherever they are . . . [M]ost commonwealths are afflicted with vagabonds, idlers, and ruffians who corrupt good citizens by their deeds and their example. There is no means of getting rid of such vermin save by the censor.[82]

The desire to know 'how many' was thus part and parcel of the desire to exercise sovereign authority. The census pins people down to a time, a place and a class, and creates the possibility of tracking them over time, space and classes: it is the classic police operation.

To describe it as the classic police operation is not to refer to the census merely as a form of control, but to hint at its role in the *fabrication of social order*. This becomes clear the more we consider the way statistics and the census work in the wider logic of statecraft. For state officials to be able to comprehend an otherwise complex reality, that reality must be made comprehensible. One of the ways this was done historically was through the invention of permanent patronyms as a means for the state to know its citizens. As Marc Bloch and, more recently, James Scott have shown, until at least the fourteenth century the vast majority of Europeans did not have permanent surnames. But the increasing intensity of state activity combined with the mobility of new forms of property simultaneously parallelled and necessitated the development of permanent patronyms. Tracing property ownership, collecting taxes, maintaining court records, performing police work, subduing indigenous populations, conscripting soldiers and generally maintaining a healthy social body by controlling epidemics were all made easier with greater clarity of full names and, following those, fixed addresses: 'Thus in Europe, long after the demise of feudal society, the permanent family name, which today is held in common by men often devoid of any feeling of solidarity, was the creation not of the spirit of kinship but of the institution most fundamentally opposed to that spirit – the sovereign state'.[83]

The invention of permanent, inherited patronyms was a crucial step in establishing the necessary preconditions for modern statecraft: 'in almost every case it was a state project, designed to allow officials to identify, unambiguously, the majority of its citizens'.[84] Like other apparently prepolitical relations, names turn out to be deeply enmeshed in the political administration of civil society by the state. Permanent patronyms were constituted politically, and thus went far in helping to fashion a legible and thus knowable people.[85] As a consequence, the more the body politic was opened to greater parts of the population – the more the early-modern body politic became a modern social body – the more the state sought to register its citizens. This is part of the intertextual and cross-institutional link between the 'statistical idea' and the 'sanitary idea' noted in the previous chapter.[86] For the state to render the social body clean and hygienic, it had to *know* precisely who, what and where the 'problem' lay.

Moreover, this logic reduces reality to a limited number of select and schematic categories allowing summary descriptions, comparisons and aggregation. Statistics does not merely generate information, but rather generates its own subdivisions and rearrangements, and determines the classifications within which people come to think of themselves.[87] It is relevant to note the shifting referential of 'classification' in the nineteenth century. In the eighteenth century and first half of the nineteenth century 'classification' meant the ordering of information in taxonomies. By the late nineteenth century, however, it came to mean knowledge placed under the special jurisdiction of the state.[88] It is the categories of classification that profoundly shape the way the state imagines its territory and thinks about the social body under its dominion. What is at stake here are new forms of knowledge produced through the development of political administration. It is here, in the generation of new categories by the state, that the real regime of power/knowledge lies (*contra* Foucault and his followers).

For the state there are virtually no epistemological categories other than those that are contained in official documents standardized for the purpose of knowing the social world. While the categories which emerge appear to be merely a way of representing and interpreting the world, there is far more at stake, for the mechanisms and analysis through which the state thinks are not merely modes of representation but are also modes of *construction*. That is, they do not merely interpret reality, but *define* it by imposing a classificatory order on a social world otherwise perceived as disorderly.[89] The practice of assembling and classifying figures was and remains not merely a mode of understanding and representing populations but an instrument for regulating and transforming them, for shaping the social world. From the state's point of view, it is only with the myriad taxonomic classifications employed by the state that social order becomes intelligible and thus obtainable; without such practices the world is, in the mind of the state, disorder writ large. The figures collected, manipulated and presented and, more importantly, the *categories* in terms of which they were (and are) collected, manipulated and presented, have thus been integral to projects aimed at the political administration of civil society or, as we might now say following the argument thus far, the statistical constitution of the social body. One meaning of 'information' offered by the *Oxford English Dictionary* is 'the giving of a form or character to something . . . *e.g.* of the body by the soul'. In this reading, information accumulated by the state is used to help *form* – that is, *to give shape to* – the social body. Two examples concerning 'unemployment' and 'youth' in Britain illustrate the point in the domestic context.

Although 'unemployment' and 'unemployed' existed within the semantic frame of reference in the early nineteenth century – in trade union, radical and Owenite writings of the 1820s and 1830s, for example – it is only in the 1880s that 'unemployment' became a central category for understanding the social world. The late nineteenth-century shift away from questions concerning pauperism and towards questions concerning poverty was simultaneously a shift towards the administrative recognition of the working class. In this process a new category emerged – 'unemployment' – distinguishable from 'idle' and used to describe a social situation rather than a personal condition. Unemployment as an administrative category emerged through the work of political economists, such as Alfred Marshall, to finally take on widespread use and acceptance by 1895. Thus the first global reference to unemployed manual workers appeared in official documents in 1887; prior to this all the trades of the workers were simply listed. With the emergence of unemployment as a category of state administration the whole population can be regarded as existing on a plane of equivalence. On this plane each individual can be treated equally, as opposed to one of a series of groups, and thus becomes an individual object of administration and statistical calculation. This plane of equivalence, this category which became a central prism through which the social world of the twentieth century was viewed, was a product of state administration. The period in which 'unemployment' emerged as an *object of discourse* is the period in which it became a *category of state administration*.[90]

A similar point can be made concerning the category 'youth'. Part of the logic of the Employment and Training Act (1948) in Britain, for example, was the need to decide what to call the emergent employment scheme for the young working class and, as a consequence, what to call the young working class. Debates concerning the Bill focused on this as a central issue:

> We are dealing with young people from the ages of 15 to 18. They have left school and gone into work, and they consider themselves, rightly or wrongly, to have become adults. It does not help to . . . call them in bold letters 'juveniles'. There is nothing that will discourage and repel them more from coming forward to make use of these services. I would suggest that the Bill be amended and that the word 'juvenile' be eliminated altogether.

Debate regarding the best category to be used continued in both the Commons, the Lords and in Committee: 'in Committee we had a great deal of discussion about this word "juvenile" '. In the event, the word 'youth' was chosen, with the final reading of the Bill incorporating several amendments deleting 'juvenile' and inserting 'youth'. A new category was born, and with it a new means of classifying a section of the working class, for whom it was designed.[91] And whereas the category 'youth' had been designed in 1948 to attract young people into the notion of capitalist work, the rethinking of 'youth' in the 1980s was designed to attract them into the notion of training. Either way, it was a means of administering a group of people according to shifting regimes of accumulation. Ideologically presented as a biological-cum-psychological state, the category 'youth' was in fact *constructed* by the state as a means of constituting a section of the working class as bona fide proletarians in the making. In the case of both 'youth' and 'unemployment' it is important to note that the logic of state administration follows the logic of capital; it is the logic of capital imposed by the state.

Far from being 'natural' phenomena, 'unemployment' and 'youth' are state-generated categories through which the social world is perceived and through which it is structured by state institutions. The state constitutes what it claims to merely observe and analyse. At the same time, members of civil society come to *imagine* themselves through the categories which the state has generated for their administration. The same categories generated by the state are the ones which become tools in the crafting of modern subjectivity. A range of examples beyond 'unemployment' and 'youth' and from outside the British context might be given. David Campbell notes that in Yugoslavia the term 'Muslim' was not a separate category until the 1961 census, from when it had only 'quasi-national status', being fully established as a national category in the 1971 census. The effect was to establish 'Muslim' as a marker of identity, a fault line around which politics could then come to revolve. Similarly, Paul Starr comments on the statistical amalgamation into the category 'Hispanic' of groups as different as Cuban Americans, Puerto Ricans and Mexican Americans in the USA, an amalgamation which both reflected a political mobilization and advanced it. In Rwanda the categories 'Hutu' and 'Tutsi' had been fairly amorphous until the Belgian powers established them as central categories for colonial administration, and thus pushed individuals into accepting a certain classificatory identity.[92] And following Bernard Cohn's work on the colonial census there now exists a wealth of research on the ways in which the (racial) categories generated by what Benedict Anderson calls the 'classifying mind' of the colonial state helped create many of the social forms they purported to describe and measure.[93]

As much as the categories generated by the state's demand for knowledge of its own body shape the way the state imagines its territory and the civil society it seeks to order, it is also the case that the categories in question are meant to shape our way of comprehending the world. By establishing the categories through which its citizens come to imagine the world, the state makes a decisive contribution to the production and reproduction of the ideological and intellectual instruments in the construction of social reality. The categories generated in this way reiterate Pierre Bourdieu's suggestion that the act of naming helps to establish the structure of the world, and does so all the more significantly the more the act is authorized; that is, the more the act stems from established authority. The social process of classification is a deeply political rite of institution and an integral dimension of the class struggle, not least in its ability to shape the way classes are constituted: 'Through the framing it imposes upon practices, the state establishes and inculcates common forms and categories of perception and appreciation, social frameworks of perceptions, of understanding or of memory'.[94] This is what Bourdieu calls 'symbolic violence', a form of violence in which the state incarnates itself simultaneously in objectivity – in the form of specific organizational structures and mechanisms – and in subjectivity – in the form of mental structures and categories of perception and thought. Which is to say two things: first, that the efficacy of the state may lie as much in the ways in which it shapes our imagination as in the direct use of force and coercion. Second, that as much as the state encourages us to think in certain ways, its categories are designed to discipline the dialectical imagination: to the extent that modern social science merely adopts such categories as part of its research agenda, it reveals its inherently uncritical nature – its 'eyes down hands up' approach to the gifts of the state – doing little more than ratifying as a sociological issue a category devised by the state for the administration of civil society.

Arcana imperii: secrecy, privacy, idiocy

One reason the state is so obsessed with information is because of its permanent state of fear about what may or may not be happening – within its territory, beyond its borders, in the minds of those who oppose it as a threat. If in its search for (bodily) order the state appears to suffer from hypochondria, then in its search for (mental) stability it appears to suffer from paranoia. The Greek *paranoia* designates a deranged or distracted mind; for Freud, more specifically, the essential characteristics of the paranoid are an extreme distrust of others and, as a consequence, a perceived enmity towards those distrusted. Indifference slides easily into hate, 'stranger' slides into 'enemy'.[95] The facets of what Richard Hofstadter describes as the paranoid style of American politics – the assumption that there exists 'a vast, insidious, preternaturally effective international conspiratorial network designed to perpetrate acts of the most fiendish character' – permeate the state and its modes of operation.[96] The state therefore distrusts and treats with enmity more or less all that it encounters. I shall spell out the implications of this for the foreigner as stranger in Chapter 4. For the moment let us note that the state's paranoia means that anyone outside the state who challenges it or comes close to unravelling its knot of comprehensive intelligence is by definition an enemy – a 'security risk' – about whom yet more information must be obtained. This also explains why security measures themselves are often intelligence-gathering devices. For example, in Britain the Defence of the Realm Act (1798) was initially intended to collect information from every parish on how many men would defend the state, their level of fitness and what weapons they possessed, while the Prevention of Terrorism (Temporary Provisions) Act (first passed in 1974 and then every subsequent year, and used to justify most intrusions of privacy), was first and foremost an intelligence-gathering act.

State paranoia works in two directions. First, it means that the state is always assuming that there is something going on which it does not know about but which it should know about – hence the perpetual search for knowledge. Second, the state seeks to protect its knowledge from those who it regards as not having a *bona fide* reason to share it. The first point raises the question of privacy; the second raises the question of secrecy. I shall spend a little time with these two ideas because together they form part of a certain tendency within the bourgeois democratic imagination concerning state power. This tendency runs something like this: privacy is a democratic virtue; with its roots in the late-eighteenth century 'democratic revolutions' to its institutionalization in the various declarations on human rights now in existence, the right to privacy is a principle which can be used to defend us from the state and protect our liberties. At the same time, those holding such a view argue that secrecy in politics is a bad thing – the higher the degree of secrecy the state operates with, the less democratic it is.

Let me say a little more about the historical background to this before taking the argument any further. The idea that 'privacy' is a political virtue developed with the rise of capitalism, the consolidation of the state and the increasing dominance of liberal ideas concerning the public-private distinction. With the breakdown of feudalism the powers which had been the carriers of 'publicness' – the Church, the prince, the nobility – disintegrated into private elements on the one hand and public ones on the other. 'Private' came to imply exclusion from the sphere of the state apparatus and referred to an individual without public office or official position, while 'public' came to refer to the state that had developed, under absolutism, into an entity having an objective existence compared to the person of the ruler:

> The public (*das Publikum, le public*), was the 'public authority' (*öffentliche Gewalt*) in contrast to everything 'private' (*Privatwesen*). The servants of the state were *öffentliche Personen*, public persons, or *personnes publiques*; they were incumbent in some official position, their official business was 'public' (*öffentliches Amt, service public*), and government buildings and institutions were called 'public'. On the other hand, there were private individuals, private offices, private businesses, and private homes . . . The authorities were contrasted with the subjects excluded from them; the former served, so it was said, the public welfare, while the latter pursued their private interests.[97]

Moreover, 'the private' came to be thought of as both the basis of judging 'public' affairs and a sphere which needed to be protected from public authority. At the same time, however, 'the public' also gradually came to refer to the collection of otherwise private individuals, understood as together forming *a* public; hence the term 'public opinion'. These two notions of 'public' – official authority on the one hand and a collection of private individuals on the other – together gave rise to the notion of *publicity*. The public sphere was to be a sphere of reasoned argument – hence Kant's definition of enlightenment as 'the *public* use of man's reason'.[98] On this basis a certain rationality was expected to inhere in the law, a rationality in which what is right converged with what is just. This claim was made against absolutist forms of rule in which the sovereign exercised power and passed laws by decrees and edicts. For the public to engage in reasoned debate about legislative and executive action, such action must be made under 'free and open examination'.[99] Thus the principle of publicity could be used not just as part of the argument for rational debate, but could be turned against the established authorities.

This principle of publicity had a clear target: it was explicitly held up in opposition to the practice of secrets of state. For Kant, 'each individual requires to be convinced by reason that the coercion which prevails is lawful . . . Obedience without the spirit of freedom is the cause of all *secret societies*'; for Bentham arguments for publicity were simultaneously arguments against secrecy; for Paine 'mystery and secrecy on one side, is opposed to candour and openness on the other'.[100] The German term for 'public sphere' (*Öffentlichkeit*) captures this demand for publicity: the word was formed after the French and its original version was *Publizität*; the sphere is 'open' and therefore neither private nor secret. 'Publicity' was therefore pitched against the reliance of sovereign authority on secrets of state: 'just as secrecy was supposed to serve the maintenance of sovereignty based on *voluntas*, so publicity was supposed to serve the promotion of legislation based on *ratio*'.[101]

We therefore have two processes which have gone hand in hand. On the one hand, an increased stress on privacy; on the other, a demand for limiting state secrecy. As Georg Simmel notes, central details of state have lost their secrecy in the same measure in which the individual has gained the possibility of withdrawal into privacy. What is public became more public, while that which is private became ever more private.[102] This defence of the privacy of the private sphere and a demand for a reduction of the secrecy (or increasing the 'openness') of the public sphere has become a central feature of bourgeois ideology in its defence of liberal democracy. In this view, the democratic society is the one with an entrenched defence of privacy, preferably in a codified constitution, and in which as little of the affairs of state are carried out in secret as possible. These issues have received a new lease of life in recent years with many liberal democracies aiming to further entrench the 'right' to privacy and to move to more 'open' (i.e. less secretive) government – the Blair and Clinton regimes being the most obvious examples. These are moves which many on the Left have praised as progressive, radical and modernizing. In the rest of this chapter I shall build on the argument in the earlier sections and suggest that despite their ostensibly radical appearance and obvious appeal, demands for 'privacy' and 'open government' are in fact severely limited when being used to challenge the various forms of power which we may set ourselves against. These limitations reside in a combination of historical and political naivety. The outcome of this naivety, I shall suggest, is that it weakens rather than strengthens real opposition to state power.

Why do states keep secrets? The answer given by states themselves is that they need to protect themselves from enemies. But why do states keep *so many* secrets? Why do they keep secret information which often turns out to be either trivial or worthless, even to the enemy? One of the most common ways to answer this question has been to put state secrecy down to a quirk of political culture. Peter Hennessy, for example, suggests that secrecy is 'incorporated into the culture . . . [it is] as much a part of the English landscape as the Cotswolds. It goes with the grain of our society' – so much so that it can be traced back over 700 years. This position has been reiterated most recently by Tony Blair in his comments on the 'entrenched culture of secrecy' in Britain by way of introducing part of the move to 'open government'.[103] Despite the appeal to a particular feature of British political culture, the same idea has been used to explain secrecy in other countries.[104] But such claims to political culture in fact serve to conceal the real issue: that what is shrouded by the cloak of secrecy is nothing less than the *essence of the state*. As Weber notes, the tendency toward secrecy within the state has little to do with national culture and everything to do with the material nature of state power.[105] As with the state's desire for knowledge, the desire for secrecy is more important than the secrets themselves. Let me flesh this out with a little more detail.

In opening his *Patriarcha* (1680) Robert Filmer comments that he will 'have nothing to do to meddle with mysteries of the present state. Such *arcana imperii*, or cabinet councils, the vulgar may not pry into. An implicit faith is given to the meanest artificer in his own craft. How much more is it, then, due to a prince in the profound secrets of government'. Filmer had in mind comments such as that made by James I in his first appearance before the Star Chamber in 1616: 'the mysterie of the King's power, is not lawfull to be disputed; for that is to wade into the weaknesse of Princes, and to take away the mysticall reverence'.[106] James I was articulating the thoughts of other monarchs, repeated by a great many politicians since, and accepted by writers such as Filmer, that sovereignty is a mystery, to be piously accepted with a mystical reverence rather than explained to the subjects. The references to *arcana imperii* and mystery are early-modern versions of what we now know as *state secrecy*. *Arcanum* is another word for 'secret', derived from the Indo-European root *arek*, meaning to hold, contain or guard, but *arcanum imperii* also played on the aura of the sacredness of the *arcana ecclesiae*, transferring this aura from the Church and religious figures to the state and its officials. *Arcanum imperii* thus gives us 'secrets of state' or 'mysteries of state'.

The word 'secret' first came into use during the fifteenth century. Drawn from the Latin *secretus*, the past participle of *secerno* meaning 'to separate, to divide, to set apart', it has been suggested that the word 'secret' originates with the sifting of grain, whose purpose is to separate the edible from the inedible, the good from the bad. The separation is effected by a hole, the function of which is to allow something to pass or not to pass depending on the relation between the object's shape and the size of the hole. The word thus bespeaks discernment, the ability to make decisions and the capacity to sort out and draw distinctions. More to the point, the word bespeaks knowledge and a relation to others based on the dissimulation of that knowledge.[107] As we have seen, the doctrine of reason of state held that political knowledge was produced and developed not through public debate but by the sovereign body and its key officials. It is for this reason that all the writers well-versed in reason of state insist on the centrality of secrecy: Guicciardini comments that secrecy is a necessary feature of government; Botero claims that 'no quality is more necessary to those who conduct important negotiations in peace or war than the ability to observe secrecy'; Bocalini suggests that 'secrecy is no less necessary for the well-ordering of States, than good council'; and Francis Bacon has it that 'Concerning Government, it is a part of knowledge secret and retired, in both these respects in which things are deemed secret; for some things are secret because they are hard to know, and some because they are not fit to utter. We see all governments are obscure and invisible'. (Centuries later the wall of the US Joint Military Intelligence College, the training ground for American security and intelligence personnel, displayed an excerpt from a note from George Washington to Elis Dayton: 'upon secrecy, success depends'.)[108]

As such, the concept of 'official secrets' is typical of the mechanisms of political administration through which the state organizes civil society, as both Marx and Weber recognized: 'The general spirit of the bureaucracy is the *secret*, the mystery, preserved within itself by the hierarchy and against the outside world by being a closed corporation'. Out of this spirit arises the idea of 'official secrets', a product of the striving for power.[109] It is for this reason that secrets are kept even though they appear to be entirely harmless pieces of information the revelation of which would be of absolutely no use to any person or institution, either friend or enemy. Secrecy thus becomes part of the ritual of state power. As Malcolm Muggeridge noted regarding his time in the British Secret Service, 'secrecy is as essential to Intelligence as vestments and incense to a Mass, or darkness to a Spiritualist seance, and must at all costs be maintained, quite irrespective of whether or not it serves any purpose'.[110] And it is also for this reason that the state refuses to allow groups within civil society, especially opposition groups, to have secrets of their own. Any group which aims to retain some secrecy will of course be placed under surveillance and infiltrated by the state: reason of state, national security and the search for knowledge demands nothing less.[111] Secrecy, in other words, is part and parcel of state reason, facilitating the claims to omnipotence by the state; it renders the prince 'like a God', as Botero puts it.[112] And even where this impetus is not realized it plays a fundamental role in furthering the designs of the state. It bestows, legitimates and barricades state power.

Ironically, nothing proves this more than the attempts in recent years to achieve 'open government' – an idea proclaimed on both sides of the Atlantic in the 1990s. A few examples will suffice. In Britain the Ministry of Defence (MoD) reports on hydrodynamics are in theory available to the public as part of the new open government initiatives. In 1998 a Liberal Democrat MP asked the MoD for a list of the titles of its technical reports on hydrodynamics – without the list it is virtually impossible to know what papers exist to read. John Spellar, the Labour Defence Minister replied: 'I am withholding the information. While the individual reports are unclassified, a composite list gives a broader picture and is classified'. The research itself has been made public, but we are not allowed to know what research exists in the first place – a composite picture of all the research, in the simple form of a list of publications, remains secret. Similarly, the Industry Minister, when asked which companies had breached government guidelines on trading with dictatorships (after British companies had been caught selling electronic batons to Saudi Arabia), replied that the government could not name names for fear of harming the competitive position of the companies in question. When it comes to companies known by the government to be breaking the law, secrecy must be maintained; under a regime of open government, crimes committed by capital can be kept secret.

The annual reports of Parliament's committees dealing with issues concerning secrecy contain an enormous range of glaring deletions. In November 2000 the Commons Defence Committee issued a special report following media pressure to reduce secrecy and move to a more 'open' style of government. Group Captain Stephen Lloyd was asked how dependent the ministry was on US military intelligence. The answer was '***'. Asked whether the US makes available any of the material it gives to Britain to any other ally, the answer is '***'. Would US intelligence be available in an operation in which the USA was not involved? Answer, '***'. Likewise the Intelligence and Security Committee reported in 1998 that 'we also questioned the agencies closely on *** work on Iraq, and the extent of intelligence sharing with *** principal allies'. The same Committee's 2000 report claimed that 'the UK needs to be *** to ensure that the UK remains ***'. Commenting on intelligence failures in Kosovo, the 2000 report suggests that 'GCHQ did comment that ***, ***, ***. The committee is concerned that ***, ***. The foreign secretary stated that ***'. And so on. When asked if the range of censored passages in the report for the year 2000 showed that the secrecy was becoming even more prevalent, the Chair of the Committee replied that in fact the opposite is true – that they show just how much more open the government now is. From this it might be deduced that the British state is unable to actually distinguish between open government and secret government. In fact, the correct interpretation would be that the state has come to *define openness* in terms of its own *need for secrecy and knowledge*, as the following example illustrates.

Academics asking questions to the Health and Safety Executive (HSE) concerning industrial accidents suffered by North Sea riggers were to be monitored. The HSE warned its staff that 'we wish to monitor those who appear to have an interest in HSE activities and who may be looking to exploit replies received in ways unfavourable to the HSE'. And the memo concluded that 'any contact with these people should be reported to the Open Government Unit'. Not content with reasserting the need for secrecy in a world of open government and freedom of information, 'open government' is now a *synonym* for 'secret intelligence gathering'.[113]

In America – a state whose widely-admired written constitution was drafted in secrecy and provides a constitutional right to state secrecy (in Article 1, Section 5) – the Information Security Oversight Office, part of the National Archives and Records Administration which keeps records of classified information, summarized in 1996 the trend for that year as witnessing a decrease in secrecy and secret documents: the number of original classification authorities decreased by 959 to 4420, and the number of reported original classification decisions decreased by 62,000 to 105,163. But the report then gives the year's 'derivative' as opposed to original classification decisions ('derivative' refers to documents classified because they are incorporated, paraphrased, restated or otherwise referred to in classified information). Reported derivative classification decisions increased by 2.2 million to over 5.5 million. Thus the age of 'open government' and the attempt to bring an end to excessive secrecy resulted in a 62 per cent *increase* in new secret documents.[114]

That the intelligence forces of the US state has produced close to 6 million classified documents per annum since the end of the cold war suggests that the secrets are being kept less from any foreign enemy and more from the citizens and their elected representatives. Symbolically, secrecy proclaims that there are those who can be trusted with certain knowledge and those who cannot. Secrecy here connects up with the doctrine of reason of state in a compelling and dangerous way. Most appeals to secrecy by the state are accepted as legitimate by most citizens on the grounds of reason of state: we cannot release this information because of the advantage it may give our enemies; we cannot tell you any more for reasons of state. Conversely, most appeals to reason of state are accepted as legitimate by most citizens because of the imagined threat to security, but no more can be said about this threat due to the secret knowledge we have. Some writers have noted that secrecy thus becomes a powerful tool enabling dominant groups within the state to delegitimize their opponents and that this shows that secrecy constitutes the basic paradox of democratic politics.[115] But this is being too generous. The point is rather that the state imagines its citizens as untrustworthy – they are objects of information rather than subjects with knowledge.[116]

The argument can be pushed a little further. When the term *arcana* first came to be widely used in the sixteenth century, it was often used as a Latin equivalent of *sophismata*, a term that appears several times in Aristotle's *Politics* (e.g. at 1297a and 1308a). Michael Donaldson explains that *sophismata* refers to institutional arrangements that seem to offer political rights or power to those outside the ruling group without actually doing so, as, for example, in oligarchies where the common people are *permitted* to bear arms and to participate in assemblies but the nobles are *required* to do so. Such practices have the effect of disenfranchising the group whose participation is optional, while at the same time allowing them to feel that they have had a choice in the matter. Such methods, called 'republicae mysteria et arcana', are legitimate and do not constitute a defrauding of good citizens so much as a 'certain concealment of the mysteries' which is permissible when practised with an eye to avoiding the downfall of the state.[117]

Arcana therefore suggests not only secrecy but also tradition – in the form of an ancient and mysterious body of knowledge – of which the subjects are encouraged to think of themselves as part but are also encouraged not to participate in due to their lack of knowledge (the reading of the Bible and Mass in Latin rather than the language of the people is a perfect example). The tradition is thus theirs, but also not theirs; like the arcane knowledge held by the Church and incomprehensible to the uninitiated, it suggests belonging but inspires awe. The *arcana imperii* therefore refer not only to, in modern terminology, 'official secrets', but to instruments and practices for the justification of power; a power which individuals are encouraged to imagine themselves as part of but which none the less appears as essentially mysterious: James I's 'mysticall reverence'. *Arcana imperii* are thus not only secrets but are the *simulacra imperii* – the creation of illusions of power, a 'devising of the means whereby the plebs will be content' as Donaldson puts it. The importance of the *contempt of the people* to reason of state arguments here comes to the fore.[118] Like the doctrine of reason of state of which it is part, *arcana imperii* constitute a key device in which subjection is legitimated by clothing the body politic in a mysterious veil.

One of the features of the history of secrecy is that it has a peculiar relation to privacy. Where the Latin form of secrecy is *secretus* (to separate from, divide from), the Latin form of privacy is *privatus*, meaning 'to free from'. Historically, the notions were so close that Samuel Johnson saw the two words as interchangeable, defining privacy as 'state of being secret; secrecy' and secrecy as 'privacy; state of being hidden'.[119] At some point, however, the two words were drawn far enough apart for them to be treated separately: privacy became a good thing, secrecy became a bad thing. But one of the implications in what I have been arguing is that because of the state's perpetual paranoia concerning knowledge, it will always be engaged in actions that infringe privacy, no matter how hard we try to stop it. The very activities which are most frequently said to infringe our privacy are the very activities through which the state expresses its need and desire to *know* its population. It is part and parcel of the state's search for knowledge that it will infringe our privacy at every possible turn and will keep such infringements as secret as it can.[120] By way of ending this chapter with a (more) polemical conclusion, I want to push this argument one step further by highlighting the limits of the liberal political imagination in this area.

As I suggested earlier, privacy became a central trope of bourgeois democracy's claim to superiority. John Stuart Mill contrasts ancient commonwealths which sought 'the regulation of every part of private conduct by public authority' with the 'modern world [in which] political communities . . . prevented so great an interference by law in the details of private life'. Similarly, Alexis de Tocqueville claims that 'to taste the pleasures of private life' one must follow the Americans and beware the political encroachments in these pleasures, for 'as the extent of political society expands, one must expect the sphere of private life to contract'.[121] From arguments such as these the idea of privacy has become one of the central tropes within debates about bourgeois democracy: defenders like to say that bourgeois democracy's liberal nature protects privacy better than any other system, while many of its Leftist critics have argued that it fails to protect privacy enough. Rather than take sides here, a broader point needs to be made. Hannah Arendt points out that it is easy to forget quite how significant a historical and ideological transformation was effected by liberal democracy in the defence of privacy. Historically, privacy had been a negative state – the state of privation, of being deprived. For the Greeks, those experiencing privacy were being deprived, and what they were being deprived of was participation in the *polis*:

> To live an entirely private life means above all to be deprived of things essential to a truly human life: to be deprived of the reality that comes from being seen and heard by others, to be deprived of an 'objective' relationship with them that comes from being related to and separated from them through the intermediary of a common world of things, to be deprived of the possibility of achieving something more permanent than life itself. The privation of privacy lies in the absence of others.[122]

To Arendt's point we should add that it is just as easy to forget how big a *political* demand is made on us when we accept the idea of privacy as a central organizing feature of our politics.

In most of the literature on privacy the idea is related to the rise of individualism. There is a well-known argument that individualism as a theory and the idea of the person as an individual have their origins in the rise of capitalism.[123] Putting privacy in this context reveals an important if rather obvious point: that the defence of privacy historically went hand in hand with its defence of capital. In other words, in helping shape a particular defence of the individual, 'privacy' was ideologically functional to the consolidation of the power of capital. No better evidence for this point can be found than Adam Smith's *Wealth of Nations*, in which 'private' gets used more times than 'wealth'.[124] 'Private', after all, is a word most frequently conjoined with 'property'. And it is worth reminding ourselves that when conjoined with 'property', 'private' by no means necessarily refers to a human individual, but also to exclusionary property rights claimed by corporate bodies which (or rather 'who', for reasons we will encounter in the next chapter) can then appear as *bona fide* persons in law. This tells us that as much as 'privacy' may be used to defend individual human rights, it can just as easily be used to defend the corporate rights of capital: the right, for example, to extract a surplus from wage-labour or to put the interests of shareholders above the safety of workers or consumers. And as we shall see, these rights are created and defended by the state.

As a principle around which we might organize resistance to forms of oppression, then, it has to be noted that privacy can be used as much by certain structures of power as against them. Moreover, as an essentially liberal concept, privacy does little more than demand certain *individual* liberties. In and of itself this has had some success, of course, and it would be churlish to claim otherwise. But the small-scale victories achieved by marching under the banner of privacy do little to mitigate against the large-scale defeat I have been discussing here, a defeat that continues to be consolidated in the minutiae of legislative and executive action. Thus some 200 years after first being articulated as a human right, the insistence on privacy has not stopped the British state from passing the Regulation of Investigatory Powers Act (2000) allowing it to monitor email and internet traffic through 'black boxes' placed inside service provider systems (and note that a secret code embedded in Microsoft software enables US security services to spy on everybody in the world who uses Windows and the internet); nor has it stopped the British state from building a £25 million email surveillance centre at MI5; nor has it stopped British intelligence elites from searching for ways to log and store for seven years every phone call made in Britain; nor has it stopped the number of warrants issued in England and Wales for telephone tapping and mail opening from reaching the highest figure (1763 in 1997–8) since records began; nor has it stopped the current regime from pushing through the new Terrorism Acts of 2000 and 2001 enabling state agencies to treat as 'terrorist' all forms of 'protesting' organizations and individuals, including trade unions and pacifist organizations, or even just individuals wearing t-shirts or badges with slogans on, and thus subject them to ongoing surveillance.[125] There is nothing peculiarly British about such developments – a plethora of examples from other states could be given, not least the recent 'Proved Appropriate Tools Required to Intercept and Obstruct Terrorism (PATRIOT) Act' in the USA. However futile these attempts may turn out to be, they reveal the contempt for privacy held by those within the state and their willingness to infringe even the basic rudiments of 'private' life – since 'an information war has no front line', as the 1998 US Defence Department Report put it,[126] no state will ever be willing to see a 'private' space as a limit on its power.

More important, however, is the fact that even where successfully used to limit state power, the mantra of privacy rests on a political imagination in which human beings are split between *public* and *private* selves. This has obviously historically been integral to *political* emancipation, but in doing so it has come to *tie us* to both capital and the state rather than liberate us from them. The 'right to privacy' in this sense merely confirms the processes of individualization and commodification in which we find ourselves and which we should be struggling against. It confirms the individualism of bourgeois society by proffering legal confirmation that we can indeed assert our egos against the state; and it confirms the commodification of modern society because it reinforces the prevalence of a concept which can just as easily be used by corporate power in its struggle to create a world after its own image.

To put the above in another way: what 'privacy' manifestly fails to do as an organizing concept is to imagine any grounds for *collective* resistance – to either state or capital. This is precisely what capital and the state want us to do: they want us to remain rooted in the legacy of the eighteenth-century Robinsonades, to choose the life of what the Greeks thought of as the idiot – a life of 'one's own' (*idion*) – instead of a life in collective pursuit of a rational society. They want us to imagine being up against power – the social power of capital as well as the political power of the state – as (private) individuals rather than as a collective subject; in other words, they want us to be idiots. In this sense, to insist on privacy is to play into the hands of the political power of the state and the social power of capital, for not only can the state grant the right to privacy while simultaneously infringing it at every turn, but it can do so by dealing with us as private individuals protecting our own rather than as a collective subject aiming to achieve something 'more permanent than life itself' (in Arendt's terms): change of a more lasting, world historical importance.

3   The personality of the state

The astute reader will have noticed that the previous chapter never really got round to dealing with the question of mind head-on, so to speak. Instead, a complex of terms associated with mind came to the fore: will, reason, intelligence. We have not left the question of mind entirely, however, but we can only return to it via a discussion of a different yet related aspect of the statist imaginary: the idea of the personality of the state.

That the state may be considered a 'person' or 'personality' appears at first sight as an affront to our political sensibilities. We are told time and again that one of the key features of the modern state is its *impersonal* nature – that no single person or group of persons either is, or controls, the state – and that in modernity legitimacy rests heavily on the assumption of the impersonality of state power. The state may be a collection of institutions, an ideological construct, a social relation – anything *but* a person. Yet if we take one of the earliest statements in the theory of the state, Hobbes' *Leviathan*, we find that the question of personality is crucial. The most frequently discussed aspect of *Leviathan*, Part II 'Of Common-wealth', in which he discusses the causes and generation of a commonwealth, the rights of sovereigns, the liberties of subjects, the power of law and the myriad other topics which have become the key discussion points of the discipline of politics, follows the argument in the final chapter of Part I, 'Of Persons, Authors, and things Personated'. As David Gauthier has pointed out, the chapter bears no obvious relation to what has gone before, nor is there any explanation of the uses to which the concepts it introduces are to be put. Indeed, it initially appears as a kind of appendix to the psychology of man outlined in the previous chapters rather than as part of Hobbes' arguments concerning sovereignty and power.[1] But as it turns out, the chapter is crucial to what follows because it introduces the concepts of person and authorization. For Hobbes, the fundamental questions concerning authority – How is it constituted? What are its limits? – can only be answered when some other, conceptually prior, questions have been answered: What is authorization and, relatedly, Who or what can authorize? This in turn begs a broader question: What is an author? And a final question: How is it that the mass of individuals in a state of nature can collectively form the sovereign through covenant? Hobbes' answers to these questions reveal him to be a theorist not just of the modern state, but of the state as a particular kind of person.

The argument in this chapter takes Hobbes' arguments as the starting point, in order to unpick the role that personification plays in the statist political imagination. I shall argue that although the idea of the 'person' of power may appear as anachronistic as the idea of the body politic, rooted in pre-modern forms of political association now long gone, this is far from the case. Instead, I shall suggest that thinking through the political issues concerning the question of personality helps raise for us some of the key issues of state power. Readers non-conversant with Hobbes' work may find the first section overly technical. For the sake of clarity, let me spell out what I aim to achieve. I aim to draw out two points: first, to show that what is at stake in the discussion of person and personality is the convergence of unity and domination in the political form of the state. Second, in the sections which follow I aim to show how this convergence penetrated the image of *social* power, in the guise of the *persona* of corporate capital. For this dimension of the statist imaginary alerts us to the fact that the social world as well as the political world is dominated by *non-human persons*. As I shall show via a detour through contemporary company law, the question of the 'person' thus takes us into the everyday world of social and political power.

Hobbes' person

Hobbes' answers to the questions concerning authorization raised above rest heavily on his conception of a person, and come to the fore in Chapter 16 of *Leviathan*: 'A Person, is he, *whose words or actions are considered, either as his own, or as representing the words or actions of an other man, or of any other thing to whom they are attributed, whether Truly or by Fiction*'.[2] Thus 'to *Personate*, is to *Act*, or *Represent* himselfe, or an other; and he that acteth another, is said to beare his Person, or act in his name'.[3] Hobbes thus distinguishes between two types of person – the natural person, whose words or actions are 'considered as his owne', and the 'feigned' or 'artificial' person, who is 'considered as representing the words and actions of an other'.[4] An artificial person is a real man or group of men, considered as representing some other man, or group of men, or thing.

The reference to 'acting another' indicates that Hobbes' ideas concerning representation are part and parcel of his appropriation of the terminology from the stage. The English 'person' originated from the Latin *persona*, which in turn originated from the Greek, where it referred to the mask worn by actors on the stage:[5]

> The word Person is latine: instead whereof the Greeks have πρόσωπον, which signifies the *Face*, as *Persona* in latine signifies the *disguise*, or *outward appearance* of a man, counterfeited on the Stage; and sometimes more particularly that part of it, which disguiseth the face, as a Mask or Visard: And from the Stage, hath been translated to any Representer of speech and action, as well in Tribunalls, as Theaters. So that a *Person*, is the same that an *Actor* is, both on the Stage and in common Conversation.[6]

It is the same theatrical terminology which provides Hobbes with his account of persons as authors and actors:

> Of Persons Artificiall, some have their words and actions *Owned* by those whom they represent. And then the Person is the *Actor*; and he that owneth his words and actions, is the Author: In which case the Actor acteth by Authority. For that which in speaking of goods and possessions, is called an *Owner*, and in latine *Dominus*, in Greek χύριος, speaking of Actions, is called an Author. And as the Right of possession, is called Dominion; so the Right of doing any Action, is called Authority.[7]

What gives an actor – that is, a representative – authority is the covenant the actor makes with the author. That is, the person who authorizes the action. In other words, to act by authority of another is to have been commissioned or licensed to do so; and such a commission of licence takes the form of a voluntary transfer of right.

How does this help us get at the idea of the person of the state? As we have seen, Hobbes distinguishes between natural and feigned or artificial persons: 'When they [a person's actions] are considered as his owne, then is he called a *Naturall Person*: And when they are considered as representing the words and actions of an other, then he is a *Feigned* or *Artificiall person*'.[8] The flow of the last sentence suggests that the artificial person is the representative, an interpretation endorsed by Hobbes' comment later in the chapter that 'Of Persons Artificiall, some have their words and actions *Owned* by those whom they represent'. And the later *De Homine* also makes the point clear: 'Because the concept of person is of use in civil affairs, it can be defined as follows: *a person is he to whom the words and actions of men are attributed, either his own or another's*: if his own, the person is *natural*; if another's it is *artificial*.'[9]

It is clear from this that some natural persons can also act as artificial persons, by being representative of others. But Hobbes' principal interest lies in artificial persons who are not natural persons at all – that is, persons capable of being represented but incapable of acting themselves. Some human beings such as 'Children, Fooles, and Mad-men', fall into this category, as do certain 'inanimate things' such as 'a Church, an Hospital, a Bridge'. These cannot be authors, but they can be represented. In fact Hobbes notes that 'there are few things that are uncapable of being represented by Fiction'.[10] The point here, however, is that this process of representation is one of 'personation': churches, hospitals and bridges are *personated* by rectors, masters and over-seers. Similarly, 'a Multitude of men, are made *One* Person, when they are by one man, or one Person, Represented'. In translating the text into Latin, Hobbes is more explicit, stating that since there are few things incapable of being represented, 'there are few things incapable of being persons'.[11] And in *De Homine* the position is even clearer: 'Even an inanimate thing can be a person, that is, it can have possessions and other goods, and can act in law'.[12]

It is at this point that Hobbes begins to consider the mechanism by which a state is constituted. As we have seen, a multitude is made one by being represented. Because 'the Multitude naturally is not *One*, but *Many*' it is the representer rather than the represented that constitutes the many into a unity. 'It is the *Unity* of the Represented, not the *Unity* of the Represented, that maketh the Person *One*. And it is the Representer that beareth the Person, and but one Person'.[13] It is on the basis of this argument that Hobbes can then open Part II of *Leviathan*, 'Of Common-wealth', and spell out the origin and nature of the sovereign state:

> The only way to erect such a Common Power, as may be able to defend them from the invasion of Forraigners, and the injuries of one another, and thereby to secure them in such sort, as that by their owne industrie, and by the fruites of the Earth, they may nourish themselves and live contentedly; is ... to appoint one Man, or Assembly of men, to beare their Person. This is more than Consent, or Concord; it is a reall Unitie of them all, in one and the same Person ... This done, the Multitude so united in one Person, is called a Common-wealth, in latine Civitas.[14]

Thus the state 'is *One Person*' – 'the greatest of humane Powers' created via an act of authorization.[15] The concept of person is thus crucial to Hobbes' thinking, for the state can only arise out of the capacity of artificial persons to represent natural persons; a state is therefore only a state when a group of natural persons is represented by the same artificial person.

It is important to note the relation between this person in question and the sovereign. The common interpretation that the person brought into existence by mutual covenant is the sovereign cannot be right, since it is clear that the name of the person created by the transformation of the multitude into one person is not 'sovereign' but 'state' (or 'commonwealth' or 'civitas', Hobbes' other terms for 'state'). For Hobbes, the sovereign 'carryeth this Person'.[16] Thus sovereigns are not the proprietors of their sovereignty. Rather, they are holders of offices with duties attached. This means that, on the one hand, the sovereign – which may be a natural person (monarchy) or an assembly of natural persons (democracy or aristocracy) – is the representative of the subjects, 'the Person representative of all and every one of the Multitude'.[17] On the other hand, it also means that the sovereign is 'always the representative of the Common-wealth'; that is, the sovereign is representative of another person: the '*Persona Civitas*, the Person of the Common-wealth' – the state.[18] Indeed, the sovereign mediates between two types of person – the person of the state and the persons that make up the multitude. It is for this reason that once Hobbes embarks on his arguments concerning the sovereign power he has recourse to descriptions of the sovereign as 'bearing', 'carrying', 'presenting' or 'representing' the person, and that this terminology is at its peak in Chapters 17 through to 19.[19]

There is an irony in the fact that this idea of the person of the state is developed in a text which can be taken as one of the most crucial contributions to the theory not just of the state, but of the state as an *im*personal force. The modern assumption is that the state requires a categorical separation between person and office. For this to happen, the state has to be radically abstracted from the persons who govern through it. This is the distinction between Machiavelli and Hobbes. Whereas for the former the state is still an essentially personal force, being the property of the prince, the latter provides the classic statement of modern state power: the state is *impersonal*, in the sense that it is *not the property* of any one person or group of persons. And yet Hobbes none the less has recourse to the category of the person. It is almost as though having expelled the notion of personality in one sense, Hobbes had to allow it in through the back door in another guise. The crucial political question is: Why? One answer might be that the authoritarian tropes in Hobbes' work lend themselves so naturally to absolutist monarchy that Hobbes was led to think about authority in terms of individual persons; another answer might be that Hobbes' imagination is here revealed as still essentially pre-modern. But neither of these answers seem right. We know that Hobbes believed that his arguments applied to more than monarchical states, and that in any case he conceives the body politic as sometimes mechanical and sometimes monstrous, a conception that would not sit easily with the monarch. More tellingly, if Hobbes' position here is pre-modern, then why is it that writers as diverse as Kant,[20] Rousseau,[21] Hegel,[22] a range of lesser German political theorists with a juridical bent,[23] and, as we shall see towards the end of this chapter, even those who sought to move beyond state sovereignty such as the pluralists, all utilized the notion of the person when imagining power?

A better answer would seem to lie in the implications contained in the notion of person. As we saw in Chapter 1, the person of the state shares with other persons a corporeal existence as the body politic. But as we also saw in Chapter 1, there is something fundamentally different about this particular person: this person is nothing less than the mortal God to which we owe *our unity as a people*: 'A Multitude of men, are made *One* person, when they are by one man, or one Person, Represented; so that it be done with the consent of every one of that Multitude in particular. For it is the *Unity* of the Representer, not the *Unity* of the Represented, that maketh the Person *One* . . . And *Unity* cannot otherwise be understood in Multitude'.[24] Hobbes is here no doubt playing on one of the roots of *persona* in *per se una* – 'united in itself',[25] but the general effect is to produce an image in which the central theme is the *convergence of unity and domination*.[26] In terms of the former, Hobbes makes the point that 'this is more than Consent, or Concord; *it is a reall Unitie of them all*, in one and the same Person'.[27] Hobbes' conception of the person of the state *vis-à-vis* the multitude is made in order to *deny* the multitude its *own* subjectivity – to deny it a unity independent of the state. Indeed, in Hobbes' theory the political function of the multitude is to *cancel* itself – it can only become a collective by handing its power over to the person of the state.[28] Hobbes simultaneously denies the multitude its own personality by having it generate the personality of the state. In so doing the person of the state comes to stand above all other persons, both natural and artificial. The state thus simultaneously becomes the *grounds of the unity* of the multitude. On the other hand, and in terms of the latter, as the mechanism for the defence of the multitude against violence and disorder the person of the state also becomes the *grounds of their domination*. The 'terror' through which the state rules is founded on the unity the state provides. If the state failed to perform this task the multitude could unite against it – the function of the unity provided by the state is thus to keep 'the people from uniting into a body able to oppose' it.[29]

In adopting the terminology of personification, the state is thus imagined as an entity which shares in the discourse of subjectivity, producing a particular political effect – the corporate identity of the state – and facilitating the process of incorporation so central to the trope of order. The person of the state thus not only forms the basis of the convergence of domination and unity, but does so by figuring domination *as* unity. At the same time, however, it also serves to legitimize the practices through which the state comes to dominate civil society – authority in the form of the person.

In the rest of this chapter I shall argue that what such an imagination does is to simultaneously take from and develop the main structural forms of *social* domination: the power of capital. The argument will then lead us back into the question of the personality – and thus the mind – of the state. While this argument will sometimes resemble a state-derivation position, in which aspects of the capitalist state are derived from the commodity-relation, I am in fact arguing that the notion of the person has been one way in which the *parallel* forms of power in contemporary society – capital and the state – have been imagined.

The personification of capital

In capitalist society, individuals are related directly to each other via social relations founded on commodity-production. They relate to each other not as members of society but as owners of determined things – that is, as 'social representatives' of the different factors of production. In his critique of political economy, Marx describes this as the process of personification. He makes a point of stating in the preface to the first edition of *Capital* that 'individuals are dealt with here only in so far as they are the personifications of economic categories, the bearers [*Träger*] of particular class-relations and interests', a point reiterated throughout the three volumes: 'except as capital personified, the capitalist has no historical value'; 'the capitalist simply personifies industrial capital'; 'he [the capitalist] represents capital only as functioning capital . . . [he] is its personification in so far as it functions'.[30] The significance of this point is reinforced throughout the three volumes.[31]

With this notion of personification, Marx understands the process through which the existence of a thing with a predetermined social form, such as capital, enables the owners to appear in a particular form – a 'capitalist' – and to thus enter concrete production relations with other people.[32] This notion has tended to be passed over in commentaries on Marx as little more than a simple methodological device: Marx is interested in capital as a social process of exploitation and domination, and so wishes to sideline the decisions of individual capitalists; each individual capitalist is thus treated solely as though they were the personification of capital. I will argue here that in the process of employing this methodological device, Marx inadvertently hits an important nail on the head. What he misses, however, is a far more important target for the nail itself. I will therefore twist Marx's formulations and argue that part of the process of personification enables *things* to appear as *non-human persons*, and that this process, achieved via a transformation of company law, has been fundamental to the consolidation of the social power of corporate capital.[33]

We have seen that Hobbes' account of persons was consciously rooted in the etymology of the stage, and commentators have tended to highlight this feature. But it is easy to overplay Hobbes theatrical terminology at the cost of another far more important link – with private property. Marx appeared to grasp this connection, where personification is linked to the *economic stage*: 'we shall find, in general, that the characters who appear on the economic stage are merely personifications of economic relations; it is as the bearers of these economic relations that they come into contact with each other'; the capitalist and wage-labourer are 'specific social characters'.[34] The link Marx makes here between the stage and socio-economic roles prompts us to consider whether that which initially appears in Hobbes' work as 'theatrical' terminology may in fact be nothing less than the terminology of private property.

For example, we have seen that the terms 'author' and, relatedly, 'authorization', are crucial to Hobbes' argument. The modern meaning of the term 'author' appears relatively late. In Latin, *auctor* originally designates the person who intervenes in the case of a minor or a person who, for whatever reason, does not have the capacity to authorize a legally valid act; thus *auctoritas patrum* is the ratification that the senators bring to a popular resolution to make it valid and obligatory in all cases. But the oldest meanings of the term also include *vendor* in the act of transferring property. The seller is said to be *auctor* in so far as their will, merging with that of the buyer, validates and legitimates the property at issue. The transfer of property thus appears as a convergence of at least two parties in a process in which the right of the acquirer is always founded on that of the seller, who becomes the buyers *auctor*. The *Digest* of Roman law thus notes that *non debeo melioris condicioni esse, quam auctor meus, a quo ius in me transit* [my right to property is, in a necessary and sufficient fashion, founded on that of the buyer, who 'authorizes' it]. In any case, what is essential is the idea of a relationship between two subjects in which one acts as *auctor* for the other: *auctor meus* is the name given by the buyer to the current seller, who renders the property legitimate.[35]

This concept of the *auctor* in Roman law is thus connected to the elementary form of private property – *persona-res*. Part of the inspiration for Hobbes' account of the person of the state was the *Digest* of Roman law. Book XIV of the *Digest* opens by considering the implications of the fact that owners of various kinds of property – specifically, the owners of ships and shops – can appoint other persons to serve as their captains or managers. The law describes the circumstances in which one might be liable for the consequences of actions performed on your behalf when you have appointed someone as your agent, and in particular the responsibility for them.[36] We have already seen that where in *Leviathan* Hobbes identifies the stage as a source of his ideas concerning the person, he also comments that the same issue of 'authorizing' is central to property ownership: 'the Actor acteth by Authority. For that which in speaking of goods and possessions, is called an *Owner*, and in latine *Dominus*, in Greek χύριοζ, speaking of Actions, is called an Author. And as the Right of possession, is called Dominion; so the Right of doing any Action, is called Authority'. In *De Cive* his example of civil persons who are not cities is 'the companies of merchants'. And *De Homine* also spells out the link between the state as person and private property: 'Even an inanimate thing can be a person, that is, it can have possessions and other goods, and can act in law, as in the case of a temple, a bridge, or of anything whatsoever that needs money for its upkeep'.[37]

Now, at first sight *persona-res* as the elementary form of property appears to imply a self-contained structure of a person and a thing. But as Geoff Kay and James Mott point out, it is far more than that, for in a society where private property is the universal mode of appropriation, the legal form *persona-res* is the very sinew that binds society together; the *'persona'* in question is nothing less than an abstract owner of commodities raised to the heavens.[38] As capital developed in the industrial age, however, it became clear that this classical legal form of property was inadequate for the capital form. Teasing out some of the issues involved in this development will enable us to make more sense of the question of personality.[39]

Prior to 1832 in Britain, corporate status was only possible through Royal Charter or special statute. The defeat of the landed aristocracy meant that reform of the legal structure of capital could take place on the scale required. The Joint Stock Companies Registration and Regulation Act (1844) laid down three principles that have remained central to company law. It drew a clear distinction between joint stock companies and private partnerships by providing for the registration of all new companies with more than 25 members or with transferable shares; it provided for full publicity, as a safeguard against fraud; and it provided for incorporation through the act of registration alone rather than a special Act or Charter. At this stage, however, limited liability, the other crucial aspect of company law, was still absent, and remained so until the Joint Stock Companies Act (1856) and then the Companies Acts (1862) allowed incorporation with limited liability to be obtained by just seven persons signing and registering a memorandum of association. Even though this was intended to apply to joint stock companies it became clear that by reducing to seven the number of persons required to form an association, and not specifying a minimum number of shares, the scope of the company legal form could potentially include small partnerships and one-man enterprises, so long as seven persons could be found among whom company shares could be divided. The decision of the House of Lords in *Salomon v. Salomon and Co. Ltd* (1897) validated the one-man enterprise[40] and the Limited Partnerships Act (1907) formally defined and recognized the private company as the legal form of capital. The historic significance of this for the intensification of capital accumulation was enormous. The joint-stock company is often interpreted as either a measure of convenience designed to protect the interests of individual investors, or as a key moment in the developing separation between ownership and control. But both these interpretations fail to grasp its real significance, which lies in the fact that what was being developed was a special legal subjectivity for capital, arising from the nature of capital as such.[41]

To grasp the nature of this special legal subjectivity we need to distinguish between the company as an economic and a legal form. By 1855 the company legal form (i.e. incorporation with limited liability) was confined to the joint-stock company economic form and deliberately withheld from economic partnerships and one-man enterprises. Yet by 1914 the company legal form had become the normal form of enterprise in English manufacturing despite the fact that the joint-stock company was subordinate to partnerships. Thus the triumph of the company legal form was due to private partnerships turning themselves into private limited companies: by 1914, 75 per cent of companies were 'private' and thus not organized on a joint-stock basis. The meaning attached to the term 'company' was thus transformed: from denoting an association of a particular *economic* nature with no connotations as to legal form, it had come to signify an association of a particular *legal* status with no connotations as to *economic* form. The company, in other words, had taken on the legal status of the corporation.[42] Between 1844 and 1914, then, the company or corporate form was constituted as the legal subjectivity of capital.

This legal subjectivity had two components. On the one hand there was the constitution of a new legal body, the incorporated company. It is often claimed that *Salomon* v. *Salomon* opened the path for the recognition of the incorporated company as a separate legal entity. In fact the real shift occurred in the wording of the 1856 and 1862 Acts. The 1856 Act regarded persons as forming *themselves* into an incorporated company. The 1862 Act saw persons as forming a company *by them* but not *of them*. The earlier Act identified the company with the members, the later Act identified the company as something separate from and external to them – from then on, companies have been referred to as 'it' rather than 'they'. On the other hand there was the constitution of a new form of property, the share, the legal nature of which had simultaneously been reconceptualized. In the eighteenth and early nineteenth centuries ownership of a 'share' was taken to mean ownership of a share of the company's assets. By the time private companies had been placed on a statutory basis (in 1907) the share had been fully constituted as property in its own right, and in a host of cases the courts found that shareholders in incorporated companies had interests only in the profits and not the assets. The essential link between the corporation as a separate legal subject and the share as a form of property is that the shareholder has no property in or right to any particular asset of a company other than the share; ownership of a share of stock in British Telecom gives the holder no right to go off with a telephone box. All the shareholder can claim as a right is to have the assets of the company administered in accordance with the constitution of the company – to attend annual meetings, receive the annual report, to vote on certain matters and, crucially, a right to a share in the surplus value produced through the company's consumption of labour power.[43] Thus the link between shares and assets had been broken, a process which helped define the company as a new legal subject: the property of the company is *precisely the property of the company*, not of the shareholders. In effect, the development of company law had produced a new form of legal subject, the private corporation, and a new form of property, the share. A dual separation was effected between companies and their shareholders, and shareholders and their shares.

That the property of the company is the property of the company and not the shareholders is a necessary corollary of the company form. Limited liability established the corporation as a new and independent legal subject every bit as real in law as the new personal subjects of the classic legal form, *though totally removed from those subjects*.[44] The corporation is the real or active owner of the capital it employs: where this capital is the object of property, the corporation is the subject. On the other hand, the corporation comprises nothing but capital – the investments of shareholders – so that capital is present at both poles of property, as both subject and object. This is the characteristic legal form of capital corresponding adequately to its economic form.[45]

The point is that this legal subject took to the stage as a fully-fledged legal *persona*, a point which, by the late nineteenth century, states in capitalist societies made great efforts to make clear: in 1889 the British 'Interpretation Act' (an 'Act for consolidating the enactments relating to the Construction of Acts of Parliament and for further shortening the Language used in Acts of Parliament') stated that 'in the Act and in every Act passed after the commencement of this Act the expression "person" shall, unless the contrary intention appears, include any body of persons corporate or unincorporate', while in 1886 in *Santa Clara County* v. *Southern Pacific Railroad* the US Supreme Court held that 'a corporation is a person, within the meaning of the Fourteenth Amendment'.[46]

There is a direct parallel here with Hobbes' account of the state. On the one hand, capital becomes an 'utterly impersonal class force',[47] in the same way that Hobbes' emergent state was an impersonal political force. On the other hand, this new legal subjectivity for capital was imagined and shaped through the language of the person, in much the same way that Hobbes' state was conceptualized as a person. More pertinent, however, is the fact that the person generated for and by the company form replicates the convergence of unity and domination found in Hobbes' account of the person of the state. The corporate form allows disparate capitals or investors to act as a *unity* on the juridical stage. At the same time, however, and of course also in part because of this unity, the corporation has come to *dominate* the very society which generates it. The *person of the corporation* thus *replicates state power* through its *unity as the basis for domination*. Moreover, we should add that this legal form was constituted for capital by the state, a point to which I return below.

In a way, then, one is tempted to reverse Marx's famous formula regarding the fetishism of the commodity. Marx comments that the commodity possesses not just a value-in-use, but also a value-in-exchange; as such it takes on a social form. What in fact 'is nothing but the definite social relation between men themselves' assumes 'the fantastic form of a relation between things'.[48] In fact, in contemporary capitalism one might argue that the objective market 'relations between things' assumes the form of 'relations between persons'.[49] And just as for Marx the fetishism of the world of commodities arises from the peculiar social character of the world of labour which produces them, so we might say that the fetishism of the world of persons arises from the peculiar legal character of the world of capital which produces them. Either way, the process of the personification of capital that I have been describing is the flip side of a process in which natural persons come to be treated as commodities. In a capitalist society the worker, as *human* subject, sells labour as an object. As relations of production are reified so things are personified – human subjects become objects and objects become subjects – an irrational, 'bewitched, distorted and upside-down world' in which 'Monsieur le Capital' takes the form of a social character – a *dramatis personae* on the economic stage, no less.[50]

Nothing illustrates this bewitched, distorted and upside-down world more directly than the way 'crimes' committed by capital are dealt with by the state. When in *Salomon* v. *Salomon* the House of Lords held that a corporation is a person distinct from the individual persons who compose it, it also held that corporations, unlike human persons, could not commit torts which demand a guilty intention, nor crimes which require *mens rea*. In doing so it raised an issue stretching back to Pope Innocent IV at the Council of Lyon in 1245 and forward to debates about corporate manslaughter in the twenty-first century: can we speak of the mind of the corporation? Asking this question will, in a roundabout way, return us to the question of mind in the previous chapter. In *Edwards* v. *Midland Railway* (1880) an action for malicious prosecution against the railway company, the defendants claimed that 'a corporation, not being possessed of a mind, could not be liable for malicious prosecution, which involved a mental state'. Justice Fry conceded that 'great evils will arise if, on the ground that a corporation can have no mind, and therefore can have no malice, a corporation were able to escape from that liability'. Referring to the ruling in an earlier case concerning the same railway company which held that 'it must be shown that the defendant was actuated by animus in his mind', the judge held that 'it is equally absurd to suppose that a body corporate can do a thing willfully, which implies will; intentionally, which implies intention; and maliciously, which implies malice. They are all acts of the mind, and one is no more capable of being done by a corporation . . . than the other'. The same position was held well into the twentieth century: in *Continental Tyre and Rubber Co., Ltd* v. *Daimler Co. Ltd* (1915) the Court of Appeal argued that 'the artificial legal person called the corporation has no physical existence. It exists only in contemplation of law . . . It has no mind other than the minds of the corporators'; in *R.* v. *Cory Bros* (1927) the court found that a railway company was not guilty of a criminal offence if it erected an electric fence against which an employee fell and was killed, since a company cannot have *mens rea*; and in 1944 Lord Caldecott claimed that 'the real point which we have to decide . . . is . . . whether a company is capable of an act of will or a state of mind'.[51]

Attempts have recently been made to overcome such problems by conceding that the company does in fact have a mind. In a landmark ruling in 1956 Lord Denning claimed that companies 'may in many ways be likened to a human body. They have a brain and a nerve centre which controls what they do. They also have hands which hold the tools and act in accordance with directions from the centre'. As a consequence, he decided, one can indeed speak of the corporate mind. But in a crucial caveat the identification of such a mind rested on identifying the minds of its *actual human* controllers, replicating the point made by the Court of Appeal in the *Continental Tyre* v. *Daimler* case: 'Some of the people in the company are mere servants and agents who are nothing more than hands to do the work and cannot be said to represent the mind or will. Others are directors and managers who represent the directing mind and will of the company, and control what they do. The state of mind of these managers is the state of mind of the company and is treated by the law as such'.[52] The caveat was crucial because, while it appeared to identify the mind of the corporation, it also made it virtually impossible for corporations to be convicted for serious crimes. Thus in the preliminary ruling in 1990 in the case bought against P&O European Ferries for the sinking of the *Herald of Free Enterprise* in 1987 Mr Justice Turner said that 'where a corporation, through the controlling mind of one of its agents, does an act which fulfils the prerequisites of the crime of manslaughter . . . it as well as its controlling mind or minds, is properly indictable for the crime of manslaughter'.[53] The problem is that this identifies the company with the mind of its controllers. In this particular case, when the prosecution against the five senior employees collapsed, the case against the company went too.

In the philosophy of mind much is made of the issue of will and intentionality. If we speak of companies in the way that the law *requires* us to, of a company possessing will and thus intentionality (the company pursuing X, desiring Y or achieving Z), then clearly we are conceding the fact that the company is an agent with intentions. As Peter French has argued:

> For a corporation to be treated as [an] agent it must be the case that some things that happen, some events, are describable in a way that makes certain sentences true, sentences that say that some of the things a corporation does were intended by the corporation itself. That is not accomplished if attributing intentions to a corporation is only a shorthand way of attributing intentions to the biological persons who comprise it e.g. its board of directors.

If we are to take seriously the idea that the corporation possesses juridical personality, then corporate actions cannot be identified with the actions of human individuals. As such, it does not always make sense to hold a human being responsible for the offences committed by the corporation.[54] It seems clear, for example, that in the case of the *Herald of Free Enterprise* there was widespread knowledge, in the industry and among state personnel, that the roll-on, roll-off ferries then in operation needed redesigning. One had capsized in 1982 killing six people and a paper at the 1985 conference of the Royal Institute of Naval Architects pointed out that a much bigger disaster was likely to happen if the proposed redesign, incorporating new bulkheads which would enable passengers to escape, did not take place. In the light of this it is easy to see why some might think that P&O ferries *intentionally* ignored the need for change. Similarly, in 1970 Ford released their new Pinto car. Tests had shown Ford that rear-end collisions would very easily rupture the fuel system, with the consequence that the car was likely to burst into flames. A cost-benefit analysis told them that installing the appropriate safety measures would cost $135 million, while prospective lawsuits resulting from fatalities and injuries would be unlikely to top $50 million. It is estimated that between 500 and 900 people lost their lives, usually by being burnt to death as a result. The indictment for reckless homicide in 1978 failed. Again, it might be thought that it was fairly easy to show that the company had *intentionally* ignored the necessary safety measures; the law thought otherwise.

One might add to these examples thousands of others, including deliberate cost-cutting measures ignoring health and safety concerning workers as well as consumers, measures resulting in the injuries and deaths – some in 'accidents', some over a prolonged period of poisoning – of countless numbers of workers. In the case of Britain alone the HSE have estimated that 40 per cent of the 2286 deaths at work since 1997 have been due to corporate failings and the official figures for the number of deaths at work in Britain rose by 32 per cent in 2001. In addition, in Britain alone in the last 15 years over 450 people have died in seven major disasters (193 at Zeebrugge, 31 in the King's Cross fire, 35 in the Clapham train crash, 51 in the sinking of the *Marchioness*, 96 at Hillsborough stadium, 7 in the Southall rail crash, 31 in the Ladbroke Grove rail crash and 7 at Potters Bar). No 'person' has been successfully prosecuted for any of these.[55] Frederick Engels was quite clear about how this should be viewed: it should count as murder, pure and simple – 'disguised, malicious murder against which none can defend himself, which does not seem what it is, because no man sees the murderer, because the death of the victim seems a natural one, since the offence is more one of omission than of commission. But murder it remains'.[56] It is symptomatic of the nature of bourgeois law that the simplicity of this position would be laughed out of court.

It is often pointed out that the only criminal penalty that can be realistically imposed on a company in English law is a fine and/or compensation order. Because a company is a creature of the law with no physical existence, it cannot be tried for murder (or treason) as the only punishments available to the court on conviction are life imprisonment or death. Company law allows companies to wind up voluntarily, which may appear to be the equivalent of the death of an individual person, but in fact is more the equivalent of suicide in which the assets have been distributed before death.[57] Although the possibility of prosecution for corporate manslaughter exists, cases are almost doomed to fail except in respect of one-man or very small companies in which the 'controlling mind' can be easily identified (hence the failure to successfully prosecute P&O, noted above). Moves to introduce a new offence of 'corporate killing' have been mooted in Britain, but it is unlikely that this will ever be as strong a law as is needed. This seems to show that although corporations appear to be persons, they escape any suggestion that they have agency when it comes to harms for which *some person* should be identified as responsible.

The law, in other words, works in a way which is far more accommodating to corporate persons than human ones. The law which granted the modern corporation fully-fledged status as a juridical person has been reluctant to admit that the same persons can commit illegal acts and recognizable harms; the corporation is a person when it comes to the advantages of law, but a 'nonperson' when it comes to crimes seemingly committed by it. The special privilege which used to arise with each act of incorporation has been replaced by a generalized privilege which to all intents and purposes places corporations as a whole above certain laws, giving them a status above the other (human) persons of civil society. The individualizing nature of bourgeois law constructs the corporation as a person but then resists punishing it on the grounds that it is not a person at all but a collective which has no mind *per se*: the state *personalizes* capital, but doesn't *punish* it as a person. It punishes it (*when* it does) as capital – as something different to (human) persons.[58] *Apropos* of attacks on 'welfare scroungers' and 'the idle poor', one might say that it is the corporation that has acquired plenty of rights but few responsibilities.[59] In Marxist terms we might say that the unity of the corporate *persona* created by the state has helped consolidate the domination of capital over everyday life. Capital has used the corporate form to its advantage by avoiding one of the most obvious disadvantages of being a legal person – namely, responsibility for one's acts. The outcome has been the tendency to treat 'crimes' committed by corporations as mere failures to follow regulations and procedures and thus not 'crimes' at all: the ruling class has defined capital as beyond incrimination. But then this should not surprise us: as with bourgeois law in general, the corporation is, after all, constructed as a person for the purposes of capital accumulation and not for the purposes of justice.

It has been argued that 'while . . . the charge of corporate manslaughter remains a highly difficult one to pursue successfully, there are no insuperable problems intrinsic to law to the effective criminalisation of such offences; . . . what is commonly lacking is political will'.[60] Maybe so; but any such 'political will' would have to be rooted not in the current structures through which mainstream politics is organized – political parties and reformist groups – but in a movement that would be willing to challenge the whole edifice on which

political and social power is structured: the state and the individualizing tendencies of bourgeois law, as well as capital itself. Moreover, from the point of
view of the Left, any real challenge to capital would have to take on board the
fact that it uses the *persona* as the veil of power. Edmund Burke once defended
the authority of the state by insisting that 'there is a secret veil to be drawn
over the beginnings of all governments';[61] unsurprisingly, the same principle
is used to defend the domination exercised by capital, for corporate personality is known as the 'veil' that capital wears. 'Veil' here is modern parlance for
the older 'mask', and reminds us once again of the connection with the stage.
While the law has occasionally been willing to 'pierce' or 'look behind' the
veil of personality – and capital continues to resist all such lifting – in general
the veil is allowed to remain in place.[62] Like the more traditional 'mask', it
is the state that supplies the corporate veil – it is a piece of costume from the
theatre of European statecraft.

The revenge of sovereignty

Historically, one response to the problems generated by the corporate *persona*
was to deny that such creatures are persons at all. To this end the corporation
has been variously described as a fraud, myth, pretended association, a bubble,
artificial, a cloak, a metaphysical conception, a simulacrum and a hollow
sham. Most significantly, it has been described as a fiction.[63] Dealing with this
issue will take us back to the wider argument concerning state power.

 The idea of the 'fictional' person stems from the theological debate about
the nature of the *universitas*. The term *universitas* derived from Roman law, and
referred to the corporate collective at large. Canonists applied this legal notion
to the various ecclesiastical bodies, such as the chapters and congregations, as
well as to the whole Church – the 'universal' Church. At the same time, civic
parallels to the religious bodies such as cities or guilds also emerged as entities
with rights and duties as a 'person' with a corporate form independent of their
inhabitants.[64] Searching for a phrase which captured the nature of religious
corporations, such as the cathedral church, and their civil parallels, the idea
developed that they were some form of subject with rights – a person, that is,
but of a 'fictitious' nature: 'one person composed of many'. According to Otto
Gierke, the first person to use the phrase '*persona ficta*' was Sinibald Fieschi,
who in 1243 became Pope Innocent IV. At the Council of Lyon in 1245 he
forbade the excommunication of a *universitas* and later justified his action on
the grounds that the *universitates* were 'names of law' only and not of persons.
He argued that the *universitas* was a person without a body and, as such, was an
imaginary 'represented person' (*persona repraesentata*) or a 'fictitious person'
(*persona ficta*). Innocent thought that the corporation was in some ways a
person, but a person by fiction and only by fiction. Thus besides 'natural

persons' the law knows as 'subjects' of proprietary rights certain fictitious or artificial persons. Moreover, such persons had to be distinguished from the group of natural persons who constituted the membership. From this there arose the possibility of treating every *universitas* as a juristic person, or subject of rights, but doing so in a way that distinguished such a person from every 'natural' person. That this person was 'fictitious' did not affect its political significance. One might say that just as the corporation was a fiction made real, so the *persona ficta* gave legal reality to the corporate person.[65] According to this 'Fiction Theory', as it became known, the only real person is the individual human person; but just as a legal capacity may be denied to many individual humans – historically some were given no personality, such as slaves, while others were given only partial personality, such as women, and even today states restrict personality in various ways, such as the French penalty of 'civil death' in which an offender is deprived of enough civil rights to prevent them from being a *bona fide* person in law – so it may also be transferred to something other than the individual human. Thus a juristic person is 'artificially' created; such corporate persons are 'artificial' subjects existing by means of pure fiction. The Fiction Theory thereby assumes that the group occupies a space in law, but only as some kind of artificial or fictitious person, possessing a legal status only by virtue of a concession granted by the state (hence it led into what was known as the 'Concession Theory' which is generally indifferent to the 'reality' of the corporate body, insisting instead that the legal power of the body is derived).

The Fiction Theory trundled along through the centuries more or less unopposed, becoming part of the common-sense of Roman law. In the late nineteenth and early twentieth centuries, however, the theory came under fire, most notably from those who offered a 'realist' account of the nature of groups and associations – an account which asserted the very 'real' nature of groups as opposed to their 'fictitious' nature. In England such writers became lumped together under the label 'English pluralists'. Although the pluralists were a politically diverse range of writers – 'the pluralist theory of the state is in itself pluralistic', noted Carl Schmitt[66] – including to varying degrees F.W. Maitland, John Figgis, Ernest Barker, Harold Laski and G.D.H. Cole, and although their ultimate political concerns were different, they shared the view that the Fiction Theory suffered from the same defects as Natural Law Theory: both tended to downplay the social and thus legal significance of groups. Otto Gierke, whose four-volume work on the nature of group life in early modern Germany was one of the pluralists' major sources, had argued that the ecclesiastical theory of the corporation arose from the desire to safeguard natural law as the source of right and obligation.[67] The prevalent natural law tendency was (and remains) the tendency to confer rights and duties on either individuals or the state, since the sovereignty of the state and the sovereignty of the individual were on their way to becoming the two axioms around which political theory would revolve. Forms of association, ranging from the most minor corporation to the state itself, could then been seen as arising from, and ultimately reducible to, agreements between the members – hence the contract. In this view corporations, and the state itself, are nothing more than the union of members at any given time. The problem with such a view is that it fails to do justice to the fact that the membership changes over time, but the group retains some form of identity. This was the basis for Innocent IV's action in 1245: he was acting on the implication that the *universitas* was a person/body which thrives on succession and, owing to its successive self-generation, cannot die. An excommunication which was extended to the whole body corporate would also affect the innocent members, and those who would later become members. Thus the Church – and any body which replicated its corporate form – remained the Church even if all its members died and were replaced by others. In other words, the essential feature of all corporate bodies was not that they were a plurality of persons collected in one body, but that they were a plurality in succession. This is an argument which both parallels and sustains that which we saw concerning the body politic in Chapter 1. Moreover, the natural law tendency was also considered to be unable to deal with the fact that corporations can act, make decisions and have rights. That is, the natural law view fails to take account of the fact that corporations are historical beings with minds of their own.

What the pluralists saw as the natural law tendency to dismiss the significance of group life was replicated, so they thought, in the Fiction Theory.[68] The pluralist view was that corporate personality is no more than a form of legal fiction and the concessionist view that a corporation is no more than a legal construct of the state had a damaging effect, since both deny the capacity for associations and groups to decide for themselves how to develop. Against this the pluralists argued that the law ought to recognize the very 'real' nature of groups and associations. What Gierke offered the pluralists was a historical view of associations as personalities in their own right – *real* bodies with a life of their own. 'Our German fellowship is no fiction,' Gierke was said to tell us, 'but a living organism and a real person, with body and members and a will of its own'.[69] For John Figgis, for example, groups and associations between the individual and the state 'live with a real life', and it would 'seem wiser to treat all these great and small corporate entities which make up our national life as real, as living beings, i.e. practically as persons.'[70] The question was therefore whether

> corporate societies [are] to be conceived as real personalities or ficti-
> tious ones, *i.e.* is their union to be throughout of such a nature that it
> has a life greater than the mere sum of the individuals composing the
> body; that it is not merely a matter of contract; that in action it has
> the marks of mind and will which we attribute to personality; that

> this corporate life and personality grows up naturally and inevitably out of any union of men for permanent ends, and is not withheld or granted at the pleasure of the State?[71]

The outcome was the view that 'the group is a person', nothing other than a 'right-and-duty bearing unit' like all other persons. The legal implications of this were clear: 'if n men unite themselves in an organized body, jurisprudence, unless it wishes to pulverize the group, must see $n + 1$ persons'.[72]

For the most part the pluralists were driven not by the nature of capital but by the legal form given to other forms of association (and on this score they notably failed to even begin to consider Gierke's comments on the 'despotism of capital').[73] Figgis' main concern, for example, was the nature of the legal recognition given to churches following the Free Church of Scotland case, while Laski was driven by the corporate status of trade unions as discussed in the *Taff Vale* case of 1901. The point here, however, is that against the Fiction and Concession Theories, the pluralists posited a 'realist' view. From this it would appear that there is an option: we think of groups and associations as either real or as fictitious.

But there is a frustrating sense in which the debates about both the 'fictitious person' and the distinction between 'natural' and 'artificial' persons miss two crucial points, both of which take us back to the question of the state.

First, the debates partly obscure the fact that it is the state which decides who or what is to be considered as possessing legal subjectivity. When it comes to the law of persons, distinctions between the real and the fictitious/ artificial (or imaginary/pretend/unreal/less-than-real and so on) are without foundation. 'English law has liked its persons to be real', as Maitland puts it, and we may follow English law here, but the law does not meet our wishes.[74] The idea that legal subjects have 'personality' applies to *all* legal persons, 'natural' or otherwise. In other words, legal personality for *all* creatures is a concession made by the state. All legal persons are born of the law. Group personality merely looks more like a legal fabrication rather than a 'natural' growth. As Frederick Pollock pointed out in an essay presented to Gierke, the word 'artificial' when used to frame discussion of personality meant not 'fictitious' but more 'in accordance with the rules of art'; this would explain Hobbes' 'by Art is created that great Leviathan'. The derivation of 'fiction' from *fingere* plays less on the modern sense of mere *feigning* and more on the original sense of *creating* or *fashioning*.[75] Thus Barker suggests that legal personality is a juristic creation, a legally created capacity of sustaining rights and duties for subjects which are also legal creations themselves. But being 'creations' does not mean that they are not real.[76] It is for this reason that law treats all persons equally – at least formally. Even the 'natural'/'real' person can never be a person 'outside the law'; when it comes to persons, there is no 'outside the law'.

The issue at the heart of the debate about the *persona ficta* may appear to be a question of 'legal metaphysics', an indulgence in 'metaphysical subtleties', or a hunting of 'communal ghosts',[77] but actually strikes at the heart of the question of state power concerning the ways in which the state fashions civil society. Such a fashioning, which we began to address in previous chapters, can now be seen to extend to the construction of corporate persons and the powers they are granted *vis-à-vis* the rest of civil society. Wherever the state attributes rights or duties to an entity or institution, it makes a person of, or recognizes a person in, that entity or institution. As a consequence, it is true to say that 'the corporate personality has no existence beyond that which the state chooses to give it'.[78] The state makes it what it is. It is for this reason that we might say that the corporation is a creature of the state – into its nostrils the state breathes life, as Maitland puts it. This is one of the ways by which the state participates in the fabrication of social order, populating civil society with creatures of its own devising, artificial but nonetheless self-determining corporate persons, ascribing 'interests' to them and deciding when their sufferings are recognizable 'harms'. The state populates civil society with new legal subjects, *structured in its own image* – that is, it populates civil society with *persons of its own making*.

One classic definition has it that a corporation is a franchise[79] and a franchise is a portion of the state's power in the hands of a subject. The fact that a special act of the state legislature is no longer required for each instance of incorporation may give the appearance that where the state was once the moving force behind the 'private' development of banks, roads, canals and other institutions vital to the development of capital, it now stands by as individuals form new corporations independently ('naturally', 'organically', 'privately') of the state.[80] But the truth is that the need for the sanction of the state *has never been abandoned*, and nor could it be. What has changed is that the process of incorporation now takes place under the everyday and mundane processes of company and administrative law rather than requiring extraordinary legislative action. While Hobbes may be overstepping the mark in claiming that a person 'constituted by the state bear its person, so that *it hath no will except that of the state*',[81] he is none the less right to insist that the state is the *author* of such entities, in the sense that whatever *authority* they have stems from the state.

The fact that the corporation, as legal subject, has some crucial features distinguishing it from human legal subjects – it cannot marry or vote, for example, or, for those with a theological bent, it has 'no soul to be saved or body to be kicked' and thus cannot be excommunicated – should not therefore lead us to describe it as a fiction or as artificial. The law does not write fiction.[82] What distinguishes corporations as persons from human persons is less important than the fact that each corporation is a *bona fide persona* in law, able to form contracts and own property; the contract, after all, presupposes that the contracting parties *recognize* each other as persons and owners of property. In taking the form of persons in law capital-as-corporation is the worthy cousin of the public corporations.[83] Early specimens of the joint-stock company were so closely related to the state as to be immediate instruments of policy, for in granting 'economic' rights to the corporation the state granted it a degree of sovereign authority too. The first trading corporations were granted criminal and civil jurisdiction over all persons belonging to the company or living under it, including the right to use direct force.[84] For example, 'in return for a trade monopoly the [English East India] Company was given the task of performing all those acts of government in those regions under its jurisdiction', while the charter of the Dutch East India Company 'bestowed upon the company the right to exercise in this region all the privileges, prerogatives, and powers usually held by sovereign states'.[85] And in the light of the argument in the previous chapter, it should be pointed out that corporations such as the East India Company 'undertook a massive intellectual campaign to transform a land of incomprehensible spectacle into an empire of knowledge'.[86] Far from having the appearance of being an independent creature within the 'private' sphere, it was blindingly obvious that the corporation was to all intents and purposes a creature and organ of the state, formed by the state, given its powers and purposes by the state and subject to dissolution by the state. It was, in other words, a major mechanism through which the state began to administer civil society politically.

It is thus unsurprising to find that despite the altered situation corporations find themselves in – the modern 'economic' or 'private' corporation no longer has such an immediate relation to state policy as the early joint-stock corporations, and the special act of state required to bring them into being has been replaced by the more mundane processes of political administration – the granting of corporate status still gives the corporation many of the characteristics of state power. This explains why both state and corporation were historically understood through the same category of 'body politic'. Historically, virtually all the Charters creating corporations described them in terms such as 'one body corporate and politic', 'a body politic [whose] members give common consent' and so on.[87] The logic of the corporate form followed and continues to follow that of the state: 'the corporation is the attempt of civil society to become the state', as the young Marx put it.[88] Or as Paul Hirst argues, companies are not self-governing associations freely formed of citizens, but are largely unaccountable hierarchical authorities with few special legal obligations other than the most obvious ones; in other words, *companies are analogous to sovereign states*.[89]

The second crucial point missed in the debate about the 'fiction' and the distinction between 'natural' and 'artificial' persons concerns the personality of the state itself, and this will allow me to bring the argument in this and the previous chapter full circle. In general the pluralists intended their work to be a critique of the absolutist tendencies they saw existing within the sovereign state.[90] As Figgis put it, 'the great *Leviathan* of Hobbes, the *plenitudo potestatis* of the canonists, the *arcana imperii*, the sovereignty of Austin, are all names of the same thing – the unlimited and illimitable power of the law-giver in the State'.[91] For the pluralists, the embodiment of sovereignty in the modern state was a problem because it necessarily undermined autonomous associations, and a society in which autonomous groups mediating between the citizens and the state are undermined tends towards the tyrannical. Thus the battle for the liberty of the individual had been incorporated into the battle for the liberty of the group: 'No longer do we write *The Man versus the State*: we write *The Group versus the State*'.[92] Unless state sovereignty was limited *vis-à-vis* groups, it would not be limited *vis-à-vis* individuals. It is precisely because the pluralists set themselves against state sovereignty in this way that the most vehement critique of their position came with Carl Schmitt's work *The Concept of the Political* (1932). For Schmitt, because the definition of the political is the opposition between friend and enemy, it is the essence of the sovereign body to engage in a decisive decision about who *is* the enemy. Since this body is the state, the state cannot allow a range of plural loyalties within it; nor can it allow itself to be understood as nothing more than yet another association. Schmitt therefore sees in pluralism the antithesis of his own views: 'Pluralism consists in denying the sovereignty of the political entity by stressing time and again the individual lives in numerous different social entities and associations'. As such, 'a pluralist theory is either the theory of state which arrives at the unity of state by a federalism of social associations or a theory of the dissolution or rebuttal of the state'.[93]

Schmitt is certainly right to point out that the pluralists meant their arguments to be worked against state sovereignty. But in itself this is hardly much of an insight, since the pluralists made that point clearly themselves. What is more interesting is that Schmitt, driven by his fierce desire to reassert the principle of sovereignty, completely missed one of the implications of the pluralist case, an implication which in fact *assists* in the assertion of sovereign state power. Put simply, the implication is that if it is feasible, or even necessary, to recognize the corporate personality of the group or association, then surely this same argument can be applied to the state? Indeed, surely this argument *must* be applied to the state? In other words, one outcome of the pluralist argument could well be that the *state* be thought of as a person in its own right. If one is to say that the corporation was a fiction made real and the *persona ficta* gave legal reality to the corporate person, then it is also the case that this argument applies equally to the corporate body known as the state. As Gierke points out, the doctrine of *persona ficta* was used not only to grapple with the corporate 'Right-Subjectivity' of the Church and other bodies such as cities, but also to grapple with the 'Right-Subjectivity' of the state. The Roman doctrine of corporations and, within that, the idea of the *persona ficta*,

was from the outset seen as an apt lever for those forces which were transforming the medieval polity into the modern state. Yet political theory never
really took up this point, since the question of legal personality became
focused on what in the political imagination became understood as a 'private'
figure: 'On the one part the concept of Legal Personality was confined always
more definitely within the boundary of Private Law . . . On the other part, the
Theory of the State had at its command no instrument which would enable it
to put into legal terms the organic nature of the State'.[94] Those writers who
did argue such a case, from Baldus in the fourteenth century, to Hobbes in the
seventeenth (as we have seen) and a host of others from then onwards, fell
into a (diverse) minority. Instead political theory allowed the idea of the
personality of the state to be torn asunder: in a monarchy it was absorbed by
the visible occupant, while in a republic it was embodied in the sovereign
assembly. Historically, the consequence was that the various institutions of
the state became separate corporate persons in the same way that universities
had – in Britain, for example, the Postmaster General became a 'body corporate' in 1840, the Treasurer of Public Charities in 1853, the Solicitor to the
Treasury in 1876, and so on – but in general there existed a resistance to
thinking of the state as a whole in such a way.[95] This is partly because of the
concerted attempt over the centuries to *depersonalize* power. But the process
of piecemeal incorporation of particular parts of the state was nothing less
than 'an awkward endeavor to ignore the personality of the greatest body
corporate and politic that has ever existed'.[96] And yet if the political imagination allows us to speak of collective and corporate personality, as it clearly
does, then it follows that 'the greatest of artificial persons, politically speaking, is the State'.[97]

On occasion, the pluralists themselves seemed to notice that their arguments did lead them in such a direction. While some, such as Figgis, were at
best ambiguous concerning state personality – at times he simply denied that
this followed from the idea of group personality – others were forced to concede the point. Laski, for example, asserts that 'the reality of the State's personality is a compulsion we may not resist', and while he later retreated from this
position he could never quite give up the idea of the 'will of the state' on which
the whole foundation of personality is based.[98] For MacIver 'the state . . . has
the essential character of a corporation'.[99] That the state must be imagined as a
personality in its own right would seem to follow from the logic of the corporate form. As Maitland put it, with typical understatement: the 'uncomfortable
suspicion that the State itself is but a questionably real person may not be
easily dispelled'.[100] Maitland recognized the political implications of the theory of group personality because his historical sensibility was such that he saw
how closely entwined were theories of the state and theories of the corporation. He saw that 'the individualism which dissolves the company into its
component shareholders is not likely to stop at that exploit, and the State's

possession of a real will is insecure if no other groups may have wills of their own'.[101] Although this form was historically connected with the idea of the body politic, by the nineteenth century it was increasingly seen in terms of its real dynamic, namely the juridical constitution of the main actors in civil society, and was eventually consolidated as part of international law, which is founded on the idea of the state as person. The Montevideo Convention on Rights and Duties of States (1933), for example, established that a permanent population, a defined territory, a government and a capacity to enter into relations with other states establishes the state 'as a person of international law'.[102]

This is inherent in the doctrine notion of legal personality upon which the corporate form relies: just as we say that 'McDonalds intends to X' so we say that 'Britain aims to achieve Y'. Like the body politic metaphor, the doctrine of the corporate personality could never have served the project of state power unless it had not been able to oscillate between notions of capital hierarchy and juridical association. The fact that the doctrine was forged in the laboratory of private law and is thus integral to the model of private property did not stop it from becoming included in the strategic field of the state and the statist imagination; indeed, it merely shows the degree to which statecraft and capital are inextricably linked. The idea of the corporate *persona* is one of the ways the corporation and the state replicate each other, both able to act 'independently' of their members – autonomous subjects in their own right, possessing both will and intention.[103]

This parallel helps shed a little light on the idea of the mind of the state. Like the corporation, the state's 'corporate veil' allows it to avoid recriminations for acts which it intentionally carries out. Take the way states accused of crimes against humanity have been dealt with. While we speak of crimes against humanity carried out by the German state, the Chilean state, the Yugoslav state and so on, the legal subjects tried for such crimes are not the German or Yugoslav states as such but their 'controlling minds'. To make this point is not to try and exonerate Eichmann, Pinochet, Milosevic, or anyone else. Rather it is to point to the fact that the corporate persona behind which the state operates encourages the kind of mystification that we saw attached to the personification of capital and the kind of 'mystery of state' we saw defended in the previous chapter. The idea of personality is part of the 'secret veil' (Burke) drawn over the state. The idea of the legal *persona* attached to corporate or collective entities thus shows that the conjunction of domination and unity inherent in the terminology of personification is applicable to both capitalist enterprises and the state itself. (It is for these reasons that questions of 'workers control', first established by the communist and socialist traditions, touch at the heart of any serious political theory.)

What is important here is not the fact that the pluralists only half-recognized the point; this chapter has not been written as a critique of pluralism. Rather, what is important is the point itself and its implications concerning the state. The pluralists tended to desire some kind of liberal democratic regime operating under a rule of law; in some cases a federal and/or socialist structure was envisaged – Gierke's *Rechtsstaat* with differences of detail according to the particular politics of the pluralist in question. What they failed to realize was that when applied to the state, as it had to be, the doctrine of group personality was poorly served by the addition of liberal or socialist constitutional ideas. Like the doctrine of reason of state, the doctrine of the personality of the state encourages the view that the state is an entity in its own right with a will of its own. It thus tends to place the state above the plane of normal legal responsibility on the grounds that such a person has no superior to whom to answer.[104] Thus the political and philosophical strategy employed by the pluralists to enhance the power of non-state associations and thereby limit the power of the state was a strategy that turned out to have been incredibly useful in *enhancing* state power. For once one concedes corporate personality in the way that capitalist states had done, and had had to do as a matter of historical necessity in order to promote the intensification of capital accumulation, one has also to concede corporate personality to the state. And once this is done, it becomes easy to argue that the *state's will transcends the will of all others*. Combined with the conjunction of unity and/as domination it becomes clear that the political imagination here operates a doctrine which again feeds into certain authoritarian political positions.[105] At its worst it ends in the political discourse of fascism. (This is the implication missed by Schmitt, despite his ambition to defend the fascist assertion of sovereignty against the 'chaos' of pluralism.)

Mussolini and Gentile saw this and built on it. In their attempt to 'reaffirm the State as the true reality of the individual', and establish that for fascism 'everything is in the state, and . . . nothing has value outside the State', they adopted the very notion of corporate personality and applied it to the state: 'this higher personality is truly the nation in so far as it is the State . . . The Fascist State, is the highest and most powerful form of personality'.[106] With the example of Mussolini's Italy well established and the Nazis gearing up for the seizure of power, Barker and Laski eventually recognized this. Whereas Maitland's introduction to his selection from Gierke was written from the relative safety of 1900, and Figgis' work on churches in the modern state written a decade later, Barker and Laski had before them rather more telling historical evidence: 'If groups are to be the beneficiaries of this theory [of personality], the greatest group may well be the greatest, and even the only, beneficiary'.[107] Or as Laski was to put it, it was only with hindsight that he realized that in taking up the mantle of personality he was, in fact, 'taking a side which was bound to have reactionary results', for 'the affirmation that corporate personality was real [led] to the exaltation of the state-personality above all others'.[108] Barker again:

> Italy has embraced the theory of real Group-personality . . . The Corporative State [being] a structure of many elements . . . But there seems to be little personality, and no autonomy, in the corporate groups contained in the Italian State; and if we read *La Dottrina del Fascismo* we can hardly doubt that the one Group-person which is really intended to act is the Italian nation as 'integrally realized' in the Fascist State of Italy.[109]

Commenting on the Stock Exchange's decision not to incorporate in 1877, Maitland noted that 'in England you cannot incorporate people who do not want incorporation'.[110] That may have been true in 1877 (or 1904 when Maitland was writing), but it could hardly be said of late-1920s Italy or Germany after 1933.

What Barker and Laski came to realize, then, was that the consequences of imagining corporate power as person were and are enormous. For in developing the idea of the corporate personality in order to expunge the notion of sovereignty from political theory, sovereignty came back, and with a vengeance.[111] We might say that it is nothing less than Hobbes' revenge. For Hobbes, and the statist imaginary in general, the state can possess the legal form of personality in a way that 'society' cannot – the people/multitude require the state as the grounds of their unity. And just as we saw with the image of the body politic, a political imagination dependent on anthropomorphic concepts tends towards authoritarian and reactionary politics. Sovereignty thus comes back in its starkest – that is, fascist – form.

In *Gravity's Rainbow* (1973) Thomas Pynchon has one of his characters point out that one of the dearest hopes of social democracy through the twentieth century was that the increasing rationalization and modernization of society would leave no room for something as terrible as charisma – the personality of the leader as worshiped through the *Führer*-principle or the cult of the *Duce*.[112] But fascism had a far greater personality to worship: the (nation-) state And this personality was provided for it through a conjunction of the bourgeois state form and the legal subjectivity forged for the benefit of contemporary capital. The statist political imaginary did the rest of the work.

4   The home of the state

In the modern world, the globe is dominated by states. Virtually every land mass that is not uninhabitable, and even most of those that are, is the territory of one state or another.[1] How this situation came about, and the fact that it continues, is telling. Inherent in the very idea of the state is the idea of space. The domination and administration of a particular space imagined as a territorial container requiring occupation by a political apparatus first emerged in Europe in the same period in which the concept of 'state' came to the fore. The term 'state' is an etymological hybrid, combining roots from *estate*, referring to land and the property rights over that land, and *status*, referring to authority and the rights associated with a certain standing. In the earliest idiom, the state was thought to represent the territorially grounded object of the property rights of sovereign monarchs embodied in a particular *dominium*. In feudal law the same word, *dominium*, stood for both '*ownership*' and '*lordship*'.[2] At the same time, *dominion* involved a conjunction of *domain* (space) and *domination* (power). As a form of property right, then, sovereignty is the highest, most complete right of ownership, combining both perfect title and possession. Thus the origins of the modern state as a body with its own domain are based not solely on sovereignty, but upon specific property rights, of which sovereignty comprises a distinct set.[3] The state could thus see in a particular domain, including the persons within it, its own property.

Sticking with etymology for the moment, it should be noted that the word 'territory' also came into its own in the fifteenth century. Territory has been defined as 'a portion of geographical space that coincides with the spatial extent of a government's jurisdiction . . . the physical container and support of the body politic organized under a governmental structure'. As such, it is often presented as the 'link between space and politics'.[4] Similarly, one of the preconditions underlying the authority and unity of the state since its inception has been that the supreme authority within each independent *regnum* should be recognized as having no rivals within its own territories as a law-making power and an object of allegiance. And the word 'frontier' (*frontière*) originally referred to the façade of a building or the front line of the army, but in the sixteenth century came to mean the boundaries or borders of a particular space and has been associated with state borders ever since.[5]

The contrast between the political organization of space in modernity and that of pre-modern society is stark. Under the feudal system of rule, boundaries overlapped and multiple authorities existed within any particular region; communities were united by allegiance and personal obligation rather than abstract conceptions of individuality or citizenship within a geographically circumscribed territory. Space was thus organized concentrically around many centres depending on personal-political affiliations constituted as a natural hierarchy, formalized by God and centring around precedence and honour. The key question concerning sovereignty was less that of space and more that of time, as we saw in Chapter 1. As sovereignty shifted from the person of the monarch to the institutions of the state, an important shift took place concerning sovereignty and space. As the contest between the Church and the emergent state was gradually resolved in favour of the latter, the concepts and symbols of secular power took on spatial connotations. The body politic came to be understood as continuous not only in time, but also in space; it became connected, in other words, with the concept of territory.[6] The plurality of hierarchical bonds was replaced with an exclusive identity based upon membership in a common territorial space with a singular centre and established territorial boundaries defined by the sovereign powers and recognized as such within a developing international state system. This development was encouraged by the natural law critique of feudal space: there was no political space in the state of nature, but in creating civil society the social contract authorized just such a political space, whether bounded by absolute authority (Hobbes), private property (Locke) or the general will (Rousseau). Such emergent political space not only separated the modern polity from feudalism, but did so by creating a territorial grounding within which constitutional discourse and political exchange could take place.[7]

Thus in the modern state system the overlapping frontier is as anathema as the idea of multiple sovereign bodies within a territory. An edict of Pope Alexander VI in 1492 gave impetus to the idea of a spatially divided earth by drawing lines delineating the parts of the globe and specifying which part 'belonged' to which European power; this was formalized in the seventeenth century with the Peace of Westphalia (1648), strengthened in the eighteenth century with the emphasis on territorial unity in the French and American Revolutions, and consolidated in the twentieth century with an international state system which became so entrenched that the territorial state eventually became the political form to be adopted by all nations.[8] The 'modernization' of politics was thus as much a process of territorialization as it was a process of secularization and rationalization.[9] The form of sovereign power that developed in Europe from the sixteenth century onward conceived space as bounded. 'Sovereignty' implies 'space', and control of a territory became the foundation of sovereignty.[10] Concomitantly, as we saw in the previous chapter, a defined territory is integral to the recognition of a state as a *bona fide* person in international law. For the modern polity the division of territorial sovereignty between states must be most explicit at the point where the fields of power interface – there must be no overlap and no uncertainty about the borders of the territory: 'modern sovereignty resides precisely on the limit'.[11] This requires a new kind of political geography in which neither overlapping margin nor multiple sovereignty is permitted. (It is precisely because of this exclusive territoriality that embassies exist. Having created mutually exclusive territories, states found that there was little space left for the conduct of diplomacy. The outcome was little islands of alien sovereignty within the state's territory: the embassy.)[12] At the same time, it requires the permanent policing of territorial boundaries. States become and remain 'sovereign' not just in the sense that they are all-powerful within their territories, but also because they police the borders of a particular space and claim to 'represent' the citizens within those borders.

The practical consequence has been that the earth's surface is inscribed in a new way – according to the territorial ambitions of the modern state. The intellectual consequence has been that space assumes an absolute priority in the statist political imaginary. The 'imagined place' of the body politic (Hobbes)[13] thus takes on political meaning as a clue to the nature of the state. Without this essential conjunction of space and politics, sovereignty would lose its meaning. As such, we might say that the statist political imaginary is necessarily a *territorial* imaginary. Territory and state power are thus mutually constitutive (a fact which assists the understanding of the state as an organic body politic).

In recent years there has been a considerable body of work across the social sciences using the notion of space and ideas connected with the spatial: the use of concepts of core and periphery in world-system and dependency theory; the revival of geopolitics, critical geopolitics and the general theme of inside/outside in international relations; a sharp increase in attention paid to the relationship between space and social theory among radical geographers; the development of arguments concerning time-space compression in social theory; the rise of theories of 'globalization' and, in particular, its effects on the spatial ordering of the world; the attempts within international political economics to grapple with the spatial significance of transnational practices; the attention paid to spatial issues in macrosociology. More generally, there has been a huge increase in the use of the metaphors of 'mapping', 'borders', 'locations' and related notions. While this chapter touches on some of the themes raised in this literature, its aim is to explore the way political practices concerning space and representations of space are dialectically interwoven. In part this has been inspired by Lefebvre's comments on the three dimensions of spatial production: material spatial practice, embracing production and reproduction; representations of space, involving conceptions of space; and representational spaces, incorporating space as directly lived through its associated images and symbols.[14] Lefebvre's work is useful because it creates an opening for an exploration of the shifts between material practices concerning space and the imagination of space which works alongside it. It is also a crucial addition to the work of macrosociologists and political theorists who have agreed that the state consists of military control over a territory but who have failed to explicate the ways in which this shapes our representations of space and thus our understanding of ourselves as situated in this or that particular space.[15]

My concern in this chapter is therefore twofold. First, the intention is to explore the ways in which the fabrication of *social* order is simultaneously the fabrication of *spatial* order. To explore, in other words, the way the social body is a geographically as well as a politically constituted realm (what we might call the geography of order). The second intention is to explore the way this fabrication of spatial order is imagined or given meaning. Lefebvre's work points us towards the material configuration of space in the framing of the activities of state, but it also helps draw our attention to the relation between spatialization and identity – where 'identity' refers to the identity of both the state and its subject-citizens – and in particular the conceptions and images through which identities are formed. In previous chapters we have encountered the way individual identity is shaped through various state practices. In this chapter I shall develop the argument by exploring the distinctive ecology of belonging which connects territory, subjectivity and the state in the broader context of both the material and symbolic organization of space and thus the political collective – as, for example, in the persistent identification of place with 'community'.[16]

The guiding link is the notion of 'home'. That the notion of 'home' plays a crucial role in our self-understanding as political citizens and subjects goes without saying. As Anthony Smith notes, such a self-understanding involves more than merely identifying a people with a particular stretch of the earth's surface: 'the earth in question cannot be just anywhere; it is not any stretch of land. It is, and must be, the "historic" land, the "homeland" '. As such 'the homeland becomes a repository of historic memories and associations, the place where "our" sages, saints and heroes lived, worked, prayed and fought. All this makes the homeland unique'.[17] Similarly, many writers have identified a politics of 'homelessness' as a key characteristic of the modern world.[18] Finally, the notion of home has been eulogized to the extent that in political terms it is treated as a sanctuary, mythically expected to be beyond the violence that saturates the political realm.[19] 'There's no place like home', as Dorothy puts it in escaping the land of Oz. One of the broader intentions of this chapter is to explore the ways in which imaginary identification of a homeland is shot through with territorial assumptions about the state as the ground of home, and to connect these with the political dimensions of space more generally. What this means, in effect, is that we shall be considering the importance of the imaginary homeland as it has taken the form of the territorial state.

The terror of territory

The idea of the homeland presupposes the territorializing impulse inherent in the modern state. The notion of 'territory' is derived from *terra* (of earth, and thus a domain), but also from *terrēre*, meaning to frighten, and *territōrium*, referring to a place from which people are warned off. And the notion of region derives from the Latin *regere* (to rule) with its connotations of military power. Territory is land occupied and maintained through terror; a region is space ruled through force. The secret of territoriality is thus violence: the force necessary for the production of space and the terror crucial to the creation of boundaries. It is not just that sovereignty implies space, but that 'it implies a space against which violence, whether latent or overt, is directed – a space established and constituted by violence'.[20] As the macrosociologists noted earlier have pointed out time and again, it is the use of physical force in controlling a territory that is the key to the state, for without it any claim to a territory would mean nothing. A founding violence, and continuous creation by violent means, are the hallmarks of the state.

As is well known, part of the construction of the state's territory took the form of defining the *legitimate use* of violence – this is the key to Weber's famous definition of the state as involving a monopoly over the means of violence. To do this the distinction between the 'legitimate' use of force *by the state* and the 'illegitimate' use of force *by non-state actors* had to be made coherent and acceptable to the members of states. During its early history, the state exercised violence alongside and often in conjunction with a range of 'non-state' or 'semi-state' organizations (these terms are misleading because 'state' itself had not been fully developed, but for the sake of the argument we will leave that issue aside). Piracy and banditry, for example, were once entirely legitimate practices within the state system, bringing as they did revenue to both the sovereign and private investors and weakening enemies by attacking their ships. Piracy on the seas was conducted with the full cooperation and support of cities and states, while banditry, as a form of terrestrial piracy, was conducted with the continual aid of lords. International agreements now have it that piracy, as an act of violence divorced from the authority of any state, is a crime. To reach this state of affairs required a campaign against piracy which relied on a change in the state's attitude from one in which non-state violence was an exploitable resource to one in which it was a practice to be eliminated. The catalyst appears to have been a clash of British interests in the eighteenth century, when the British East India Company began demanding British Royal Navy protection against British pirates who were operating in collusion with British colonists to plunder British commerce in the East. When the Navy was sent to patrol the eastern waters, the pirates moved to the Bahamas. Suppressing piracy in American waters in turn pushed the pirates back to Madagascar. Since other states and companies of other states found themselves in the same situation, a broader and lasting solution to the problem was sought, and an agreement was reached among the European powers that each state was responsible for controlling piracy in its own waters. But this required that states distance themselves from piratical acts:

> No clear norm could develop, much less be universalized, until the state system produced a clear definition of what constituted piracy. *And this was impossible so long as states continued to regard individual violence as an exploitable resource.* Simply put, piracy could not be expunged until it was defined, and it could not be defined until it was distinguished from state-sponsored or -sanctioned individual violence.[21]

Distinguishing piracy from state-sponsored or -sanctioned violence required that states be defined as the sole legitimate organization in the exercise of violence, a process that only occurred towards the end of the eighteenth century. By challenging the state's claim to a monopoly of the means of violence within a particular territory, piracy and banditry threatened the state system as a whole. Crucially, the delegitimization of piracy relied on pirates being defined as *stateless* persons – persons, that is, for whose actions no state could be held responsible.

Similarly, the word 'bandit' derives from the Italian *bandire*, meaning to exile or banish, and thus contains the notion of frontier or border within its very meaning. A bandit is by definition one who exists on the physical borders of the state as well as at the edge of law. In struggling against banditry, states were thus involved in a struggle over the *frontiers of territory* as well as the *exercise of violence*: 'Bandits contributed to the demarcation of territorial states and were partly responsible for the consolidation of state power [through] the "border effect". Boundaries took on concrete form in space through the interactions between border guards and bandits who seized upon the jurisdictional ambiguity of these liminal zones as cover for their depredations'.[22] It is because the bandit throws down a challenge to law, state violence and the territorial imaginary that the state sees in the bandit not just a criminal but a political opponent and, conversely, why many bandits become 'primitive rebels'.[23]

In a contemporaneous development, mercenarism was also gradually eradicated. It is often claimed that the absolutist states of the sixteenth and seventeenth centuries pioneered the professional army. But such armies were far from being the kind of national conscription force which are now the norm. Rather, they were a mixed mass constructed from the 'foreign' and 'professional' soldiers then available to any state. The *condottieri* hired by the fifteenth-century Italian city-states were essentially contractors – a *condotta* was a contract to make war for a particular sovereign. The German *Unternehmer* conveys the same commercial tone, while etymologically 'soldier' means 'one who serves in an army for pay' not 'one who serves his country'. The extent of mercenarism and its significance to the state is illustrated by Janice Thomson:

> In the eighteenth century, all the major European armies relied heavily on foreign mercenaries for troops. Half the Prussian army was comprised of mercenaries. Foreigners constituted one-third of the French army. Britain used 18,000 mercenaries in the American war for Independence and 33,000 mercenaries in its 1793 war with France . . . The last instance in which a state raised an army of foreigners was in 1854, when Britain hired 16,500 German, Italian, and Swiss mercenaries for the Crimean war.[24]

For several reasons, however, states gradually stopped hiring their soldiers and sailors from anywhere, and began substituting them with standing armies based on conscription. Following the example of the French Revolution and the Napoleon regime, in which huge effective armies were raised from within France, the practice of mercenarism gradually died out through the nineteenth century. One factor was sheer cost: states began to realize that fighting forces could be constructed more cheaply from their 'own' citizens. But a further factor was reliability: states realized that an armed force whose relation to the state was purely contractual often dragged its feet and was always ready to rebel; its 'own' citizens, however, were more reliable.

To form mass national armies, states therefore had to lay claim to a *monopoly* on the acts of military violence carried out by their own citizens. The US Neutrality Act of 1794, for example, prevented citizens of the USA from enlisting in the service of a foreign state, and prohibited all persons in the USA from 'setting on foot' military expeditions against states with which the USA was at peace. Such practices of neutrality soon became the standard for other states. In other words, to prevent those individuals increasingly seen as being the state's own citizens from breaking this perceived allegiance, states prevented their citizens from either joining the armies of foreign states or forming their own armies.[25] On the one side, then, states began to develop an international code on mercenarism. Only at this point does mercenarism become mercenarism – just as 'contraband usually becomes contraband when rulers decide to monopolize the distribution of the commodity in question',[26] so mercenarism only becomes mercenarism when states decide to use and monopolize the exercise of violence by their own citizens. This was crucial to states' claim to a monopoly over the means of legitimate violence within their own borders. (It is also one reason, though by no means the only reason, why states felt threatened by the International Brigade in Spain in the 1930s.)

On the other side, however, to legitimize this monopoly, states had to foster a national consciousness among their citizens, in order that they would more easily imagine that allegiance to the state of which they were a member was stronger than any allegiance formed through contract. Perry Anderson suggests that the most obvious reason for the mercenary phenomenon was, of course, the natural refusal of the noble class to arm its own peasantry; the nobility understood that it was impossible to train its subjects in the art of war and to simultaneously keep them obedient.[27] By the late eighteenth century, the semi-disciplined peasantry had been more or less converted into a working class, jointly disciplined through a combination of the new rules of wage-labour and the rationalization of the legal process. The point to add here is that this discipline began to be internalized through the ideological trope of national interest and identity. The newly-emergent 'citizens' were expected to imagine themselves as part of a community held together by and through the state. It is this imagination which has meant that many people are now more repulsed by the mercenary, and especially the citizen who fights against their own state, than by the genuinely foreign enemy. This 'nationalization of the masses' was in Lefebvre's terms both material and representational. It was a component of both the politically centralizing tendencies of the bourgeois class and the ideological tendency to imagine political formations in national rather than international terms. This can be understood as the ideological generation of 'one national class interest' (in Marxist terms) or 'national identity' (in sociological parlance). Either way, what is at stake is the generation of a subjectivity rooted in a political imaginary centred on the state and its national institutions. It is partly for this reason that writers on nationalism stress the importance of the late eighteenth century for the forming of the nation-state. The emergent national 'pathos' (Weber) which became part of the ideology of the bourgeois revolution was a product of the imagined community embodied in the state's territory.

Little is heard these days of the bandit, pirate or mercenary, but the struggle to delegitimize their practices was central to the struggle over the means of violence and thus to the consolidation of the notion of territory. They were the unwitting instruments of history, as Carlo Levi puts it, in that their existence acted as a major catalyst in the shaping of the state, a process in which they themselves were (almost) swept from history.[28] One effect of this ideological isolation of non-state violence from other modalities of violence has been to endow state violence with a special sanctity. Since the Peace of Westphalia the state system has seen non-intervention in a state's domestic affairs as the corollary of the ideological commitment to the protection of state sovereignty. As Cynthia Weber has shown, in modern global political discourse, 'intervention' generally implies a violation of state sovereignty: 'Intervention discourse begins by positing a sovereign state with boundaries that might be violated and then regards transgressions of these boundaries as a problem'.[29] In violating sovereignty, intervention is thus a violation of the norms of the international state system and the sanctity of the state. As a consequence, intervention comes to function as an *alibi* for the actions carried out in the name of the sovereign state, to such an extent that states use their claim to territorial sovereignty to legitimize genocidal practices against peoples under their rule. The United Nations (UN) has generated for itself a humanitarian air, refusing a seat on the General Assembly to such states, but in accepting the state's claim to sovereign territorial control the UN has effectively condoned the sacrifice of human beings to the demands of the territorial state and thus genocide as a standard exercise of sovereign power. It should be remembered that the liberal democratic states waged war on Nazi Germany not because it was committing genocide but because it was breaking out of what were thought to be its territorial limits; had the Nazis stuck to killing Jews, gypsies and communists within internationally sanctioned German borders, no state would have intervened to stop them.[30]

Conversely, while state violence has been endowed with a special sanctity, non-state violence is either invested with a unique danger – compare the language used to describe acts of violence carried out by the Palestinians, for example, with that used to describe acts of violence carried out by the Israeli state[31] – or it is ignored entirely. Identifying 120 wars in 1987 Bernard Nietschmann found that only 3 per cent involved conflict between two sovereign territorial states; the vast bulk were struggles between states and insurgent groups or nations. Yet these struggles receive very little media or academic attention. One reason for this is that the statist imaginary is so deeply entrenched in our political and intellectual culture that the predominant tendency is 'to consider struggles against the state to be illegitimate or invisible . . . [They are] hidden from view because the fighting is against peoples and countries that are often not even on the map. In this war only one-half of the geography is shown and only one side of the fighting has a name'.[32] This last point is only half the story, however, since the 'other' side of the fighting, when it is mentioned, often goes under a generic name intended to capture the unique danger of non-state violence: 'terrorism'.

'Terrorism' retains part of the original double meaning of territory, in that it refers not only to violence, but to space too. Things are usually labelled 'terrorist' when the acts of violence in question are not sanctioned by the state. Where they have been sanctioned by a state then they always take place outside of that particular state's territories (and usually result in the state in question being labelled a 'rogue state'). What this means, in effect, is that 'terrorism' is in fact *generated* by the international state system; it is the 'other' generated by the system of states. As Connolly notes, terrorism 'allows the state and the interstate system to protect the logic of sovereignty in the international sphere while veiling their inability to modify systemic conditions that generate violence by non-state agents'.[33] Thus while terrorism threatens the state, the threat is ultimately a superficial one, since the production of 'terrorism' ultimately serves to protect and strengthen the identity of particular states and the state system as a whole by reinforcing the enactment of state violence and legitimizing the surveillance techniques discussed in Chapter 2.

The state system and the statist political imaginary together use terrorism to effect a political rationalization of violence under the firm control of the state. In this context, the declaration of a war on terrorism by the US state and its allies in 2001 proves nothing other than the state's own misunderstanding of the world it has created. (And note that such a declaration was immediately expanded to include designated states which could then properly be confronted.) The standard Left-liberal critique of the category 'terrorism' is to point to the lack of any internationally agreed definition of the term (the UN, the North Atlantic Treaty Organization – NATO – and the European Union – EU – have all struggled to come up with an acceptable definition); or to point to the contradiction involved in the once denigrated 'terrorist' being fêted as 'world statesman' (Mandela), or to the once-celebrated 'freedom fighter' being castigated as 'terrorist' (Bin Laden); or, finally, to point to the hypocrisy of western liberal democracies training and funding armed rebellions in some parts of the globe while objecting to them elsewhere. While pertinent, these arguments miss the central point, which is that terrorism is defined according to the demands of the *raison d'État* of hegemonic powers. States define terrorism according to their own interests, and the predominant interests are necessarily those of the hegemonic forces. This then consolidates the state's claim to a monopoly of violence: terrorism will only end, says the state, when you all fully obey the demand to use violence only when we say so. As such, terrorism turns out to be the lifeblood of state terror.

Such obedience as demanded by the state has traditionally been offered in exchange for protection. The state attempts to 'set before mens eyes the mutuall Relation between Protection and Obedience', as Hobbes puts it.[34] This mutual relation has remained a key trope throughout western thought concerning the state. But what is meant by 'protection'? Charles Tilly has noted that the word sounds two contrasting tones. One is comforting, calling up images of a friendly shelter against danger and a form of security or safety provided by a powerful friend, a large insurance policy, a sturdy roof or a bulwark against terrorism. The other, however, is more ominous, evoking the racket in which a local strong man forces merchants to pay tribute in order to avoid damage. In the second scenario, of course, the dangers are often imaginary: the strong man encourages the imagination of danger and may even threaten the danger himself in order to prove that it really does exist. The state's provision of protection plays on the first meaning of the term – recall how crucial the ideas of 'security' and 'welfare' are to statecraft – but the state could equally be said to be providing 'protection' in the second sense of the term:

> To the extent that the threats against which a given government protects its citizens are imaginary or are consequences of its own activities, the government has organized a protection racket. Since governments themselves commonly simulate, stimulate, or even fabricate threats of external war and since the repressive and extractive activities of governments often constitute the largest current threats to the livelihoods of their own citizens, many governments operate in essentially the same way as racketeers.[35]

The state, in other words, is a protection racket – and like all protection rackets it is a process of domination in which the 'protected' become evermore subordinated to the 'protector'. But this begs a question: who is to be protected? Better still: who is *not* to be protected? And what about those who appear to be 'protected' by no state at all?

The scum of the earth, or, once more on the dirty social body

In the political order of modernity, one of the key ways in which citizens are said to be protected is through the existence of a set of rights. The French Revolution is taken to be the historically definitive statement of the rights of man, rights which have since been claimed to be universal. But the 1789 Declaration in which the rights were outlined was in fact a *Declaration of the Rights of Man and Citizen*. There was and remains a crucial political ambiguity in the very title of the document: are the rights in question ascribable to all humans as humans, or to citizens as members of a particular political territory? The distinction is crucial, for it raises the question of political form, and still resonates through contemporary debates concerning human rights. The declarations of human rights in the late eighteenth century were meant to provide protection in an era in which individuals were no longer protected by the estates to which they were born. As 'inalienable' rights they were meant to be independent of all government. And yet it soon became clear that such rights were simultaneously articulated as achievable only through the political form of a nation-state (as Edmund Burke was at pains to show). Since such rights were achievable only through the state, the rights of 'man' as universal subject were in fact to play second fiddle, if they were allowed to play at all, to the rights of the citizen as a member of a state.

This in turn begged (and continues to beg) a crucial question: if rights are granted to citizens of states, what happens to those with no state? That is, in a world divided into states, what happens to those who belong to no territory? It is because of issues such as these that many have agreed with Michael Walzer's suggestion that 'statelessness is a condition of infinite danger'.[36] The stateless individual appears to be cut off from the communal provision of protection, welfare and security structured through the political form of the state. Later in this chapter I will explore some of the implications of such danger. First, however, I want to flip Walzer's formulation around and pose another question: what if statelessness is also imagined as dangerous to the state itself? What if statelessness turns out to be a condition of infinite danger because the state imagines the stateless as *inherently dangerous to the state*? Answering this question will tell us something about the ideological importance of the territorial dimension of the statist imaginary and the material effects of the geography of order.

In the modern political imagination a distinction is often made between the national and international or domestic and foreign: the 'inside' and 'outside' of order. This is reflected in the claims to disciplinary distinction made by those working on 'international relations'. Where 'inside' the state rational democratic processes may function, 'outside' the territorial boundaries of the state rational government is thought impossible: anarchy is said to prevail. The account of the territorial imaginary and the geography of order being developed here operates across the inside/outside divide; in fact, the territorial imaginary and geography of order points to the fact that, as we saw in Chapter 1, the distinction between inside and outside is a political fiction: borders are always imagined as inherently unstable. But it is a political fiction that has material effects. The geography of order points to the *outside* in that it assumes that global order is brought about through the territorial state system – because order is founded on territory, those who for one reason or another cannot or will not be placed within the system are thought to be a threat. It also works in terms of the *inside* in that it assumes that internal order is brought about by the state knowing where individuals are located – those who for one reason or another have no fixed place are thus equally thought to be a threat. The real effect of the political fiction is thus the fabrication of the enemy figure.

One of Hegel's insights into the nature of state power was to point out that since the state functions as an individual subject, and since individuality necessarily contains its own negation, the state will necessarily generate enemies: 'Even if a number of states join together as a family, this league, in its individuality, must generate opposition and create an enemy'.[37] Such an insight has been used by some writers to help shape the definition of the political: 'The specific political distinction to which political actions and motives can be reduced is that between friend and enemy', comments Carl Schmitt.[38] But in such accounts the political comes to be much more about 'enemies' than 'friends', since it is through the enemy that the identity of the collective is forged and through the fight against the enemy that the unity of the body politic is reproduced. As Bill Clinton put it in one of his more Schmittian moments: 'the painful lesson is that you define yourself by who you fight'.[39] On a more mundane level, however, what follows from the generation of enemies by the state is that members of other states appear as strangers and thus as *potential* enemies. While in everyday language we now distinguish between the enemy and the stranger, in a number of ancient languages the two were named by a single word, and it is easy to see how this connection is still present. Its most obvious manifestation appears in the work of those on the political Right. Schmitt, for example, comments that 'the political enemy need not be morally evil or aesthetically ugly; he need not appear as an economic competitor, and it may even be advantageous to engage with him in business transactions'; the point is that the enemy 'is . . . the other, the stranger; and it is sufficient for his nature that he is, in a specially intense way, existentially something different and alien'.[40] Those from other (enemy) states thus appear as strangers (enemies) to the state.

It is for this reason that border issues (i.e. the points of entry to the body politic) are saturated with so much political tension. The fact that individuals may leave their own state does not generate a right to enter another state; nor do they possess the right to leave their own state, since the passport can at any time be confiscated (according to reason of state). Two stories run by the *Guardian* on 29 August 2001 illustrate the point. 'Stranded Refugees Start Hunger Strike' documents the case of 438 asylum seekers stranded on a ship in the Indian Ocean. Having fled their designated homeland, the refugees discovered that no country would actually let them in. Meanwhile, 'Police Clampdown on Munich Match' documents the case of the 537 banning orders served against known or potential football hooligans (45 of the 537 had no previous convictions) preventing them from traveling to Germany for a football match.

More generally, immigration and emigration are politically asymmetrical. The UN Convention on Refugees (1952) asserts that the right to leave is a universal right, but says nothing about the right to entry. Citizens alone enjoy unconditional rights to remain and reside in the territory of the state, including the right to re-enter should they leave. The space of the state is their territory; the land of the state is their (home)land. In contrast, rights pertaining to the entry and residence of non-citizens are never unconditional. Some non-citizens have no such rights, while others are subject to exclusion or deportation in certain circumstances. To reiterate a point made in Chapter 2, the passport is not a ticket of entrance or exit, but a document that first and foremost certifies identity and citizenship and only secondarily permits travel. This is why the French movement for the legalization of all 'illegal immigrants' has taken the name *sans-papiers* – undocumented people. It is because the state has a fundamental interest in territorial closure that it can never allow an unconditional right to travel. Thus the border becomes a site through which the stabilization of order is attempted, with a whole panoply of legal and administrative mechanisms existing to regulate the movement of persons. The bottom line, of course, is that non-citizens may be excluded or expelled as a matter of course and by virtue of political will: again, the only reason needed is *raison d'État*.

The 'ban' is symptomatic of this connection between sovereignty and territory. The ban designates exclusion from a territory, but also refers to the command and insignia of the sovereign power. The banned are not merely set outside the law but rather are *abandoned* by it, an abandonment that has the full force of state violence to implement it (physical exclusion) and which identifies a territory within which the ban holds: one who has been banned is outside the juridical order of this or that particular state.[41] But as the territorial jurisdictions of modern states have come to exhaust the inhabitable surface of the earth, a person cannot now be expelled from one territory without being expelled into another, cannot be denied entry into one territory without having to remain in another. For this reason all humans are compelled to identify a particular space as 'home'. Those who have abandoned their own 'home', such as the 438 asylum seekers just mentioned, may find themselves banned by all states. The varying degrees of territorial closure against citizens and types of non-citizen is thus essential to the state *qua* state.

In general, states coordinate and rationalize their expulsion practices according to two basic principles: first, that a state can expel into the territory of another state only a person belonging to that state; and second, that a state is obliged to admit into its territory those who are previously defined as its own members.[42] The foundations of this inter-state system of political administration are illustrative of the fact that at the deepest level all states are *profoundly illiberal*, for in tying particular persons to particular states by virtue of the morally arbitrary accident of birth, the very institution of citizenship serves as a powerful instrument of social closure.[43] And it is this illiberal tendency which makes it urgent for the system to be able to establish who counts as member of which state; just who can count which part of the globe as home. At the most general level this results in explicit membership rules. At a more mundane level, it provides part of the *raison d'être* for the state's knowledge practices outlined in Chapter 2. For the state to know for sure which human individuals have a legitimate claim to permanent residence, it has to know just who is a *bona fide* member and is thus impelled to keep tabs on its citizens: the refugee is often a problem because of lack of cards and documents.

Because of the state's desire to know its population, it also desires the ability to *fix* people in space, in exactly the same way that the state itself is fixed. The birth of the modern state was simultaneously the birth of a tendency in which the territorial imaginary of the state was used to embrace the dispersed populations of the modern world. History, in that sense, has been written from the sedentary point of view and in the name of the unified territorial state apparatus.[44] Because of this, those persons who for one reason or another appear to be nomads – that is stateless – are always problematized by the state. The refugee, for example, is one who lacks the citizen's unproblematic grounding within a territorial space and so lacks the effective representation and 'protection' of a state. As Nevzat Soguk argues, while the citizen remains forever rooted in a particular territorial space, the refugee is uprooted, dislocated, displaced, forced out, or self-displaced from the community of citizens. In a world imagined to be composed of mutually exclusive, territorially bound spaces, the refugee figures only as an aberration of the proper subjectivity of citizenship; lacking the posited qualities of the citizen, the refugee does not properly belong anywhere.[45] The same point is also true of the vagabond – as a person without a place the vagabond figures as an 'internal refugee'.

In the statist imaginary this lack of belonging and absence of territorial grounding on the part of refugees and nomadic peoples is viewed as a form of homelessness, and the search for homelands by groups as different as the Palestinians, the Kurds, the Sikhs and others is suggestive of the centrality of territory to the political imaginary of diasporic populations and stateless peoples.[46] It is also suggestive of the ways in which the notion of 'home' is connected to state-centric notions of territorial sovereignty. And with its strong emotional content, the idea of 'home' is easily manipulated by ruling classes. Witness, as just one example, the way that the apartheid state of South Africa generated the idea of 'homelands' for various South African populations.

It is therefore clear that statelessness is imagined as a condition of infinite danger *to the state*. At the same time, however, 'statelessness' has actually been *functional* to the statist political imaginary in allowing the state system to protect the logic of state sovereignty. As Soguk shows, in its historical articulations and transformations the figure of the refugee has in fact been instrumental to the task of statecraft, for it has been important to the *enabling* of a specific imagination of the world. And that imagination is of the world organized in terms of the posited subjectivities, relations and institutions of the territorial state. In the political discourse surrounding the refugee one finds the statist or 'statized' imagination of the world presented as the presumed 'normal' world in which people live, and the territorial state posited as the natural 'order of things'. The space of the refugee is a point of reference for innumerable rearticulations of state sovereignty in various fields of political conduct – human rights, democracy, humanitarian intervention, security, international law. The territorial state is thus offered as the necessary system around which a 'normal' life is to be established and developed. Because of this, official organizations and political pronouncements treat the refugee as an abnormality, rooted in the refugee's absence of a home; the refugee's problem, in other words, is the absence of the state and the solution is a return to the state. This state-centric or statist imagination is thus built into refugee discourse. International refugee programmes and refugee discourse, for example, take for granted the state as the centre of the political universe. While purportedly concentrating on the problem of the refugee, refugee programmes are in fact intimately involved in the active production and stabilization of the territorial being of the modern citizen. There is an 'already there' quality in such programmes' representations of both state and refugee. The League of Nations High Commissioner for Refugees (LNHCR), for example, which emerged in the period following World War I to deal with the human displacement caused by the war, and the UN High Commissioner for Refugees (UNHCR) which replaced it, are presented in mainstream political discourse and official documentation as organizations concerned with non-political inter-governmental (i.e. cross-state) relief work. They have constructed the refugee as an ahistorical universal humanitarian subject; as a consequence, interventions around the refugee tend to be imagined as 'humanitarian'. On one level, the League of Nations and UN have thus depoliticized the refugee category.[47]

At another level, however, the actions of the League of Nations and the UN have been supremely political, in that they have served to consolidate the idea of the territorial state as the norm. In two conferences held in August and September 1921, the League of Nations formalized the problem of post-war human displacement as a 'refugee problem' and presented it in statist terms. The refugee was formally agreed to be a problem and the solution was formally agreed to lie in the return of refugees to a state they could call home. In other words, despite its inter-governmental and non-political appearance, the League operated to impose a *statist ontology* on the identity of the refugee. Such an ontology was developed in the following year with the invention of a new legal document for refugees that officially documented the displaced person as a refugee. A League of Nations conference in July 1922 agreed to create a special identity certificate for refugees and stateless persons, subsequently adopted by more than 50 states. The informal name given to the 'certificate of identity' – the 'Nansen passport' (after the first Commissioner, Fridtjof Nansen) – is revealing for what it tells us about the role the certificate was expected to play: it was nothing less than a substitute for the national passport held by *bona fide* citizens of territorial states, at the very time when states had begun resurrecting the national passport system more generally. While it was presented as a humanitarian attempt to provide refugees with the same measure of protection as those with 'normal' passports, the certificate replicated one of the key documents of identity through which states administer their own citizens. The identity certificates issued by the League of Nations sought to document otherwise stateless individuals through a refugee version of the passport. The League thus not only replicated one of the key practices of statecraft, but did so with the active collusion of states themselves, without which the system would have been unworkable. As Soguk points out, the certificate of identity 'enabled a set of practices that orchestrated the state into existence as a representative agent, representing and protecting what are seen as the a priori *normal* relations of governance'.[48] The state could thus be imagined and presented as a corrective agent, intervening in a set of events which are seen as deviating from the normal conditions of order. Of course, the refugee is here documented as a stateless person and thus a 'non-citizen'. This is made clear by the discussions concerning a suggestion to change the name of the 'identity certificate' to 'passport'. Those states that were willing to accept the change would do so only on the proviso that 'for refugees' was added to the name 'passport'.

The LNHCR and, following that, the UNHCR, therefore worked through the question of refugees in fundamentally statist terms, despite their supposedly non-political air. That the refugee was presented as a problem for states and the solution was thought to lie in the state should not surprise us. Since both organizations have been bodies with states as members – the 'nation' in their titles is designed to mislead – and which receive the overwhelming part of their funds from states, they have conceptualized and administered refugees within the logic of statism and a statist imagery of life. The UN thus implicitly treats the state as the proper subject of political life, and casts the modern citizen as, 'naturally', a member of a territorially bounded state. A 'home' imagined and identified as a particular state is posited as the normal condition of lived experience. Out of this a refugee is defined negatively as a homeless person who lacks the citizen's unproblematic grounding within a specific territory and thus the protection of a specific state. The UN defines itself as the instrument of its member states and, like its members, is pathologically incapable of imagining anything other than a state-centred solution to any problem generated by modernity.

A parallel argument can be made concerning the idea of the foreigner. In the process of inventing the national citizen and legally homogeneous national citizenry, the French Revolution also invented the foreigner. The invention of the rights of man simultaneously gave legitimacy to the concept of the foreigner; citizen and foreigner would thereafter be mutually exclusive categories. The democracy of the French Revolution was thus expected to exclude no one – *except foreigners*. One would be either citizen or foreigner; there would be no third way. As a result of this stark simplification in the political geometry of citizenship, *l'étranger* could symbolize pure extraneity in a manner that was not possible in the *ancien régime*. The revolutionary invention of the nation-state and national citizenship thus engendered the modern figure of the foreigner, not only as a legal category but as a political epithet, invested with a psychopolitical charge it formerly lacked and condensing around itself pure outsiderhood.[49] Representative of this investment is the fact that in some states foreigners who are allowed to remain in the country are officially registered as 'aliens'. From the Latin *aliengena*, 'alien' connotes 'stranger, a foreigner by birth'. The *Oxford English Dictionary* notes the first use of the term in 1330 and offers as one definition 'belonging to another person, place or family; strange, foreign, not one's own'.[50] As Marx would say: the political state is both constitutive of and constituted by alienation.

The distinction between the citizen as familiar and the foreigner as stranger was historically crucial to the process of state-building and remains crucial to the geography of order through which state power operates. As Julia Kristeva notes, the foreigner is always thought of in terms of political power and legal rights; the group to which the foreigner does not belong must therefore be a social group structured about a given kind of political power, namely the state: 'Indeed, without a social group structured about a power base and provided with legislation, that externality represented by the foreigner and most often experienced as unfavourable or at least problematical would simply not exist'.[51] Moreover, as a modern category the foreigner affords the state a space within which it can control the writing of the people through the mechanisms of political administration. The statistician-demographer Alphonse Bertillon's contribution to the *Dictionnaire des Sciences Médicales* (1878) is instructive in this regard:

> From the perspective of social accounting, a Nation is similar to a factory. Whether it is people or things that are produced, the keeping of books is subject to the same rules and obligations: One must record exactly what *enters*, what *exits*, establish the *balance* of this two-way movement and *verify*, according to the *state* of the register and the products in the store (inventory and counting), the accuracy of the account of *movements* (what comes in and what goes out).[52]

The foreigner, then, legitimizes and rationalizes the processes of political administration through which the state polices civil society. The state lays claim to a necessary knowledge of who comes into the territory and who leaves (and frequently keeps tabs on where they go when inside the territory). The monopoly over the legitimate means of violence is matched by the state's claim to what we might call a monopoly over the legitimate means of movement. Such monopoly relies on key documents such as the passport in order to effectively distinguish between citizen-subjects and foreigners.[53] It is here that the notion of the foreigner connects to that of the immigrant.

States have historically made a categorical distinction between the legal and the illegal immigrant. For the state there is a set of procedures and criteria (varying from state to state) for legal immigration. But legalities always create illegalities. Any 'unauthorized' international migration – that is, any international migration which has not been permitted by the states to and from which the individual is travelling – is specifically 'illegal'. And one of the reasons it is illegal is because the relevant documentation authorizing the travel has not been issued.[54] The existence of illegality is then used to justify even tighter administration of legal immigrants and, in turn, the administration of the population as a whole. The process is then presented as a defence of identity and the homeland – 'we need tough immigration procedures lest our identity and home come under threat' being the common refrain. As Bonnie Honig points out, this is what the politics of immigration is all about: the struggle and counter-struggle to define the terms of 'foreignness' in relation to the shifting terrain of state power by imagining the immigrant negatively as what 'we' are not.[55] The immigrant thus plays a particular social role – of the stranger/foreigner pursuing someone else's identity.

But a further reason the distinction between the citizen as familiar and the foreigner as stranger is important is because the foreigner is one of the means through which states form their image of the enemy. However strange the foreigner is or may be, they are not usually understood as a threat in the way that the refugee is. The foreigner has a home, a territorial space to which they belong; they just happen to be not 'at home' right now. Their lack of threat is witnessed by the fact that they will at some point return home, and should it be necessary they can always be expelled. The refugee on the other hand appears on the social periphery as a figure in search of a home; their 'homelessness' symbolizes the absence of statehood. Barbara Babcock has suggested that 'what is socially peripheral is often symbolically central'.[56] Nowhere is this clearer than in the figure of the refugee. Symbolically, the refugee connotes the possible pollution of the social body and, concomitantly, the introduction of discontent and disorder into the clean space of the political order. The refugee shares with the foreigner the (alien) identity of 'stranger', and both are situated on the same terrain as that which connects the stranger and the enemy. By marking negatively what 'we' are not, the move which runs foreigner → stranger → enemy helps to simultaneously constitute both the state as the focal point of political life and the foreigner as an ever-present threat. It is a move parallel to that which runs homeless/refugee → enemy. Such moves reveal the radical instability in the concept of 'human rights' and the politics of the 'homeland'.

We are now in a better position to answer the questions posed at the beginning of this section: if rights are granted to citizens of states, what happens to those with no state? That is, in a territorially divided world, what happens to those who belong to no territory? Historically, such questions became most pressing in the great displacement caused by World War I. The disruption of the war and its political aftermath created a situation of mass homelessness: thousands of peoples across Europe appeared to have been ejected from the old trinity of state-people-territory. As Hannah Arendt noted, this brought to the fore the tension between the universal and particular dimensions of citizen rights. If rights pertain to people as citizens rather than as humans, does this mean that those who appear to be non-citizens (i.e.

stateless) have no rights? Are they human beings if they are not citizens? In other words, the issue brought to the fore the perennial tension between human rights and state power.

Nowhere is this clearer than in the categorical answer to these questions provided by the Nazis. One of the major reasons for the Nazi hatred of the Jews was rooted in the idea that the Jews were a nation without a nation and, as such, were driven to occupy space within another national body. The Jew was unlike other foreigners, for not only was the Jew not at home in Germany, but the Jew was not at home anywhere. (The Gypsies shared this feature with the Jew, and thus had to share their fate). For the Nazis, being a 'foreigner' was the *essence* of being a Jew rather than a transitory state. As such, the Jew was thought to pose a double threat. Stubbornly refusing to adopt *the* mode of being, to adhere to *the* political form through which rootedness should be expressed, the Jews insisted on being a 'community' within other states. But on the other hand, being a 'non-national nation' meant that the Jews equally appeared to be an *inter*-national nation, in that their stateless condition encouraged them to drift across the borders of other, real, nations. Definitively: 'the Jewish state . . . is completely unlimited as to territory'; 'the Jewish state was never spatially limited in itself, but universally unlimited as to space'.[57] For the Nazis, this also explained the Jews' supposed propensity towards communist internationalism and intellectual cosmopolitanism. Physically, politically and intellectually, then, the Jew was considered a non-national element in a world of nations; with no nation the Jew had no home, and with no home the Jew appeared as the ultimate threat: 'Gentlemen, nothing is more dangerous for a state than people without a home', commented Robert Ley, speaking as leader of the German Labour Front to German industrialists in 1933.[58] Since the nation was to be the basis of the Nazi movement and German greatness, the medium through which rejuvenation and revitalization could occur, the nationless status of the Jews was thought to threaten this salvation from within. In 1938 the official SS newspaper, the *Schwarze Korps*, stated that since the world was increasingly faced with unidentifiable beggars as those without nationality, money and passports crossed borders, it would soon become convinced that homeless peoples were scum.[59] And in a sense he was right: other states treated the Jews exactly like scum. Dangerously strange and foreign, and dangerously without a home, the Jewish refugees undermined the geography of order created by the international state system. Shiploads of refugees therefore searched high and low for states to welcome them: 'once they had left their homeland they remained homeless, once they had left their state they became stateless; once they had been deprived of their human rights they were rightless, the scum of the earth'.[60]

The treatment of the Jews by the Nazis should not be thought of as a special case. Just as the political constitution of the enemy figure is not the work of fascist ideologues but is a ubiquitous feature of state power, so the Nazi party was far from alone in thinking that the *Heimat* could only be maintained through its identification with a specific space. The 'territorial sensibilities' expressed by the Nazis were adopted from the widely-held view which had connected the geo-body of the state to political identity and the national organism to its dwelling area. The Nazis adopted the kind of geopolitical thinking which was by then a common part of bourgeois ideology and social science, and a fundamental dimension of the statist imagination – the kind of thinking which identified the territorial state as the most fundamental political unit. In a German context, this approach centred *Raum* (space), *Lebensraum* (living space) and *Boden* (soil/ground) as the crucial motivations for political action; they merely took these ideas to their exterminationist conclusion.[61] In the inter-war period the Jews were the homeless *minorité par excellence*, but their case is representative. The Jews therefore served as both proof of and metaphor for the territorial dimension of the modern state; simultaneously, of course, they also symbolized its exclusionary and genocidal potential. As Hannah Arendt points out, in the period in question 'there was hardly a country left on the Continent that did not pass . . . some new legislation which, even if it did not use this right [of expulsion] extensively, was always phrased to allow for getting rid of a great number of its inhabitants at any opportune moment'.[62] In this sense the Jews can be seen as a paradigmatic example of the statist preoccupation with identity and territory. Thus although after World War II the problem of Jewish statelessness was solved through the colonizing impulse inherent in territorial sovereign formations – the Israeli state became a necessity in a world where only states are allowed to stake a claim to sovereignty – the problem of the stateless minority remained far from solved. Indeed, the creation of the new state merely generated a new category of Arab 'refugee' who in turn now figures as searching for a 'homeland'.

Such geopolitical thinking more or less fully consolidated the idea of the state as the ground of political identity. Statelessness became imagined as, in Walzer's terms, a condition of infinite danger, and thus as a condition to be abolished. The 1961 UN Convention on the Reduction of Statelessness (note: statelessness formally defined as a problem) insisted that 'everyone has a right to a nationality'. In doing so, it licensed a particular form of subjectivity which, as Michael Dillon points out, is inextricably linked to the state.[63] That is: everyone has a right to be a member of a state. The corollary, of course, is that no one has a right *not* to belong to a state.

The violence of cartography

One of the ways in which the Nazis developed their account of the threat to the German nation posed by the 'scum of the earth' was through an intensely political use of maps. The map was a crucial propaganda tool for the Nazis, being used to portray the 'injustice' of Europe's political geography, the extent of the Aryan race, the threat posed by world communism and the spread of the Jews. But this begs a question: what is it about the map that made it possible to use it in this way? The usual perception of the nature of maps is that they are a mirror, a graphic representation, of some aspect of the real world, and that the map presents a factual statement about geographical reality. Cartography is thus defined as a factual science.[64] But as a wealth of material from within the 'new geography' has argued at length, the map is an intensely political object and the practice of cartography has been crucial to the state and its territorial imagination.

In 1400 few people in Europe used maps, except for the Mediterranean navigators with their portolan charts; by 1600, however, maps were essential to a wide variety of professions.[65] This period was, as we have seen, the period in which the state came to the fore, and it is the emergence of the state and the need to delineate the borders of states, combined with the search for new trade routes, to which the theory and practice of cartography were committed. The early history of cartography is inseparable from the affirmation of monarchic power and a rising merchant class. Political theorists, advisers, diplomats, courtiers and spies all commended maps to statesmen, who in turn were their systematic collectors. As the abstract state replaced the personalized monarch and the nascent bourgeoisie replaced an aristocracy on the wane, so cartography remained inseparable from the affirmation of state power and integral to the fiscal, political and cultural hegemony of Europe's ruling elites. In this context the state became the principal patron of cartographic activity, and maps of the globe represent the contest between the major European powers for ownership of commercially valuable territories. As territory became more and more obviously central to the state and the multiple sovereignties of the feudal era were replaced by the unitary sovereign state, cartography – as a means of identifying the boundaries of the sovereign state's territories as well as its core features, a means of asserting ownership, sovereignty and legitimacy – emerged as a political discourse concerned with the acquisition and main-tenance of state power. The map became the perfect symbol of the state. To map a territory means to formally define space along the lines set within a particular epistemological and political experience – a way of knowing and dominating – transposing a little-known piece of concrete reality into an abstraction which serves the practical interests of the state, an operation done for and by the state.[66]

The map, then, has been an instrument of power. On a superficial level it is easy to see why the map appears to be a graphic representation of some aspect of the real world, for it presupposes the existence of borders and boundary lines. Logically this would appear to mean that boundary lines must exist *before* the map. But in reality the reverse has been true. As Winichakul comments, 'it is the concept of a nation in the modern geographical sense that requires the necessity of having boundary lines clearly demarcated. A map may not just function as a medium; it could well be the creator of the supposed reality'.[67] Sovereignty does not just imply space, it creates it; left to itself, the landscape has no political form. We need to therefore appreciate the political function of maps in *constructing* rather than merely reproducing the world and in *creating* rather than merely tracing borders. Borders are constructed through a socio-political process; to the extent that the map helps create the borders, so it helps create the thing which is being bordered: the geo-body created literally on paper.[68] Given that the world being constructed is one in which the earth's surface is carved up under the territorial ambitions of political states, mapping is a crucial instrument in concretizing the territorial desire of states onto the earth's surface, constituting the social order by shaping the way land is imagined. In fabricating the territorial foundation of order, it is no exaggeration to describe the map as a having a police function, delineating the contours of power and property through which civil society is administered.

This is abundantly clear from the wealth of research on the role of maps in the construction of colonial space and imperial domination. The imperial powers used maps as a means of shaping colonial spaces in advance. Harley has outlined how:

> The division of the world by a Pope – on a map – *preceded* the arrival of most European peoples, yet it endangered political demarcations that were and were meant to be enduring. The names New England, New France, or New Spain were placed on maps long *before* the settlement frontiers of New England, New France, or New Spain became active zones of European settlement. John Smith's well-known map of New England of 1614, with its carefully fabricated English names, *preceded* the arrival of Puritan settlers.[69]

And once in power, imperial adventurers have always been quick to utilize the map in fabricating a particular order among the indigenous population. The ability to impose names that would then take root in the territory was a key feature of the colonial process. When Columbus arrived in the 'Indies' he imposed his own names for the islands over the already existing names of the natives. When the French mapped Martinique and Guadeloupe after the Seven Years War (1756–63), the mapping was carried out with a view to the plantation system being put in place – the names of owners but not those of workers were noted – and with the need to provide information on the territory with future hostilities with England in mind. More generally, the nomadic nature of many of the native peoples of Africa, Asia and Australasia was deemed problematic to a process which needed to locate people in space, and was thus gradually eradicated. Mapping was functional to the reorganization and redistribution of space to suit such an exercise of power, and cartography, with its strategies of inscription, enclosure and hierarchization, proved a crucial technique for the acquisition, management and reinforcement of colonial power, providing a portrait of how successfully the search for territory by expansionist European states had helped them shape the New World.[70]

Cartography's predisposition towards colonialism and imperialism was derived in part from the strength of the historic tie between the discipline of geography (which became a formal discipline taught in universities in the heyday of imperial power) and the state. Far from being something already possessed by the earth, geography has been an active writing of the earth by an expanding, centralizing imperial state. State sovereignty has developed out of an almost mythical power of geographic authority, inscribing lines of antagonism and identity across the face of the earth.[71] This active writing on the part of the imperial state correlates with the fact that, as Edward Said notes, imperialism is an act of *geographical* violence through which virtually every space in the world is explored, charted and finally brought under control.[72] And once in place, the map helped to illuminate the late colonial state's style of thinking about its domain, part of the totalizing classificatory grid which the state uses to order and comprehend civil society. In helping the European powers to create a world in their own image, cartography helped stabilize the earth's surface around the territorial imaginary of the modern state.

In being used to assert and settle territorial claims, the political importance of the map is obvious: it is one of the most explicit assertions of sovereignty. But as the colonial experience suggests, the labour of power involved in mapping is a labour of identifying, bounding, naming and creating an inventory of the territory or homeland of the state. Mapmakers were historically charged with the same task as information-gatherers had concerning citizens: to make space an object of political knowledge.[73] Spatial politics in general and mapmaking in particular are thus part of the epistemological project of state power, being inextricably bound up with the intelligence-gathering propensities outlined in Chapter 2. It is impossible to undertake an accurate census or other forms of statistical administration unless there is some territorial framework on which to base the work. In cataloguing space, the map adds documentary intelligence concerning territory to the wealth of other intelligence the state holds about itself. It increases the legibility of the territory by identifying key features of the geographical order fabricated by the state. Etymologically the map is a conception of the arrangement of something as much as it is a representation of the earth's surface, while 'off the map' is defined by the *Oxford English Dictionary* as describing something 'out of existence . . . an insignificant position; of no account; obsolete'. The state's cartographic project thus helps it define who or what exists and in what order. Maps are thus a means of both physical colonization and conceptual control, involving both a cognitive paradigm as well as a practical means of political administration.

As a form of knowledge maps have therefore been shrouded in the veil of secrecy we identified in Chapter 2 as central to statecraft. Maps were historically regarded as privileged knowledge, with access given only to those close to the core of state power; map secrecy, like other forms of secrecy, came to be regarded as a prudent policy of good government. This practice of cartographic secrecy can be traced back to the sixteenth-century Spanish and Portuguese policy of *siglio*. The Spanish kept their official charts in a lockbox secured with two locks and keys held by different persons, while Prince Henry the Navigator of Portugal banned the dissemination of geographical documents and shrouded them in a veil of secrecy. Columbus' voyages yielded massive amounts of geographical information and generated a range of maps which the Spanish tried to keep secret, and his journal was also treated as a secret document (and subsequently lost). In the first decade of the sixteenth century the Castillan court established the *Casa de Contracion*, a department to oversee exploration and to house in secrecy the documents produced, including the master world map, the *Padron Real*.[74]

Such secrecy is said to be anathema to the modern democratic polity. One of the tropes of liberal democratic discourse is that 'our' maps are neutral, accurate, objective and above all open, while non-liberal democratic regimes maintain non-neutral, inaccurate, biased and above all secret maps. It is well known that Soviet street maps of Moscow used to 'overlook' the KGB building on Dzerzhinski Square, despite the fact that one could hardly miss it. But there is abundant evidence that certain forms of cartographic secrecy continue to this day in all regimes. Official mapmaking agencies have traditionally been reticent about publishing the details of military installations, for example, and even about publishing the details of the rules which govern the publication of such information. There are places which do not officially exist and which therefore cannot appear on maps. In Britain the organization responsible for maps, the Ordnance Survey, operates a system for grading certain types of building or location. A nuclear weapons establishment is graded 'S' and the Ordnance Survey ensures that such places remain 'secret' by 'vanishing' them from maps. Other vanishing sites are coded 'U' and 'F', and cover such things as GCHQ radio stations and government-owned oil terminals. Maps of Catoctin Mountain National Park in western Maryland, USA, generally camouflage Camp David, the presidential retreat. Some states, such as Greece, publish maps with large blank areas. Under the guise of 'national security', then, maps are universally censored, kept secret and falsified.[75] One response to this has been to demand 'accuracy': states should live up to the supposedly scientific nature of the cartographic endeavour by aiming to achieve the most accurate maps possible; any political interference with this is by definition wrong. But 'accuracy' here is misleading, for it assumes that maps are intended to achieve a literally accurate representation of the thing that they map. A far better notion might be one of efficiency. Maps are intended to convey the concepts or information intended by the dominant political forces, and a better question would ask how efficiently they do this.[76] That some maps may be 'inaccurate' could well be part of their efficiency.

A key component of the claim to accuracy is the map's apparently author-less condition, which renders it a neutral phenomenon. As Denis Wood argues, part of the map's power lies in the *disappearance* of the author. Author and interest become marginalized or done away with altogether, and the represented world comes to fill our vision. The apparent absence of author and interest encourages us to forget that this is a picture someone has arranged for us, chopped and manipulated, selected and coded. Soon enough the map becomes the world and the reality of the thing most commonly represented – the borders of states – becomes entrenched in the political imagination.[77]

Two things follow from this mystification. First, the map performs a crucial role in the cultural integration of the people ('one class interest' or 'national identity') by helping form an image of the state with which inhabit-ants can identify. Through the myth of unity and naturalness, maps hom-ogenize the land's inhabitants and focus their political imagination around the state. The apparently non-political weather map, to take a mundane example, takes as its point of reference the political unit: 'Thus, in Britain, the inhabitant of Kent is provided with more information about the situation in distant Westmorland than in nearby Pas-de-Calais, which is in a different nation-state. The former is assumed to be more relevant . . . [The map] is a statement of the centrality of the national sphere even in fields in which the state . . . plays no role'.[78] The constant reiteration of cartographic images of the state in, for example, rail and road maps also ensures that the shape and terri-torial outline of the state becomes clearly established. A polity imagines itself, and is imagined by others, in part through its cartographic image. The central-ity of the form of the state to the process of mapping facilitates the identifica-tion of individual citizens with a particular territorial imagination of the space with which they are expected to identify and be most concerned. Moreover, the territorial imaginary figures one's emotional roots in *this* homeland as real physical roots in *this* soil. The cartographical convention testifies to a key component of the ideology of statism: that however diverse the human experience within its borders, a unitary and natural state power predominates overall. If the administrative and statistical tabulation of the census populates the national body with fractured subjects, then the map helps enact imma-nent political units, relocating these subjects in a (re)unified body politic and thereby functioning as a crucial building block in the construction of national identity.

Second, in obliterating significant political questions the map serves to *naturalize* the historically contingent. Pierre Bourdieu comments that 'every established order tends to produce . . . the naturalization of its own arbitrariness'.[79] By encouraging a belief in the naturalness of the nation the cartographic enterprise encourages the state to see and think of its territory in terms of 'natural' boundaries, and thus its very existence is naturalized. The intensely *political* and *violent* processes through which borders are established and social order is fabricated are obliterated: the social order established by the state appears as a natural order established by geography. The map thus plays an important role in the ruling-class tendency to erase from the political imagination the violence and bloodshed out of which the state was born: territory and terror are ideologically torn asunder. Map, territory and power become mutually implicated in one another as the map encourages a primordialist thesis about the autochthonous state, depoliticizing and ideologically mystifying the original violence through which the state and its territory were shaped. Actions conducted under *raison d'État* appear to contain the interests not of an arbitrarily configured political power, but of 'natural' (biological, organic) needs. The great achievement of this naturalization is to have depoliticized inter-state rivalry into a set of natural geographical 'facts of life'.

As a consequence, the map helps to mask the violence that brings the state into being and the interests that sustain the ideological preponderance of the state system. Borders may be drawn in blood, but the blood never appears on the page. It is the repetitive impact of the image of the territory mapped that lends credence to the claims of control; that is the way of myth. From the perspective of myth, the delineation of the state's borders is of the essence. Outside the world of maps, states carry on a precarious existence for, as I have been arguing, to map a state is to assert its territorial expression; to leave a state off a map is to deny its existence. Thus the map is crucial to the recognition of the state as an international subject, for an unmapped state is an unrecognized one, and vice versa. As a crucial political technology of space, the map simultaneously illustrates the territorial imperative which gave birth to and sustains the state, and yet also masks the inherently violent nature of that same project. In dominating the political imagination in this way the map legitimizes the great movement of territorialization through which the whole earth has been turned into an object of state ownership.

Coda

To say that the whole earth has been turned into an object of state ownership would appear to run against one of the implications of what is perhaps the master concept of our time: globalization. One can barely move in the bookshops for tomes on the topic or read a newspaper without coming across the term several times; and one can certainly not fail to notice the term slide from the lips of politicians. Perhaps the most fashionable of all concepts in the social sciences, the term has now become a catch-phrase for journalists and politicians of every stripe. It is endorsed in different disciplines, advanced by both theoretical innovators and traditionalists and found across the political spectrum.[1] I want to briefly consider the globalization thesis and the claims it makes regarding the territorial state, as a way of finishing the argument in this book.

The 'globalization thesis' asserts that the world economy is becoming more and more integrated and, as a consequence, cultural and/or national differences are breaking down; within this thesis the concept of state redundancy is usually assumed. We are told that states are unnatural or even dysfunctional actors in a global economy;[2] that states are doomed to extinction in a 'borderless world';[3] and that we are living after or at the end of the nation-state.[4] In terms of spatiality the argument is that 'territory has lost its significance' – we are witnessing the 'end of geography' rather than history.[5] On a superficial level – and it has to be said that many of the arguments about globalization are indeed superficial – such pronouncements appear as though they have history on their side: the usual list of recent transformations trawled out as evidence includes the fall of the Berlin Wall, the disintegration of the Soviet state, the development of inter- or super-state associations such as the EU and the rise of separatist movements and regional autonomy, all bound up with an overall claim about the growing power of global corporations. But while it may appear as though the sovereign state is in decline, a more nuanced view is needed.

There is little evidence, either empirical or theoretical, to suggest that the state is on its way out. The assumption that increasingly neo-liberal policies towards capital accumulation are gradually eroding the state is based on a fundamental misconception about what it means to be a sovereign state. To exercise sovereignty does not mean deciding on the detail of everything that takes place within every sphere of society; it can just as easily involve the decision that on this or that particular issue the state will, for the time being at least, stand at arm's length. In the current political conjuncture the state stands at arm's length from the process of capital accumulation (relative to the post-war period that is). To make such a choice is, however, part of the function of the state. In that sense, the global intensification of capital accumulation is an *exercise* rather than a supersession of state sovereignty. To define states and global accumulation as somehow mutually exclusive operations or in zero-sum terms is nonsensical. States have merely used their sovereignty to redefine their role *vis-à-vis* international capital.[6]

Moreover, the process of globalization has been shaped and managed *by* states, in league with international capital. In 1997, for example, some 1513 bilateral trade agreements were reached – over four a day. Likewise, the removal of controls on cross-border financial flows, the massive privatization of public assets and deregulation in other spheres have all been accomplished through state action. The liberalization of financial markets has not involved any abdication by states of their supervision of banks. On the contrary, states have promoted an array of cooperative arrangements including the founding of a bank supervisors' committee by the Group of Ten countries, summer schools of bank regulators and the articulation of internationally accepted principles and rules of banking supervision.[7] States, in other words, have played an active and fundamental role in making globalization happen. As Marxists have long argued, the capitalist system would not last a week if it were not for the state, which takes its role as the executive committee of the ruling class seriously. Just who is wielding the truncheons and water cannon against the anti-capitalist protestors if it is not the agents of the state?

The idea that globalization is bringing about the end of the state is thus clearly a myth of the highest political order. To say that we are moving towards a 'borderless world' reveals an almost unbelievable naivety. To be sure, finance capital in particular may be more mobile now, but in other ways borders are becoming even more entrenched. Witness, as just a few examples, the introduction of strict regulations concerning the entry into the EU of certain groups of people (tellingly: Africans, Asians and Caribbeans), the intensification of border patrols along the frontier between Mexico and the USA, and the fact that in 1999 Canada spent $300 million on border protection against refugees – ten times its contribution to UNHCR funds. Better still, try telling asylum seekers being returned back 'home' that we live in a borderless world. And we should remind ourselves of the importance of the passport in still rooting individuals to a particular territory.

Charles Tilly and Michael Mann have argued that the evidence is that the obituary of the state system will be hard to write; the state may be diversifying and developing, but it is far from dying.[8] But what the globalization thesis and the examples just given touch on is actually something far more subtle, something that draws our attention to the central tension within capital accumulation first pointed out by Marx. On the one hand, the capital relation is inherently a 'global' one. In the *Manifesto of the Communist Party* this is described as 'intercourse in every direction' and the generation of the 'world market': 'the need of a constantly expanding market for its products chases the bourgeoisie over the whole surface of the globe. It must nestle everywhere, settle everywhere, establish connections everywhere'.[9] In the *Grundrisse* this becomes reformulated as the 'annihilation of space' inherent in the capital relation.

> Capital by its nature drives beyond every spatial barrier. Thus the creation of the physical conditions of exchange [and] the annihilation of space by time becomes an extraordinary necessity for it . . . Thus, while capital must on one side strive to tear down every spatial barrier to intercourse, i.e. to exchange, and conquer the whole earth for its market, it strives on the other side to annihilate space with time.[10]

The particular space being annihilated is the space of the nation-state. 'National one-sidedness and narrow-mindedness become more and more impossible' as the bourgeoisie 'compels all nations, on pain of extinction, to adopt the bourgeois mode of production'.[11] On the other hand, Marx understands the historical significance of the territorial and politically centralizing tendencies of the bourgeois class. As he and Engels point out in the *Manifesto*, the necessary consequence of the bourgeoisie's subjection of the country to the rule of the city, agglomeration of the population and centralization of the means of production and property, has been political centralization: 'Independent, or but loosely connected provinces, with separate interests, laws, governments and systems of taxation, became lumped together into one nation, with one government, one code of laws, one national class interest, one frontier and one customs tariff'.[12]

Thus the success of the bourgeois class contains a foundational tension: it succeeds by simultaneously *annihilating space* through its global ambitions and by *producing territorial space* through the projection of state power across the globe. This tension has been present since the emergence of the bourgeois class and the capitalist state, and so long as capital survives there is no reason to think that this will change. For even while international capital flows ever more freely, the state continues to set itself up as the centre around which the citizen's identity and political imagination are organized. In other words, despite the incredible transworld reach and mobility of capital, border controls remain very real indeed for labour. Whatever the extent of the globalization of capital, humanity itself remains far from global – it remains rooted to the territorial ambitions of the modern state.

This leaves those on the Left with a conundrum. Any challenge to the social and economic power of the bourgeois class will have to take on the structures of territorial domination through which that class rules. Rather than an *anti*-globalization movement, what is needed is in fact a movement for *democratic globalization*, a *nonterritorial democratization* of power.[13] To operate *against* state boundaries any such movement – a 'geography of insurrection' in opposition to the geography of order[14] – would have to aim to disturb both the entrenched power of the capitalist corporations which dominate our lives and the normal operation of state-centred and territorially based sovereignty. In other words, as well as being anti-capitalist, a movement for democratic globalization would have to disrupt state-centred concepts of citizenship and belonging, state-centric definitions of political participation and democracy, and the state-focused political imagination as a whole. In the context of an anti-capitalism that currently presents itself as anti-globalization this might seem an odd claim, but in fact it is entirely consistent with one of the most important traditions of the Left, namely its internationalism. We should recall that such internationalism, embodied in Marx's injunction for workers of the world to unite, was aimed at undermining not just the socio-economic power of the capitalist class but also the political power of the territorial state. It is also entirely consistent with the fact that a movement labelled 'anti-globalization' can be co-opted for fascism: as the anti-globalization protestors fail to see, to be anti-globalization could just as easily lead to a reterritorialization of capital – that is, to *national socialism*.

Intellectually, such a movement would therefore have to encourage the view that 'the state' is only one way of organizing and imagining space. If we are to recover a sense of the range of political possibilities which exist for us then we have to think politics outside of the statist political imaginary, while at the same time addressing such an imaginary in order to undermine it. We need to start imagining, for example, an end to all nationality codes and the possibility of travelling across borders as freely as capital. It is indicative of the strength of the statist imagination that the idea of moving across the face of the earth without a passport does not come easy; it is indicative of the power of the state that practising such an idea is currently impossible, and looks like remaining so. Challenging the statist imaginary will therefore not be an easy task since, as I have tried to show, in dominating the political imagination states encourage us to think that territorially-based sovereignty (i.e. the state) is a necessary feature of political life in general and democratic society in particular. In so doing a connection is constantly reinforced between political collectivity and territorial space, nature and nation, and strangeness and danger. Moreover, any such movement comes with its own dangers, for challenging the territorial state raises the very real possibility of the kind of even more violent reterritorialization which often follows any deterritorialization.[15] And, as with the most violent reassertion of sovereignty, the most fantastic reterritorialization is the fascist state.

Notes

Introduction

1 Susan Buck-Morss, *Dreamworld and Catastrophe: The Passing of Mass Utopia in East and West* (Cambridge, MA: MIT Press, 2000), pp. 12–13.
2 Pierre Clastres, *Society Against the State: Essays in Political Anthropology* (1974), trans. Robert Hurley (New York: Zone Books, 1989), pp. 189–94.
3 Michael Walzer, 'On the role of symbolism in political thought', *Political Science Quarterly*, Vol. 82, No. 2, 1967, pp. 191–204, 194.
4 Stuart Hall, 'Blue election, election blues', *Marxism Today*, July 1987, pp. 30–35, 33.
5 Edmund Burke, *Reflections on the Revolution in France* (1790), ed. Conor Cruise O'Brien (Harmondsworth: Penguin, 1968), pp. 171, 218. Burke also comments on how the revolutionaries may imagine his own argument at pp. 85, 181.
6 Mary Wollstonecraft, *A Vindication of the Rights of Men* (1790), in *Political Writings* (Oxford: Oxford University Press, 1994), pp. 5, 14, 44, 48, 56, 57, 58, 61.
7 Thomas Paine, *Rights of Man* (1791–2), in *Rights of Man, Common Sense and Other Political Writings*, ed. Mark Philp (Oxford: Oxford University Press, 1995), pp. 132, 173, 193, 234.
8 John Barrell, *Imagining the King's Death: Figurative Treason, Fantasies of Regicide 1793–1796* (Oxford: Oxford University Press, 2000).
9 Raymond Williams, *Keywords* (London: Fontana, 1976), p. 130.
10 Michael Oakeshott, 'The vocabulary of modern European state', *Political Studies*, Vol. 23, Nos. 2–3, 1975, pp. 319–41.
11 Theodor Adorno and Max Horkheimer, *Dialectic of Enlightenment* (1944), trans. John Cumming (London: Verso, 1979), p. 211.
12 Buck-Morss, *Dreamworld and Catastrophe*, p. 17.
13 Credit here to James Holstun, *Ehud's Dagger: Class Struggle in the English Revolution* (London: Verso, 2000), p. ix.
14 Anthony Giddens, *The Third Way: The Renewal of Social Democracy* (Cambridge: Polity Press, 1998), pp. 70–7; Ulrich Beck, *Democracy Without Enemies*, trans. Mark Ritter (Cambridge: Polity Press, 1998), pp. 141–53.
15 Pierre Bourdieu, 'Rethinking the state: genesis and structure of the bureaucratic field', in George Steinmetz (ed.) *State/Culture: State-Formation after the Cultural Turn* (Ithaca, NY: Cornell University Press, 1999), p. 53.
16 Walter Benjamin, 'Theses on the philosophy of history' (1940), in *Illuminations*, trans. Harry Zohn (London: Fontana, 1973), p. 259.

Chapter 1

1 Respectively: *International Herald Tribune*, 10 August 1987; *New York Times*, 29 April 1981; *Time*, 8 December 1986. For Reagan on his bottom see Ronald Reagan, *Where's the Rest of Me?* (New York: Karz Publishers, 1965), p. 3.

2 Terry Eagleton, 'It is not quite true that I have a body', *London Review of Books*, 27 May 1993, p. 7.

3 Theodore R. Schatzki and Wolfgang Natter, 'Sociocultural bodies, bodies sociopolitical', in Theodore R. Schatzki and Wolfgang Natter (eds) *The Social and Political Body* (New York: Guilford Press, 1996), p. 1.

4 David George Hale, *The Body Politic: A Political Metaphor in Renaissance English Literature* (The Hague: Mouton, 1971), p. 137; J.A.W. Gunn, *Beyond Liberty and Property: The Process of Self-Recognition in Eighteenth-Century Political Thought* (Kingston: McGill-Queen's University Press, 1983), p. 194; E.M.W. Tillyard, *The Elizabethan World Picture* (Harmondsworth: Penguin, 1970). In contrast, Catherine A. Holland, *The Body Politic: Foundings, Citizenship, and Difference in the American Political Imagination* (London: Routledge, 2001), argues that political thought has never overcome or abandoned its pre-modern past, but has reworked 'archaisms' such as the body politic. While this is true, as I shall show later in this chapter, Holland reduces this reworked 'body politic' to a question of the individual human body, and is thus much closer to the new somatic than to my argument here.

5 Hale, *Body Politic*, p. 8; Jens Bartelson, *A Genealogy of Sovereignty* (Cambridge: Cambridge University Press, 1995), p. 210; Jonathan M. Hess, *Reconstituting the Body Politic: Enlightenment, Public Culture and the Invention of Aesthetic Autonomy* (Detroit, MI: Wayne State University Press, 1999), pp. 29, 88.

6 John of Salisbury, *Policraticus: Of the Frivolities of Courtiers and the Footprints of Philosophers*, trans. Cary Nederman (Cambridge: Cambridge University Press, 1990), Bk. V, Ch. 2, pp. 66–7.

7 Christine de Pizan, *The Book of the Body Politic* (1406), trans. Kate Langdon Forhan (Cambridge: Cambridge University Press, 1994), p. 4; see also pp. 58, 90–91.

8 Marsilius of Padua, *The Defender of Peace* (1324), trans. Alan Gewirth (New York: Harper Torchbooks, 1956), p. 326.

9 Sir John Fortescue, *In Praise of the Laws of England* (1468–71), in Shelley Lockwood (ed.) *On the Laws and Governance of England* (Cambridge: Cambridge University Press, 1997), pp. 20–1.

10 Leonard Barkin, *Nature's Work of Art: The Human Body as Image of the World* (New Haven, CT: Yale University Press, 1975), p. 74.

11 Cited in Ernst H. Kantorowicz, *The King's Two Bodies: A Study in Medieval Political Theology* (Princeton, NJ: Princeton University Press, 1957), p. 194.

12 Otto Gierke, *Political Theories of the Middle Age* (1900), trans. F.W. Maitland (Cambridge: Cambridge University Press, 1987), pp. 18–19.

13 Gierke, *Political Theories*, pp. 10–13.

14 Kantorowicz, *King's Two Bodies*, pp. 15–16, 206–8, 216–18, 231; Anton-Hermann Chroust, 'The corporate idea and the body politic in the Middle Ages', *Review of Politics*, Vol. 9, No. 4, 1947, pp. 423–52; Louis Marin, *Portrait of the King*, trans. Martha M. Houle (London: Macmillan, 1988), p. 12.

15 Ernest William Talbert, *The Problem of Order: Elizabethan Political Commonplaces and an Example of Shakespeare's Art* (Chapel Hill, NC: University of North Carolina Press, 1962), p. 19.

16 24 Henr. VIII, c.12, in J. R. Tanner, *Tudor Constitutional Documents A.D. 1485–1603, with an Historical Commentary* (Cambridge: Cambridge University Press, 1922), p. 41.

17 Thomas Starkey, *A Dialogue Between Reginald Pole and Thomas Lupset*, ed. Kathleen Burton (London: Chatto & Windus, 1948). Though not widely discussed in 'the history of political thought', Starkey's book is of crucial historical importance. Pole and Lupset were both scholars of wide reputation, Pole also being cousin to the king. J.W. Allen, *A History of Political Thought in the Sixteenth Century* (London: Methuen, 1957), p. 143, describes the book as 'by far the most remarkable piece of writing concerned with politics that was produced in England under Henry VIII, with the exception of More's *Utopia*'. More importantly, Quentin Skinner claims that perhaps the earliest instance of the term 'state' being used in an impersonal sense is in Starkey's *Dialogue*. That this occurs in the context of the idea of the body politic is of obvious significance. See *The Foundations of Modern Political Thought, Vol. 2: The Age of Reformation* (Cambridge: Cambridge University Press, 1978), p. 356.

18 Starkey, *Dialogue*, pp. 79–81, 86, 120, 127, 129, 131–3, 145, 178–80.

19 Starkey, *Dialogue*, pp. 77–8, 87, 90, 91, 108, 124, 145, 161.

20 Jens Bartelson, *The Critique of the State* (Cambridge: Cambridge University Press, 2001), p. 45.

21 Paul D. Halliday, *Dismembering the Body Politic: Partisan Politics in England's Towns, 1650–1730* (Cambridge: Cambridge University Press, 1998), pp. 3–5, 58.

22 Thomas Hobbes, *Leviathan* (1651), ed. Richard Tuck (Cambridge: Cambridge University Press, 1991), p. 128.

23 Starkey, *Dialogue*, pp. 79, 88, 123–4, 148, 168.

24 Starkey, *Dialogue*, pp. 80–3, 87–8.

25 Edmund Plowden, *Commentaries or Reports* (1571) (London: 1816), cited in Kantorowicz, *King's Two Bodies*, p. 7.

26 Kantorowicz, *King's Two Bodies*, pp. 421–5. See also Ralph Giesey, in *The Royal Funeral Ceremony in Renaissance France* (Geneva: Librarie E. Droz, 1960).

27 F.W. Maitland, 'The crown as corporation' (1901), in *The Collected Papers of Frederic William Maitland, Vol. III* (Cambridge: Cambridge University Press, 1911), p. 249.

28 J.G.A. Pocock, *The Machiavellian Moment: Florentine Political Thought and the Atlantic Republican Tradition* (Princeton, NJ: Princeton University Press, 1975), pp. 75–6; Bartelson, *Critique of the State*, p. 37.

29 Jeremy Bentham, *An Essay on Political Tactics* (1791), in John Bowing (ed.) *The Works of Jeremy Bentham, Vol. II* (Edinburgh: William Tait, 1843), p. 306. On the question of time see Marie Axton, *The Queen's Two Bodies: Drama and the Elizabethan Succession* (London: Royal Historical Society, 1977), p. 12; Bartelson, *Genealogy of Sovereignty*, p. 97; Kantorowicz, *King's Two Bodies*, p. 438.

30 Giorgio Agamben, *Homo Sacer: Sovereign Power and Bare Life*, trans. Daniel Heller-Roazen (Standford, CA: Stanford University Press, 1998), pp. 93, 101; José Gil, *Metamorphoses of the Body*, trans. Stephen Muecke (Minneapolis, MN: University of Minnesota Press, 1998), pp. 298, 311.

31 Jean Bodin, *Six Books of the Commonwealth* (1576), trans. M.J. Tooley (Oxford: Basil Blackwell, n.d.), p. 25.

32 Quentin Skinner, *The Foundations of Modern Political Thought, Vol. 1: The Renaissance* (Cambridge: Cambridge University Press, 1978), Preface; *Foundations of Modern Political Thought, Vol. 2*, pp. 356–8.

33 Carl Schmitt, *The Concept of the Political* (1932), trans. George Schwab (Chicago: University of Chicago Press, 1996), p. 42. The 'war on terrorism' declared by the USA and its allies in September 2001 was initially called 'Operation Infinite Justice'. This was withdrawn after religious groups pointed out that only God can dispense infinite justice. Commentators interpreted this as a cultural oversight (or insult) on the part of US politicians. My guess is that they knew what they were doing: they thought the state could play the part of God.

34 Otto Gierke, *Natural Law and the Theory of Society 1500 to 1800* (1913), trans. Ernest Barker (Boston, MA: Beacon Press, 1957), p. 41.

35 Michel Foucault, 'Truth and power' (1977), trans. Colin Gordon, in *Power/Knowledge: Selected Interviews and Other Writings 1972–1977* (Brighton: Harvester, 1980), p. 121.

36 I am playing here with comments by F.W. Maitland, 'Moral personality and legal personality' (1903), in *Collected Papers, Vol. III*, p. 313, and Ernst Kantorowicz, 'Mysteries of state: an absolutist concept and its late Medieval Origins', *Harvard Theological Review*, Vol. 48, 1955, pp. 65–91, p. 67.

37 For a similar question in the context of the work of Kant see Diane Morgan, *Kant Trouble: The Obscurities of the Enlightened* (London: Routledge, 2000), p. 86.

38 Georges Bataille, *The Accursed Share, Volumes II and III* (1976), trans. Robert Hurley (New York: Zone Books, 1993), p. 222.

39 Hobbes, *Leviathan*, pp. 9–10.

40 Aristotle, *The Politics*, in Stephen Everson (ed.) *The Politics and The Constitution of Athens* (Cambridge: Cambridge University Press, 1996), Bk. I, para. 1253.

41 Hobbes, *Leviathan*, pp. 269, 463.

42 Thomas Hobbes, *Elements of Philosophy. The First Section, Concerning Body*, in Sir William Molesworth (ed.) *The English Works of Thomas Hobbes, Vol. I* (London: John Bohn, 1839), p. 11.

43 John Locke, *Two Treatises of Government* (1698) (Cambridge: Cambridge University Press, 1988), Bk. II, Ch. VII, s. 93.

44 Hobbes, *Leviathan*, p. 306.

45 Hess, *Reconstituting the Body Politic*, p. 94.

46 Carl Schmitt, *The Leviathan in the State Theory of Thomas Hobbes: Meaning and Failure of a Political Symbol* (1938), trans. George Schwab and Erna Hilfstein (Westport, CT: Greenwood Press, 1996), p. 34.

47 Thomas Hobbes, *De Homine* (1658) in Hobbes, *Man and Citizen (De Homine and De Cive)*, ed. Bernard Gert (Indianapolis, IN: Hackett, 1991), p. 35.

48 Thus it is not surprising that for all their differences, Rousseau's 'democratic republicanism' turns out to resemble Hobbes' model. For Rousseau too 'the constitution of man is the work of nature; that of the State the work of art', and the 'tutelary God' that is his 'republican absolute' has little to distinguish it from Hobbes' 'mortal God' or 'God on earth'. See Jean-Jacques Rousseau, *The Social Contract* (1762), in *The Social Contract and Discourses*, trans. G.D.H. Cole (London: Dent & Sons, 1973), pp. 191, 235.

49 Locke, *Two Treatises*, Bk. II, Ch. II, s. 14; Bk. II, Ch. VII, s. 87, 89, 94; Bk. II, Ch. VIII, s. 95, 96, 97.

50 Antoine de Baecque, *The Body Politic: Corporeal Metaphor in Revolutionary France, 1770–1800*, trans. Charlotte Mandell (Stanford, CA: Stanford University Press, 1997), pp. 39, 51–9; Peter Brooks, *Body Work: Objects of Desire in Modern Narrative* (Cambridge, MA: Harvard University Press, 1993), p. 58; Robert Darnton, *The Forbidden Best-sellers of Pre-Revolutionary France* (London: Fontana, 1997), pp. 165, 241; Sarah Melzer and Kathryn Norberg (eds) *From the Royal to the Republican Body: Incorporating the Political in Seventeenth- and Eighteenth-Century France* (Berekely, CA: University of California Press, 1998); Diana Outram, *The Body and the French Revolution: Sex, Class and Political Culture* (New Haven, CT: Yale University Press, 1989), p. 74; Simon Schama, *Citizens: A Chronicle of the French Revolution* (New York: Viking, 1989), p. 205; Chantal Thomas, *The Wicked Queen: The Origins of the Myth of Marie-Antoinette*, trans. Julie Rose (New York: Zone Books, 1999), pp. 25, 50, 114. For similar points regarding an earlier context see Abby E. Zanger, *Scenes from the Marriage of Louis XIV: Nuptial Fictions and the Making of Absolutist Power* (Stanford, CA: Stanford University Press, 1997), pp. 44, 98.

51 Jonathan Gil Harris, *Foreign Bodies and the Body Politic: Discourses of Social Pathology in Early Modern England* (Cambridge: Cambridge University Press, 1998), p. 141; Gunn, *Beyond Liberty and Property*, pp. 194–5; Werner Stark, *The Fundamental Forms of Social Thought* (London: Routledge, 1962).

52 Claude Lefort, *The Political Forms of Modern Society: Bureaucracy, Democracy, Totalitarianism* (Cambridge: Polity Press, 1986), pp. 302–3; 'How did you

become a philosopher?', in Alan Montefiore (ed.) *Philosophy in France Today* (Cambridge: Cambridge University Press, 1983), p. 85; *Democracy and Political Theory*, trans. David Macey (Cambridge: Polity Press, 1988), pp. 234–5.

53 Simon Critchley, 'Re-tracing the political', in David Campbell and Michael Dillon (eds) *The Political Subject of Violence* (Manchester: Manchester University Press, 1993), p. 80. This idea of power as an 'empty space' is the same as that found in Laclau and Mouffe, who also develop it out of their reading of Lefort.

54 Philippe Lacoue-Labarthe and Jean-Luc Nancy, *Retreating the Political*, ed. Simon Sparks (London: Routledge, 1997), p. 127.

55 Ernesto Laclau and Chantal Mouffe, *Hegemony and Socialist Strategy: Towards a Radical Democratic Politics* (London: Verso, 1985), pp. 186–7; Chantal Mouffe, *The Democratic Paradox* (London: Verso, 2000), p. 2; Slavoj Žižek, *For They Know Not What They Do: Enjoyment as a Political Factor* (London: Verso, 1991), pp. 256–60; John Keane, *Václav Havel: A Political Tragedy in Six Acts* (London: Bloomsbury, 1999), pp. 501–4.

56 The key to *The King's Two Bodies* lies in its subtitle, *A Study in Medieval Political Theology*. Kantorowicz was in part responding to the intellectual origins of what he describes in the Preface as 'the horrifying experience of our own time' in which 'whole nations, the largest and the smallest, fell prey to the weirdest dogmas and in which political theologisms became genuine obsessions defying in many cases the rudiments of human and political reason'. The general reference is of course to fascism, but the more specific reference is to Schmitt's *Political Theology* (1922). In an article published two years before *The King's Two Bodies*, he is even more explicit: 'Under the impact of those exchanges between canon and civilian glossators and commentators . . . something came into being which then was called "Mysteries of State", and which today in a more generalizing sense is often termed "Political Theology" '; and he adds in a footnote that 'the expression [was] much discussed in Germany in the early 1930s' – 'Mysteries of state', p. 67.

57 Johan Heilbron, *The Rise of Social Theory*, trans. Sheila Gogol (Cambridge: Polity Press, 1995), pp. 86–8.

58 Rousseau, *Social Contract*, pp. 165, 181, 214, 248, 273.

59 Heilbron, *Rise of Social Theory*, pp. 90–1.

60 These are from Adam Smith, *Inquiry into the Nature and Causes of the Wealth of Nations* (1776), ed. R.H. Campbell, A.S. Skinner and W.B. Todd (Indianapolis, IN: Liberty Fund, 1979), pp. 144, 622, 668, 774, 782, 808.

61 Rousseau, *Social Contract*, p. 175.

62 Rousseau, *Social Contract*, pp. 176, 182, 210, 212, 235, 238. The '*Économie Politique*' of 1755 has the sovereign as representing the head of the body politic – in Jean-Jacques Rousseau, *Oeuvres Complètes, III* (Paris: Gallimard, 1964), p. 244.

63 Jean-Jacques Rousseau, *Oeuvres Complètes, III*, pp. 362, 369, 404, 427 (*Social Contract*, pp. 176, 183, 217, 238).

64 Rousseau, *Oeuvres Complètes, III*, p. 369 (*Social Contract*, p. 183).

65 Rousseau, *Oeuvres Complètes, III*, p. 370. G.D.H. Cole, for example, translates *corps social* here as 'body politic'. See *Social Contract*, p. 183.

66 Rousseau, *Oeuvres Complètes, III*, pp. 373, 380 (*Social Contract*, pp. 186, 193); see also *Oeuvres Complètes, III*, pp. 374, 396 (*Social Contract*, pp. 188, 209).

67 Jean Jacques Rousseau, *Oeuvres Complètes, IV*, p. 249. One English translation of this, by Barbara Foxley, renders 'social body' as 'community'. See *Émile* (London: Dent & Sons, 1966), p. 7.

68 Smith, *Wealth of Nations*, pp. 604, 605, 606, 674.

69 Smith, *Wealth of Nations*, p. 782. Elsewhere (p. 492) he refers to the 'great body of workmen'. More generally on the 'great body of the people' see *Wealth of Nations*, pp. 11, 14, 99, 166, 173, 493, 494, 508, 523, 524, 533, 535, 538, 586, 617, 618, 649, 684, 696, 697, 705, 765, 781, 784, 786, 787, 789, 792, 798, 804, 813, 821, 823, 835, 844, 881, 947. On the 'whole body of the people' see pp. 96, 281, 508, 509, 517, 681, 693, 696, 785, 786, 787, 813.

70 James Madison, Alexander Hamilton and John Jay, *The Federalist Papers* (1788), No. 39 (Harmondsworth: Penguin, 1987), p. 255.

71 Emmanuel Joseph Sieyès, *What is the Third Estate?* (1789), trans. M. Blondel (London: Pall Mall Press, 1963), pp. 79, 83, 109, 123, 135, 165–6; Sieyès, *Deliberations to be Taken in the Assemblies of the Bailiwicks* (1789), in Murray Forsyth (ed.) *Reason and Revolution in the Political Thought of the Abbé Sieyès* (New York: Leicester University Press, 1987), p. 81.

72 Baecque, *Body Politic*, pp. 95–102.

73 The idea of the 'body of the people' was also important to later texts defending the democratic transformations which had taken place – see, for example, Alexis de Tocqueville, *Democracy in America* (1835–40), trans. George Lawrence (New York: Fontana, 1968), pp. 10, 11, 70, 867, 889, 905.

74 Hannah Arendt, *On Revolution* (New York: Viking Press, 1965), pp. 69–86.

75 The comment is from Gunn, *Beyond Liberty and Property*, p. 210, but the sentiment is found in the work of many others.

76 See Michel Foucault, 'Body/Power' (1975), in *Power/Knowledge*, p. 55. Bryan S. Turner, in *Max Weber: From History to Modernity* (London: Routledge, 1992), p. 158, suggests that one can conceptualize the historical development of political power in terms of an oscillation between the sacred body of the sovereign and the sovereign body of the citizens. This is true, but omits the extent to which the body of the state acted as both a historically and conceptually mediating role.

77 Mark Neocleous, *Fascism* (Buckingham: Open University Press, 1997), p. 83.

78 In focusing on the causes in the body politic in Chapter 3 of the *Dialogue* (pp. 78–88), Pole and Lupset identify the causes of decay as consumption ('a great sklenderness', 'a lack of people . . . to maintain the flourishing state of

the body politic'), dropsy (in which the body is 'unwieldy, unlusty and slow'), palsy (in which some parts of the body 'be ever moving and shaking . . . but to no profit nor pleasure'), pestilence (in which the parts of the body fail to work together and are 'dissevered asunder', disproportion of some parts compared to other parts, weakness), frenzy (in which men do anything 'that cometh to [their] fancy, without any order or rule of right reason'), and gout (which is compared to 'idle gluttony'). In similar fashion, Hobbes allows the organic analogy free rein when dealing with those things that weaken a state in Chapter 29 of *Leviathan* (pp. 221–30): 'Pleurisie' (where money accumulates in too few hands, just as blood may 'get into the membrane of the breast'), 'Ague' (the difficulty of raising money), 'Hydrophobia' (a bizarre term referring to seditious literature), and the existence of too many corporations ('wormes in the entrayles of a naturall man'). Anything which Hobbes does not have a ready-made answer to gets described in biological terms. 'Mixt monarchy', for example, is a serious irregularity: 'To what Disease in the Naturall Body of man I may exactly compare this irregularity of a Common-wealth, I know not. But I have seen a man, that had another man growing out of his side, with an head, armes, breast, and stomach, of his own: If he had had another man growing out of his other side, the comparison might then have been exact'.

79   Sieyès, *What is the Third Estate?*, pp. 164, 174.
80   See for example Adolf Hitler, *Mein Kampf* (1925) (Boston: Houghton Mifflin Co., 1943), pp. 302, 304–5; Hitler, 'The mission of the Nazi Movement' (Speech to the People's Court, 26 February 1924), in Roger Griffin (ed.) *Fascism* (Oxford: Oxford University Press, 1995), p. 116; Hammer Press, 'Nazism's world crusade against the Jews' (1937), in Griffin (ed.) *Fascism*, p. 146.
81   Robert N. Proctor, *Racial Hygiene: Medicine Under the Nazis* (Cambridge, MA: Harvard University Press, 1988), pp. 194–202; *The Nazi War on Cancer* (Princeton, NJ: Princeton University Press,1999), pp. 46–7, 291.
82   F.T. Marinetti, 'Beyond communism' (1920), in *Selected Writings*, ed. R.W. Flint (London: Secker and Warburg, 1972), pp. 148–57.
83   Benito Mussolini, 'Address to the Chamber of Deputies, 26 May 1927' (the 'Ascension Day Speech'), cited in David G. Horn, *Social Bodies: Science, Reproduction, and Modernity* (Princeton, NJ: Princeton University Press, 1994), p. 46, also p. 23; Mussolini, 'Fascism's myth' (the 'Naples Speech') in Griffin (ed.) *Fascism*, p. 44.
84   Luisa Passerini, *Fascism in Popular Memory: The Cultural Experience of the Turin Working Class*, trans. Robert Lumley and Jude Bloomfield (Cambridge: Cambridge University Press, 1987), pp. 99, 223.
85   Lefort, *Political Forms of Modern Society*, p. 298.
86   Chetan Bhatt notes how for Hindu nationalists invasions of India have been thought of as 'pollution', how the cancer trope figures in their discourse, and the extent to which the 'liberation' of the social body has been inextricably linked with its 'purification'. Chetan Bhatt, *Liberation and Purity: Race, New*

Religious Movements and the Ethics of Postmodernity (London: UCL Press, 1997), pp. 70, 159, 206–11; *Hindu Nationalism: Origins, Ideologies and Modern Myths* (Oxford: Berg, 2001), pp. 114, 129–30, 143.

87 Philip Corrigan and Derek Sayer, *The Great Arch: English State Formation as Cultural Revolution* (Oxford: Blackwell, 1985), p. 129.

88 Since sociology only emerged once the social problem had been articulated, it is unsurprising that as a discipline it was first and foremost a form of biologism. The metaphor of the social body therefore came to pervade and dominate the reigning sociological theories of Henri de Saint-Simon, Charles Fourier, Auguste Comte, Herbert Spencer, Emile Durkheim and Radcliffe-Brown.

89 Mark Neocleous, *The Fabrication of Social Order: A Critical Theory of Police Power* (London: Pluto Press, 2000), pp. 84–9.

90 Edwin Chadwick, *Report on the Sanitary Condition of the Labouring Population of Great Britain* (Edinburgh: Edinburgh University Press, 1965), pp. 371, 375, 409, 413; and 'The new poor law', *Edinburgh Review*, Vol. 63, 1836, pp. 487–537, p. 498; John Stuart Mill, *Three Essays on Religion*, in *Collected Works, Vol. X: Essays on Ethics, Religion and Society*, ed. J.M. Robson (London: Routledge, 1969), p. 394.

91 Victor Hugo, *Les Misérables* (1862), trans. Charles Wilbour (London: Dent, 1958), pp. 531–48.

92 François Delaporte, *Disease and Civilization: The Cholera in Paris, 1832*, trans. Arthur Goldhammer (Cambridge, MA: MIT Press, 1986), p. 52.

93 Churchill, *Illustrated Sunday Herald*, 25 January 1920, and *The Times*, 10 November 1920; also *Collected Speeches*, Vol. 3, p. 2798, cited in Fraser J. Harbutt, *The Iron Curtain: Churchill, America, and the Origins of the Cold War* (Oxford: Oxford University Press, 1986), pp. 25–7.

94 McGrath and Humphrey cited in Joel Kovel, *Red Hunting in the Promised Land: Anticommunism and the Making of America* (London: Cassell, 1997), pp. 140, 186; Reagan, *Where's the Rest of Me?*, p. 164.

95 Kovel, *Red Hunting in the Promised Land*, p. 99.

96 George Kennan, 'The long telegram', in Thomas H. Etzold and John Lewis Gaddis (eds) *Containment: Documents on American Policy and Strategy, 1945–1950* (New York: Columbia University Press, 1978), pp. 50–63; X [George Kennan], 'The sources of Soviet conduct', *Foreign Affairs*, Vol. 25, No. 4, 1947, pp. 566–82; 'Totalitarianism in the modern world' (1953), in Heinz Lubasz (ed.) *The Development of the Modern State* (New York: Macmillan, 1964), pp. 112–13.

97 See Glenn D. Hook, 'The nuclearization of language: nuclear allergy as political metaphor', *Journal of Peace Research*, Vol. 21, No. 3, 1984, pp. 259–75, p. 262; Kovel, *Red Hunting in the Promised Land*, p. 46.

98 Mary Douglas, *Purity and Danger: An Analysis of the Concepts of Pollution and Taboo* (London: Ark, 1984), pp. 4, 115; *Natural Symbols: Explorations in Cosmology* (Harmondsworth: Penguin, 1973), pp. 98–9.

99 Mikhail Bakhtin, *Rabelais and His World* (1965), trans. Helene Iswolsky (Bloomington, IN: Indiana University Press, 1984), pp. 26, 320.

100 Claude Quétel, *History of Syphilis*, trans. Judith Braddock and Brian Pike (Cambridge: Polity Press, 1990), p. 16; Dorothy Nelkin and Sander S. Gilman, 'Placing blame for devastating disease', *Social Research* 55, 1988, pp. 361–79, p. 365; Susan Sontag, *Illness as Metaphor and Aids and its Metaphors* (Harmondsworth: Penguin, 1991), p. 133.

101 Daniel Defoe, *A Journal of the Plague Year*, ed. Anthony Burgess (Harmondsworth: Penguin, 1986), p. 23.

102 Hastings Donnan and Thomas M. Wilson, *Borders: Frontiers of Identity, Nation and State* (Oxford: Berg, 1999), p. 132; Catherine Waldby, *AIDS and the Body Politic: Biomedicine and Sexual Difference* (London: Routledge, 1996), pp. 104, 142; Nelkin and Gilman, 'Placing blame for devastating disease', p. 364.

103 Sontag, *Illness as Metaphor*, p. 77. Foucault describes the relationship as one between medical and moral concerns in *Madness and Civilization: A History of Insanity in the Age of Reason*, trans. Richard Howard (London: Tavistock Publications, 1971), p. 202.

104 Bryan S. Turner, *The Body and Society: Explorations in Social Theory* (Oxford: Blackwell, 1984), p. 114.

105 Faced with what to do with individuals who are unreasonable, Rawls states: 'That there are doctrines that reject one or more democratic freedoms is itself a permanent fact of life, or seems so. This gives us the practical task of *containing them* – like war and *disease*'. John Rawls, *Political Pluralism* (New York: Columbia University Press, 1993), p. 64, emphasis added. I am grateful to David Stevens for bringing Rawls' comment to my attention.

106 John McMurtry, *The Cancer Stage of Capitalism* (London: Pluto Press, 1999), p. 100.

107 Jacques Derrida, 'Plato's pharmacy', in *Dissemination*, trans. Barbara Johnson (London: Athlone Press, 1981), p. 133.

108 Madison, Hamilton and Jay, *Federalist Papers*, No. 38, p. 249.

109 Andrew Ross, 'Containing culture in the cold war', *Cultural Studies*, 1, 1987, pp. 328–48, p. 331.

110 See Darrow Schecter, *Sovereign States or Political Communities? Civil Society and Contemporary Politics* (Manchester: Manchester University Press, 2000), pp. 135–6.

111 Jonathan Gil Harris, for example, ends his excellent *Foreign Bodies and the Body Politic* by suggesting that the organic political analogy may be transformed into a vehicle for dissent and critique (p. 146), but does not show how this might be done. John O'Neill, *Five Bodies: The Human Shape of Modern Society* (Ithaca, NY: Cornell University Press, 1985), pp. 67–90, likewise seeks to revive and develop the idea of the body politic as a means of enhancing democracy against the modern administrative state, but when arguing against the latter fails to make any real use of the idea of the body politic. Similarly, Donna

Haraway's comment that 'it is possible to build a socialist-feminist theory of the body politic that avoids reductionism in both its forms' doesn't seem to be fulfilled in the rest of her book, *Simians, Cyborgs, and Women: The Reinvention of Nature* (London: Free Association Books, 1991), p. 10. The same criticisms might be levelled at Susan Buck-Morss' suggestion of a 'global body politic' with the Left as its 'thinking organ' – 'A global public sphere?', *Radical Philosophy*, 111, 2002, pp. 2–10.

Chapter 2

1   J.A. Hobson, *Work and Wealth: A Human Valuation* (London: Macmillan, 1914), p. 15; 'The re-statement of democracy' (1902), in *The Crisis of Liberalism: New Issues Of Democracy* (London: P.S. King and Son, 1909), p. 73; 'Review of Hobhouse's *Social Evolution and Political Theory*', *Manchester Guardian*, 22 February 1912.

2   Bernard Bosanquet, *The Philosophical Theory of the State* (London: Macmillan, 1925), pp. 6–7.

3   G.W.F. Hegel, *Philosophy of Mind*, trans. A.V. Miller (Oxford: Clarendon Press, 1971), p. 22; *Philosophy of Right* (1821), trans. T.M. Knox (Oxford: Clarendon Press, 1942), p. 156. I leave aside the question of whether 'Mind' is an appropriate translation.

4   Michel Foucault, *Discipline and Punish: The Birth of the Prison* (1975), trans. Alan Sheridan (Harmondsworth: Penguin, 1977), p. 28.

5   Bruce Anderson, 'The West's security rests safely in American hands', *Independent*, 21 January 2002.

6   Friedrich Meinecke, *Machiavellism: The Doctrine of Raison d'État and its Place in Modern History* (1957), trans. Douglas Scott (New Brunswick: Transaction Publishers, 1998), p. 1.

7   Francesco Guicciardini, *Ricordi* (1512–30), trans. as *Maxims and Reflections of a Renaissance Statesman*, trans. Mario Domandi (New York: Harper & Row, 1965), p. 54.

8   Francesco Guicciardini, *Dialogue on the Government of Florence* (1521–4), trans. Alison Brown (Cambridge: Cambridge University Press, 1994), p. 159.

9   Maurizio Viroli, *From Politics to Reason of State: The Acquisition and Transformation of the Language of Politics 1250–1600* (Cambridge: Cambridge University Press, 1992).

10 Karl Marx, 'Contribution to the critique of Hegel's philosophy of law' (1843), in Karl Marx and Frederick Engels, *Collected Works, Vol 3* (London: Lawrence & Wishart, 1975), p. 32; Marx and Engels, *The German Ideology* (1846), in *Collected Works, Vol. 5* (London: Lawrence & Wishart, 1976), p. 89; Karl Marx, 'On the Jewish question' (1843), in Marx and Engels, *Collected Works, Vol 3*, p. 167.

11 Marx, 'On the Jewish question', p. 166; Marx and Engels, *German Ideology*, p. 90.

12   Justin Rosenberg, *The Empire of Civil Society: A Critique of the Realist Theory of International Relations* (London: Verso, 1994), pp. 69, 79, 123. Rosenberg notes that what Marx is discussing is nothing less than the very state autonomy which becomes the cornerstone of realist international relations theory in the twentieth century, though the realists themselves ignore this fact. See also Mary Poovey, *A History of the Modern Fact: Problems of Knowledge in the Sciences of Wealth and Society* (Chicago: University of Chicago Press, 1998), p. 86; Gaines Post, *Studies in Medieval Legal Thought: Public Law and the State, 1100–1322* (Princeton, NJ: Princeton University Press, 1964), p. 249.

13   Niccolò Machiavelli, *The Prince* (1532), in *The Chief Works and Others, Vol. 1*, trans. Allan Gilbert (Durham, NC: Duke University Press, 1958), p. 66.

14   Niccolò Machiavelli, *Discourses on the First Decade of Titus Livius* (1513–17), in *Chief Works, Vol. 1*, p. 218.

15   It might be useful to note here that it is this fact which undermines the common assumption that 'Machiavellism' is the appropriate term to describe the doctrine. The fact that Machiavelli is so obviously the writer more than any who justifies 'evil' or immoral actions, combined with the fact that he was writing in the context of the emergence of reason of state arguments, has led many to find in his work the essence of the doctrine of reason of state. Most commentators have therefore followed Meinecke in using this as the label despite the fact that, as they all point out, Machiavelli never used the term '*raison d'État*'. But while Machiavelli can clearly be seen to hold the view that the state is not limited by conventional or Christian morality, it is far from clear that he subscribes to the view of the state as a historical subject. In *The Prince*, for example, the term *lo stato* or its plural form appears 114 times. Most of these are references to the state in a narrowly political sense concerning the general orbit of the ruler. In a fair number of these occurrences, *lo stato* occurs in association with five verbs – *acquistare, tenere, mantenere, togliere, perdere*: to acquire, to hold, to maintain, to take away, to lose. Although we now speak of the state acquiring, holding, maintaining, taking and losing a territory or power and so on, this is not how Machiavelli uses these terms. For Machiavelli it is not the state which acquires, holds, loses and so on. Rather, it is the state which is acquired, held, lost. Similarly, Machiavelli refers to the way that the state may be assaulted, disarmed, injured, occupied, conceded and won; in contrast, he never suggests that the state *does* any of these things. The reason for this is because *The Prince* was written in the tradition of advice books for princes. Machiavelli's concern was thus with what the prince could or should do *with* the state. As such, in the vast majority of references to the state in Machiavelli's *Prince*, it has things done to it, or is used to do things, rather than does things itself. Similarly, the term 'interest' seldom occurs in Machiavelli's work. In other words, for Machiavelli the state is a passive object rather than an active subject with interests of its own. What this means is that as much as Machiavelli may have propounded an ethico-political theory in tune with the

general tenor of reason of state arguments, it is somewhat misleading to use his name as the label with which to describe them. See H.C. Dowdall, 'The word "state" ', *Law Quarterly Review*, 39, 1923, pp. 98–125; J.H. Hexter, '*Il principe* and *lo stato*', *Studies in the Renaissance*, 4, 1957, pp. 113–38; Harvey C. Mansfield, 'On the Impersonality of the modern state: a comment on Machiavelli's use of *stato*', *American Political Science Review*, 77, 1983, pp. 849–56.

16 Trajano Bocalini, *I Raggvagli Di Parnasso* (1612–13), in *I Raggvagli Di Parnasso: or, Advertisements from Parnassus: In Two Centuries. With The Politick Touchstone*, trans. Henry Earl of Monmouth (London, 1669), p. 305.

17 Meinecke, *Machiavellism*, pp. 39, 49; see also William F. Church, *Richelieu and Reason of State* (Princeton, NJ: Princeton University Press, 1972), pp. 11–13, 38; Nannerle O. Keohane, *Philosophy and the State in France: The Renaissance to the Enlightenment* (Princeton, NJ: Princeton University Press, 1980), pp. 16, 31; Richard Tuck, *Philosophy and Government 1572–1651* (Cambridge: Cambridge University Press, 1993), p. xii; Viroli, *Politics to Reason of State*, pp. 238–80; Michel Foucault, ' "*Omnes and singulatim*": toward a critique of political reason' (1979), in *Power: The Essential Works, Vol. 3*, ed. James D. Faubion (London: Penguin, 2000), p. 315.

18 George L. Mosse, *The Holy Pretence: A Study in Christianity and Reason of State from William Perkins to John Winthrop* (Oxford: Basil Blackwell, 1957); C.J. Friedrich, *Constitutional Reason of State: The Survival of the Constitutional Order* (Providence, RI: Brown University Press, 1957), pp. 6, 24, 70; Church, *Richelieu and Reason of State*, pp. 44, 62–72, 163–5; Andrew Vincent, *Theories of the State* (Oxford: Blackwell, 1987), p. 71. J.A. Fernández-Santamaría, *Reason of State and Statecraft in Spanish Political Thought, 1595–1640* (London: Lanham Press, 1983), argues (pp. 5–7, 23) that in the Spanish context there were two types of reason of state, a realist ('Machiavellian') one, and an ethicist (essentially Christian) one, as the Christian thinkers themselves liked to claim. But as he himself then goes on to argue, the two strands have so much in common that it is often difficult to tell them apart.

19 Giovanni Botero, *The Reason of State*, trans. P.J. and D.P. Waley (London: Routledge, 1956), p. 3.

20 'Debate of Dec. 3, 1621', in Wallace Noteststein, Frances Helen Relf and Hartley Simpson (eds) *Commons Debates, 1621, Vol. Two* (New Haven, CT: Yale University Press, 1935), p. 492–3.

21 Machiavelli, *Discourses*, p. 218.

22 Friedrich, *Constitutional Reason of State*, p. 7; Viroli, *From Politics to Reason of State*, p. 4.

23 Scipione Ammirato, *Discorsi sopra Cornelio Tacito*, cited in Peter S. Donaldson, *Machiavelli and Mystery of State* (Cambridge: Cambridge University Press, 1988), p. 119.

24 John Locke, *Two Treatises of Government* (1690), ed. Peter Laslett (Cambridge: Cambridge University Press, 1988), II, paras. 159, 160, pp. 374–5.

25 Locke, *Two Treatises*, II, para. 147, p. 365.

26 Locke, *Two Treatises*, II, para. 147, p. 366.

27 Locke, *Two Treatises*, II, para. 147, p. 375.

28 John Locke, 'An essay on toleration' (1667), in *Political Essays*, ed. Mark Goldie (Cambridge: Cambridge University Press, 1997), pp. 142–3.

29 Sheldon Wolin, *The Presence of the Past: Essays on the State and the Constitution* (Baltimore, MD: John Hopkins University Press, 1989), pp. 167–8. John Dunn notes that Locke was taking notes from Gabriel Naudé's *Considerations Politiques sur les Coups d'Estat* (1667), a defence of reason of state, at the time of writing parts of the *Two Treatises*. See John Dunn, *The Political Thought of John Locke* (Cambridge: Cambridge University Press, 1969), p. 163. Elsewhere he adds (p. 199) that although Locke was interested in this genre of writing, that scarcely makes the *Two Treatises* an example of such writing. On the other hand, he concedes (p. 39) that the 'Essay on Toleration' contains Locke's most unequivocal assertion of the primacy of *raison d'État*.

30 Adam Smith, *Inquiry into the Nature and Causes of the Wealth of Nations,* ed. R.H. Campbell, A.S. Skinner and W.B. Todd (Indianapolis, IN: Liberty Fund, 1979), p. 539.

31 Reinhart Koselleck, *Critique and Crisis: Enlightenment and the Pathogenesis of Modern Society* (1959), (Oxford: Berg, 1988), p. 21.

32 In 1999, in the context of war in Yugoslavia, Gerhard Schröder demanded of his cabinet absolute loyalty to the western alliance: 'the western alliance is part of Germany's *raison d'État*'. Cited in Ian Traynor, 'War in europe', *Guardian*, 3 April 1999. On its use in superpower confrontation see James Der Derian, *On Diplomacy: A Genealogy of Western Estrangement* (Oxford: Blackwell, 1987), p. 205. On its use by non-superpower states, Fred Halliday reports that before he died the Ayatollah Khomeini clearly stated that even the holiest of Islamic commandments can be overridden by reason of state – 'Britain's bad record on the hostage issue', *Guardian*, 11 May 1990.

33 Mark Neocleous, *The Fabrication of Social Order: A Critical Theory of Police Power* (London: Pluto Press, 2000). Symptomatically, in its early stages the police project and reason of state amounted to much the same thing. Botero's *Reason of State* (*Della ragion di stato*), for example, was translated into German as *Johannis Boteri Grundlicher Bericht Anordnung guter Polizeien und Regiments* (1596).

34 'Few doubt that Mitterand was guilty of illegal wire-tapping, Kohl of crooked funding, Chirac of municipal rake-offs, González of complicity with assassination, Scalfaro of pocketing payments from the secret service. *Dura lex sed lex* never applies: none ever faced charges' – Perry Anderson, 'Testing formula two', *New Left Review*, 8, 2001, p. 14.

35 Max Weber, 'Religious rejections of the world and their directions' (1915), in *From Max Weber: Essays in Sociology*, trans. and ed. H.H. Gerth and C. Wright Mills (London: Routledge, 1948), p. 334.

36 Michel Foucault, 'The political technology of individuals' (1981), in Luther H. Martin, Huck Gutman and Patrick H. Hutton (eds) *Technologies of the Self* (London: Tavistock, 1988), p. 151; also 'Politics and reason', in *Politics, Philosophy, Culture: Interviews and Other Writings 1977–1984*, ed. Lawrence Kritzman (London: Routledge, 1988), pp. 76–7; ' "Omnes and Singulatim" ', pp. 316–7.

37 Thomas Hobbes, *Elements of Law, Natural and Politic* (1640), ed. Ferdinand Tönnies (London: Frank Cass, 1969), Pt. 2, Ch. 6, para. 12 (p. 157); *Leviathan* (1651), ed. Richard Tuck (Cambridge: Cambridge University Press, 1991), p. 223.

38 *Leviathan*, p. 223.

39 *Elements of Law*, Pt 2, Ch. 6, para. 13 (p. 158); *Leviathan*, p. 306.

40 Tuck, *Philosophy and Government*, p. 282; Meinecke, *Machiavellism*, pp. 210–16.

41 René Descartes, *A Discourse on Method*, trans. John Veitch (London: Dent, 1912), pp. 27, 32.

42 Koselleck, *Critique and Crisis*, pp. 25, 33–4; Jonathan M. Hess, *Reconstituting the Body Politic: Enlightenment, Public Culture and the Invention of Aesthetic Autonomy* (Detroit, MI: Wayne State University Press, 1999), pp. 93–4.

43 Cornelia Navari, 'Knowledge, the state and the state of nature', in Michael Donelan (ed.) *The Reasons of States: A Study in International Political Theory* (London: George Allen & Unwin, 1978), pp. 105–6.

44 Hobbes, *Leviathan*, p. 89.

45 Jacques Rancière, *The Names of History: On the Poetics of Knowledge*, trans. Hassan Melehy (Minneapolis, MN: University of Minnesota Press, 1994), p. 21.

46 Bruno Latour, *We Have Never Been Modern* (1991), trans. Catherine Porter (Hemel Hempstead: Harvester Wheatsheaf, 1993), p. 29.

47 Francis Bacon, 'In praise of knowledge', in *The Works of Francis Bacon, Vol. 1*, ed. Basil Montagu (London: Pickering, 1825), p. 255; see also Francis Bacon, *The Advancement of Learning* (1605), ed. G.W. Kitchin (London: Dent, 1973), p. 6.

48 Theodor Adorno and Max Horkheimer, *Dialectic of Enlightenment* (1944), trans. John Cumming (London: Verso, 1979), p. 4.

49 Thomas Richards, *The Imperial Archive: Knowledge and the Fantasy of Empire* (London: Verso, 1993), p. 74; see also Jens Bartelson, *The Critique of the State* (Cambridge: Cambridge University Press, 2001), pp. 5, 34–5, 69–75.

50 Gilles Deleuze and Félix Guattari, *A Thousand Plateaus: Capitalism and Schizophrenia* (1980), trans. Brian Massumi (London: Athlone Press, 1987), pp. 375–6.

51 Georges Bataille, *The Accursed Share, Volumes II and III* (1976), trans. Robert Hurley (New York: Zone Books, 1993), p. 222.

52 I have taken the phrase 'cult of intelligence' from Victor Marchetti and John D. Miller, *The CIA and the Cult of Intelligence* (London: Jonathan Cape, 1974).

53 Eugene Poteat, 'The use and abuse of intelligence', *Diplomacy and Statecraft*, Vol. 11, No. 2, 2000, pp. 1–16. Poteat was a former scientific intelligence officer with the CIA.

54 Daniel Defoe, 'Memorandum to Robert Harley' (1704), in *The True-Born Englishman and Other Writings* (Harmondsworth: Penguin, 1997), p. 262; Carl von Clausewitz, *On War* (1832), ed. Anatol Rapoport (Harmondsworth: Penguin, 1968), p. 120. It might be remembered here that Defoe had been a government spy when Robert Harley was Lord High Treasurer.

55 It should not be assumed that this means that politicians and political administrators are themselves intelligent, of course. As Hegel, *Philosophy of Right*, p. 8, points out, the idea that 'If God gives a man an office, he also gives him brains', is 'an old chestnut which these days will scarcely be taken seriously by anyone'.

56 Journals such as the *Intelligencer* and the *Daily Intelligencer of Court, City and County* became the preferred instruments of governments in the seventeenth century.

57 Samuel Johnson, *A Dictionary of the English Language* (1755) (London: Times Books, 1979).

58 John Michael Archer, *Sovereignty and Intelligence: Spying and Court Culture in the English Renaissance* (Stanford, CA: Stanford University Press, 1993), pp. 3, 139; Ernst H. Kantorowicz, *The King's Two Bodies: A Study in Medieval Political Theology* (Princeton, NJ: Princeton University Press, 1957), pp. 8, 271–2, 495; J.G.A. Pocock, *The Machiavellian Moment: Florentine Political Thought and the Atlantic Republican Tradition* (Princeton, NJ: Princeton University Press, 1975), pp. 21–2, 324–7, 353–4.

59 Bacon, 'In Praise of Knowledge', p. 255.

60 Norbert Elias, *The Court Society* (1969), trans. Edmund Jephcott (Oxford: Blackwell, 1983), pp. 105, 108. This is the basis of Walter Benjamin's reference to the 'intriguer', a court character who has a combination of political, anthropological and physiological knowledge: 'the sovereign intriguer is all intellect'. See Walter Benjamin, *The Origin of German Tragic Drama* (1928), trans. John Osborne (London: Verso, 1977), p. 95. It is pertinent to note here that this undermines Foucault's influential account of power and knowledge. As is well known, Foucault distinguishes the rule of sovereignty from a regime of surveillance (discipline) (e.g. *Discipline and Punish*, pp. 187–8). But in fact, the techniques of surveillance have their roots in the court politics of the pre-Enlightenment state under the rule of a personal sovereign, as Elias shows. The monarch engaged in constant surveillance of his courtiers' actions and interests, which he also used, where possible, in surveying his subjects and foreign powers. For the sovereign, the observation and supervision of people is indispensable in defending his rule. Thus it is safe to say that the practices of surveillance and discipline, far from being a mode of power categorically distinct to that of sovereignty, have their origins in sovereignty's most classic form. The pre-history of 'intelligence' shows that the relation between power and knowledge, which Foucault has done so much to highlight, becomes far more complicated than Foucault's formulations allow. Because his argument

that power produces knowledge and knowledge produces power is heavily dependent on his account of *modern* disciplinary power, the power of surveillance, Foucault was never in a position to grasp the practical conjunction of power as *sovereignty* with knowledge as *state* intelligence. His suggestion that we behead the king, noted in Chapter 1, relies on a mistaken identification of sovereignty with monarchy. Given his attempt to obliterate the concept of the state from political theory, this could only mean that his account of power/ knowledge was destined to be developed outside of any account of the state. The argument here is that we need to recognize the links not between knowledge and some ubiquitous and ill-defined 'power', but between knowledge and the state. For the broader context of these comments see Mark Neocleous, *Administering Civil Society: Towards a Theory of State Power* (London: Macmillan, 1996), Ch. 3.

61 Cited in Peter Miller, 'On the interrelations between accounting and the state', *Accounting, Organizations and Society*, Vol. 15, No. 4, 1990, pp. 315–38, p. 328.

62 The member was Nick Bentley, cited in Phillip Knightley, *The Second Oldest Profession: The Spy as Bureaucrat, Patriot, Fantasist and Whore* (London: André Deutsch, 1986), p. 199.

63 Cited in Bernard Cohn, *Colonialism and its Forms of Knowledge* (Princeton, NJ: Princeton University Press, 1996), p. 45.

64 Cited in Paul Virilio, *Strategy of Deception*, trans. Chris Turner (London: Verso, 2000), p.17.

65 Cited in Richard V. Ericson and Kevin D. Haggerty, *Policing the Risk Society* (Oxford: Clarendon Press, 1997), p. 319.

66 Mark Poster, *Foucault, Marxism and History: Mode of Production versus Mode of Information* (Cambridge: Polity Press, 1984); Scott Lash, *Critique of Information* (London: Sage, 2002).

67 Richards, *Imperial Archive*, pp. 5, 76.

68 Ian Hacking, *The Taming of Chance* (Cambridge: Cambridge University Press, 1990), pp. 4–5.

69 'The art of governing characteristic of reason of state is intimately bound up with the development of what was then called either political "statistics" or "arithmetic" ' – Foucault, ' "Omnes et Singulatim" ', p. 317.

70 Geoffrey Kay and James Mott, *Political Order and the Law of Labour* (London: Macmillan, 1982), pp. 87–91.

71 Stuart Woolf, 'Statistics and the modern state', *Comparative Studies in Society and History*, 31, 1989, pp. 588–604; Patricia Cline Cohen, *A Calculating People: The Spread of Numeracy in Early America* (New York: Routledge, 1999), pp. 150, 158; Victor L. Hilts, '*Aliis Exterendum*, or, the origins of the Statistical Society of London', *Isis*, Vol. 69, No. 246, 1978, pp. 21–43; Silvana Patriarca, *Numbers and Nationhood: Writing Statistics in Nineteenth-Century Italy* (Cambridge: Cambridge University Press, 1996), p. 51; Paul Starr, 'The sociology of official

statistics', in William Alonso and Paul Starr (eds) *The Politics of Numbers* (New York: Russell Sage Foundation, 1987), p. 15.

72 Raymond Williams, *Politics and Letters: Interviews with New Left Review* (London: Verso, 1981), p. 170, emphasis added.

73 Ian Hacking, 'Making up people', in Thomas C. Heller, Morton Sosna and David E. Wellbery (eds) *Reconstructing Individualism: Autonomy, Individuality, and the Self in Western Thought* (Stanford, CA: Stanford University Press, 1986), p. 222; 'How should we do the history of statistics?', in Graham Burchell, Colin Gordon and Peter Miller (eds) *The Foucault Effect: Studies in Governmentality* (London: Harvester Wheatsheaf, 1991), p. 188; Karl H. Metz, 'paupers and numbers: the statistical argument for social reform in Britain during the period of industrialization', in Lorenz Krüger, Lorraine Daston and Michael Heidelberger (eds) *The Probabilistic Revolution, Vol. I: Ideas in History* (Massachussets: MIT Press, 1987), p. 348.

74 The phrase is Giuseppe Sacchi's, cited in Patriarca, *Numbers and Nationhood*, p. 31.

75 Peter Buck, 'Seventeenth-century political arithmetic: civil strife and vital statistics', *Isis*, Vol. 68, No. 241, 1977, p. 76.

76 Theodore M. Porter, *The Rise of Statistical Thinking 1820–1900* (Princeton, NJ: Princeton University Press, 1986), p. 17; Nikolas Rose, *Powers of Freedom: Reframing Political Thought* (Cambridge: Cambridge University Press, 1999), pp. 197–232; Starr, 'Sociology of official statistics', p. 57.

77 Benito Mussolini, 'Il destino dei popoli' (Address to the High Council of ISTAT, 20 December 1926), cited in David Horn, *Social Bodies: Science, Reproduction, and Italian Modernity* (Princeton, NJ: Princeton University Press, 1994), pp. 54–5; Carl Ipsen, *Dictating Demography: The Problem of Population in Fascist Italy* (Cambridge: Cambridge University Press, 1996), p. 41.

78 Edwin Black, *IBM and the Holocaust: The Strategic Alliance Between Nazi Germany and America's Most Powerful Corporation* (London: Little, Brown and Company, 2001), pp. 47–51, 59, 82, 93; J. Adam Tooze, *Statistics and the Modern State, 1900–1945: The Making of Modern Economic Knowledge* (Cambridge: Cambridge University Press, 2001), pp. 19–24, 369, 177–215.

79 Black, *IBM and the Holocaust*, pp. 49, 201; Horn, *Social Bodies*, p. 55.

80 Paul Gilroy, *Between Camps: Nations, Cultures and the Allure of Race* (London: Penguin, 2000), p. 104. For the wider picture see William Seltzer and Margo Anderson, 'The dark side of numbers: the role of population data systems in human rights abuses', *Social Research*, Vol. 68, No. 2, 2001, pp. 481–513.

81 Edmund Burke, *Reflections on the Revolution in France* (1790), ed. Conor Cruise O'Brien (Harmondsworth: Penguin, 1968), p. 243.

82 Jean Bodin, *Six Books of the Commonwealth* (1576), trans. M.J. Tooley (Oxford: Basil Blackwell, 1967), pp. 181–5. See also Machiavelli, *Discourses*, pp. 528–9.

83 Marc Bloch, *Feudal Society, Vol. 1: The Growth of Ties of Dependence*, trans. L.A. Manyon (London: Routledge & Kegan Paul, 1965), p. 141.

84 James C. Scott, *Seeing Like a State* (New Haven, CT: Yale University Press, 1998), p. 65.

85 While it is the case that names have sometimes been used as a form of resistance to the state, the state has nonetheless managed to reassert its powers. For example, when the Gypsies in Bulgaria adopted Turkish, Arabic or Islamic names, the Bulgarian state responded (in 1968) by requiring all Gypsies to change their names to Boter and Levski (two Bulgarian national heroes). Jacqueline Stevens, in *Reproducing the State* (Princeton, NJ: Princeton University Press, 1999), notes that the effect of such juridical interventions is to taxonomize individuals by families and nations (pp. 160, 166). This is part of the inherently illiberal way the state assigns citizenship according to birth and ancestry, a point I develop in Chapter 4.

86 Immediately after the Reform Act of 1832, for example, the British state set about naming all its citizens through the Registration of Births, Deaths and Marriages Act (1836), which ensured that every inhabitant would appear in a public record on at least two occasions; this was quickly followed by the attempt to tie individual names to particular residences. The same period saw the emergence of the Department of Statistics at the Board of Trade (1832–3), while the Poor Law Board established in 1834 combined both the statistical and the sanitary idea in one institution.

87 Scott, *Seeing Like a State*, p. 77; Hacking, 'How should we do the history of statistics?', p. 194; 'Making up people', p. 223.

88 Richards, *Imperial Archive*, p. 6.

89 I am partly encouraged in this argument by Talal Asad, 'Ethnographic representation, statistics and modern power', *Social Research*, Vol. 61, No. 1, 1994, pp. 55–88; Jens Bartelson, *A Genealogy of Sovereignty* (Cambridge: Cambridge University Press, 1995), p. 152; Joan Wallach Scott, *Gender and the Politics of History* (New York: Columbia University Press, 1988), pp. 115, 133.

90 For a longer account see Neocleous, *Administering Civil Society*, pp. 136–8.

91 *Parliamentary Debates (Hansard)*, Vol. 449, 1947–8, 1371–95; Vol. 451, 1947–8, 218–55. On the 'youth question' as a question of class and state power see Phil Mizen, *The State, Young People and Youth Training: In and Against the Training State* (London: Mansell, 1995); on the birth of the category see Michael Neary, *Youth, Training and the Training State: The Real History of Youth Training in the Twentieth Century* (London: Macmillan, 1997).

92 David Campbell, *National Deconstruction: Violence, Identity, and Justice in Bosnia* (Minneapolis, MN: University of Minnesota Press, 1998), p.79; Starr, 'Sociology of official statistics', p. 45; Seltzer and Anderson, 'Dark side of numbers', p. 493. And for a similar argument regarding Basque identity see Jacqueline Urla, 'Cultural politics in an age of statistics: numbers, nations, and the making of Basque identity', *American Ethnologist*, Vol. 20, No. 4, 1993, pp. 818–43.

93 Bernard S. Cohn, 'The census, social structure and objectification in South Asia' (1970), in *An Anthropologist Among the Historians and Other Essays*

(Oxford: Oxford University Press, 1987), pp. 224–54; also Cohn, *Colonialism and its Forms of Knowledge*, p. 8; Benedict Anderson, *Imagined Communities: Reflections on the Origin and Spread of Nationalism* (London: Verso, 1991), pp. 163–70. For a sense of the research in this field see Arjun Appadurai, *Modernity at Large: Cultural Dimensions of Globalization* (Minneapolis, MN: University of Minnesota Press, 1996), pp. 114–35; Asad, 'Ethnographic representation', p. 76; C.A. Bayly, *Empire and Information: Intelligence Gathering and Social Communication in India, 1780–1870* (Cambridge: Cambridge University Press, 1996); Bruce Curtis, 'Official documentary systems and colonial government: from imperial sovereignty to colonial autonomy in the Canadas, 1841–1867', *Journal of Historical Sociology*, Vol. 10, No. 4, 1997, pp. 389–417; U. Kalpagam, 'The colonial state and statistical knowledge', *History of the Human Sciences*, Vol. 13, No. 2, 2000, pp. 37–55; Norbert Peabody, 'Cents, sense, census: human inventories in late precolonial and early colonial India', *Comparative Studies in Society and History*, Vol. 43, No. 4, 2001, pp. 819–50; Daniel Thorner and Alice Thorner, *Land and Labour in India* (Bombay: Asia Publishing House, 1962), pp. 131–63.

94 Pierre Bourdieu, 'Rethinking the state: genesis and structure of the bureaucratic field', in George Steinmetz (ed.) *State/Culture: State-Formation after the Cultural Turn* (Ithaca, NY: Cornell University Press, 1999), p. 68; *Language and Symbolic Power*, trans. Gino Raymond and Matthew Adamson (Cambridge: Polity Press, 1991); *The State Nobility: Elite Schools in the Field of Power*, trans. Lauretta C. Clough (Cambridge: Polity Press, 1996).

95 Sigmund Freud, 'Some neurotic mechanisms in jealousy, paranoia and homosexuality' (1922), in *The Penguin Freud Library, Vol. 10: On Psychopathology* (Harmondsworth: Penguin, 1979), p. 201.

96 Richard Hofstadter, *The Paranoid Style in American Politics and Other Essays* (London: Jonathan Cape, 1966), pp. 14, 29–38; also Gilles Deleuze and Felix Guattari, *Anti-Oedipus: Capitalism and Schizophrenia* (1972), trans. Robert Hurley, Mark Seem and Helen Lane (London: Athlone Press, 1984), pp. 9, 193; Kenneth Dean and Brian Massumi, *First and Last Emperors: The Absolute State and the Body of the Despot* (New York: Autonomedia, 1992), p. 100. And it is interesting to read Thomas Pynchon's *Gravity's Rainbow* (1973) for the observations on the 'operational paranoia' which drives the state mechanism.

97 Jürgen Habermas, *The Structural Transformation of the Public Sphere: An Inquiry into a Category of Bourgeois Society* (1962), trans. Thomas Burger (Cambridge: Polity, 1989), p. 11.

98 Immanuel Kant, 'An answer to the question: "What is Enlightenment?" ' (1784), in *Political Writings*, trans. H.B. Nisbet (Cambridge: Cambridge University Press, 1991), p. 55.

99 Immanuel Kant, *Critique of Pure Reason* (1787), trans. Norman Kemp Smith (London: Macmillan, 1929), p. 9.

100 Immanuel Kant, 'On the common saying: "This may be true in theory, but it does not apply in practice"' (1793), in *Political Writings*, p. 85; Jeremy Bentham, *An Essay on Political Tactics* (1791), in *The Works of Jeremy Bentham, Vol. II*, ed. John Bowring (Edinburgh: William Tait, 1843), pp. 310–14; Thomas Paine, *Rights of Man* (1792), in *Rights of Man, Common Sense and Other Political Writings*, ed. Mark Philp (Oxford: Oxford University Press, 1995), p. 287.

101 Habermas, *Structural Transformation*, p. 53.

102 Georg Simmel, *The Sociology of Georg Simmel*, trans. Kurt H. Wolff (Glencoe, IL: Free Press, 1950), pp. 336–7.

103 Peter Hennessy, *Whitehall* (London: Fontana Press, 1990), pp. 346–7, 349; Tony Blair, 'Preface by the prime minister', *Your Right to Know: Freedom of Information*, Cm 3818, 1997; also para. 7.2. For other examples see Gavin Drewry and Tony Butcher, *The Civil Service Today* (Oxford: Basil Blackwell, 1988), p. 175; Clive Ponting, *Secrecy in Britain* (Oxford: Basil Blackwell, 1990), pp. 42–55; David Vincent, *The Culture of Secrecy: Britain 1832–1998* (Oxford: Oxford University Press, 1998); Will Hutton, 'The state we can't escape', *Observer*, 29 October 2000.

104 For example, Daniel Patrick Moynihan, *Secrecy: The American Experience* (New Haven, CT: Yale University Press, 1998), p. 153.

105 Max Weber, *Economy and Society: An Outline of Interpretive Sociology*, ed. Guenther Roth and Claus Wittich (Berkeley, CA: University of California Press, 1978), p. 992.

106 Robert Filmer, *Patriarcha*, in *Patriarcha and Other Writings*, ed. Johann P. Sommerville (Cambridge: Cambridge University Press, 1991), pp. 3–4; James I, 'Speech in Star Chamber, 1616', in *The Political Works of James I*, ed. Charles Howard McIlwain (Cambridge, MA: Harvard University Press, 1918), p. 333.

107 Gérard Vincent, 'A History of Secrets?', in Antoine Prost and Gérard Vincent (eds) *A History of Private Life, Vol. V: Riddles of Identity in Modern Times* (Cambridge, MA: Harvard University Press, 1991), pp. 163–4; Sissela Bok, *Secrets: Concealment and Revelation* (Oxford: Oxford University Press, 1984), p. 6.

108 Guicciardini, *Dialogue*, pp. 61, 99, 163; *Maxims and Reflections*, p. 54; Botero, *Reason of State*, p. 47; Bocalini, *I Raggvagli Di Parnasso*, p. 11; Bacon, *Advancement of Learning*, p. 205. As Defoe argued, from the fact that 'intelligence abroad is so considerable' it follows that 'the most useful thing at home is secrecy' – 'Memorandum to Robert Harley', p. 264. The Washington note is cited by Julian Borger, 'The dean of deception', *Guardian*, 17 August 1999.

109 Marx, 'Contribution to the critique of hegel's philosophy of law', p. 47. It is thus unsurprising to find the mature Marx praising the Paris commune for doing away with 'the whole sham of state mysteries' – 'First draft of *The Civil War in France*' (1871), in Marx, *The First International and After*, ed. David Fernbach (Harmondsworth: Penguin, 1974), p. 251; Weber, *Economy and Society*, p. 225.

110 Malcolm Muggeridge, *Chronicles of Wasted Time, Part 2: The Infernal Grove* (London: Collins, 1973), p. 123.

111 The one group which appears to escape such covert infiltration is the Masonic lodge. Originating as a 'countervailing power' to absolutism, the Masonic lodges adopted the absolutist cloak of secrecy. This secrecy continues to this day, although the reason it is allowed is no doubt due to the fact that the Masonic lodges are so bourgeois in both form and content, and so full of members of the ruling class anyway, that the state sees them as no threat whatsoever.

112 Botero, *Reason of State*, p. 56.

113 Richard Norton-Taylor, ' "****" ' you too, pal', *Guardian*, 17 November 2000; Francis Wheen, 'Jack takes a liberty too far', *Guardian*, 8 November 2000; Nick Cohen, 'A right to know? Don't ask', *Observer*, 20 June 1999; *Cruel Britannia: Reports on the Cruel and the Preposterous* (London: Verso, 1999), p. 166.

114 Moynihan, *Secrecy*, pp. 74–5.

115 Richard Gid Powers, 'Introduction' to Moynihan, *Secrecy*, p. 19; Friedrich, *Pathology of Politics*, p. 177.

116 During the 'war on terrorism' in 2001 the USA dropped leaflets over Afghanistan as part of its 'propaganda war'. The same leaflets were not available to any non-Afghans, such as reporters. The Secretary of Defence Donald Rumsfeld explained that the message that the western allies were dropping onto the people of Afghanistan was considered secret when it came to non-Afghans. See Andrew Buncombe, 'This food is a gift from america', *Independent on Sunday*, 14 October 2001.

117 Donaldson, *Machiavelli and Mystery of State*, p. 117.

118 Donaldson, *Machiavelli and Mystery of State*, p. 127; Keohane, *Philosophy and the State in France*, p. 224.

119 Samuel Johnson, *A Dictionary of the English Language* (1755) (London: Times Books, 1979).

120 When in 1844 the British Home Office's practice of opening 'private' letters was revealed, a minor storm of public indignation was raised. The first line of defence by the Home Secretary, Sir James Graham, was simply to refuse to discuss the issue at all, on security grounds. When this proved inadequate the second line of defence was a Select Committee of the Commons – which met in secret. This then revealed that the practice had been carried on by every British government since the Commonwealth. See Charles Townshend, *Making the Peace: Public Order and Public Security in Modern Britain* (Oxford: Oxford University Press, 1993), p. 32.

121 John Stuart Mill, *On Liberty* (1859), in *Utilitarianism, On Liberty and Considerations on Representative Government*, ed. H.B. Acton (London: Dent & Sons, 1972), p. 76; Alexis de Tocqueville, *Democracy in America, Vol. 2* (1840), trans. George Lawrence (New York: Fontana, 1968), pp. 782–3; also see Isaiah Berlin, 'Two concepts of liberty' (1958), in *Four Essays on Liberty* (Oxford: Oxford University Press, 1969), p. 129.

122 Hannah Arendt, *The Human Condition* (1958) (Chicago: University of Chicago Press, 1998), p. 58; see also pp. 38, 64.

123 Nicholas Abercrombie, Stephen Hill and Bryan Turner, *Sovereign Individuals of Capitalism* (London: Allen & Unwin, 1986), p. 36.

124 The exact figures are: 'wealth' – 168 mentions; 'private' – 198 mentions.

125 Stuart Millar, Richard Norton-Taylor and Ian Black, 'Worldwide spying network is revealed', *Guardian*, 26 May 2001; Kamal Ahmed, 'Secret plan to spy on all British phone calls', *Observer*, 3 December 2000; Jane Martinson, 'Spider in the web', *Guardian*, 3 May 2000; *Statewatch*, May–August 1999; István Mészáros, *Socialism or Barbarism?* (New York: Monthly Review Press, 2001), p. 36.

126 Cited in Leo Abse, *Fellatio, Masochism, Politics and Love* (London: Robson Books, 2000), p. 80.

Chapter 3

1 David P. Gauthier, *The Logic of Leviathan: The Moral and Political Theory of Thomas Hobbes* (Oxford: Clarendon Press, 1969), p. 120.

2 Thomas Hobbes, *Leviathan* (1651), ed. Richard Tuck (Cambridge: Cambridge University Press, 1991), p. 111.

3 Hobbes, *Leviathan*, p. 112.

4 Hobbes, *Leviathan*, p. 111.

5 Ernest Barker, 'Introduction' (1934), to Otto Gierke, *Natural Law and the Theory of Society 1500 to 1800* (1913), trans. Ernest Barker (Boston, MA: Beacon Press, 1957), pp. lxx–lxxi.

6 Hobbes, *Leviathan*, p. 112. The point is reiterated in Thomas Hobbes, *De Homine* (1658), XV, in *Man and Citizen (De Homine and De Cive)*, ed. Bernard Gert (Indianapolis, IN: Hackett, 1991), p. 83. For Hobbes' use of theatrical metaphors and terminology see Christopher Pye, 'The sovereign, the theater, and the kingdome of darknesse: Hobbes and the spectacle of power', *Representations*, 8, 1984, pp. 85–106.

7 Hobbes, *Leviathan*, p. 112; see also Hobbes, *De Homine*, XV, p. 84.

8 Hobbes, *Leviathan*, p. 111. The issue of the person in Hobbes' *Leviathan* has been the subject of debate between David Runciman and Quentin Skinner. See David Runciman, *Pluralism and the Personality of the State* (Cambridge: Cambridge University Press, 1997), pp. 6–33; Quentin Skinner, 'Hobbes and the purely artificial person of the state', *Journal of Political Philosophy*, Vol. 7, No. 1, 1999, pp. 1–29; David Runciman, 'What kind of person is Hobbes' state? A Reply to Skinner', *Journal of Political Philosophy*, Vol. 8, No. 2, 2000, pp. 268–78. Also useful here is François Tricaud, 'An investigation concerning the usage of the words "person" and "persona" in the political treatises of Hobbes', in J.G. van der Bend, (ed.) *Thomas Hobbes: His View of Man* (Amsterdam: Rodopi, 1982).

9   Hobbes, *De Homine*, XV, p. 83.

10   Hobbes, *Leviathan*, p. 113.

11   Cited in Skinner, 'Hobbes and the purely artificial person', p. 17.

12   Hobbes, *De Homine*, XV, p. 85.

13   Hobbes, *Leviathan*, p. 114.

14   Hobbes, *Leviathan*, p. 120.

15   Hobbes, *Leviathan*, pp. 62, 121. See also Thomas Hobbes, *De Cive* (1642), II.5.9, in *Man and Citizen*, p. 170.

16   Hobbes, *Leviathan*, p. 121.

17   Hobbes, *Leviathan*, p. 129.

18   Hobbes, *Leviathan*, pp. 166, 183, 223.

19   Hobbes, *Leviathan*, pp. 120, 121, 122, 131, 166.

20   For Kant the state 'has its own roots, and to graft it on to another state as if it were a shoot is to terminate its existence as a moral personality' – Immanuel Kant, 'Perpetual peace' (1795), in *Political Writings*, trans. H.B. Nisbet (Cambridge: Cambridge University Press, 1991), p. 94.

21   Rousseau describes the state as a 'corporate person', '*persona ficta*', 'public person' and 'moral person' – Jean-Jacques Rousseau, *The Social Contract* (1762), in *The Social Contract and Discourses*, trans. G.D.H. Cole (London: Dent & Sons, 1973), pp. 175, 177, 186.

22   G.W.F. Hegel, *Elements of the Philosophy of Right*, trans. H.B. Nisbet, ed. Allen Wood (Cambridge: Cambridge University Press, 1991), para. 279.

23   Georg Jellinek, for example, claimed that 'the inner ground of the origin of the State is the fact that an aggregate of persons has a conscious feeling of its unity, and gives expression to this unity by organizing itself as a collective personality, and constituting itself as a volitional and active subject'; *Die Lehre von den Staatenverbindungen*, cited in Westel Woodbury Willoughby, *An Examination of the Nature of the State* (New York: Macmillan, 1896), p. 119.

24   Hobbes, *Leviathan*, p. 114.

25   A.J. Gurevich, *Categories of Medieval Culture* (1972), trans. G.L. Campbell (London: Routledge), p. 297.

26   Claire McEachern, '*Henry V* and the paradox of the body politic', *Shakespeare Quarterly*, Vol. 45, No. 1, 1994, pp. 33–56, p. 44.

27   Hobbes, *Leviathan*, p. 120, emphasis added.

28   Ellen Meiksins Wood and Neal Wood, *A Trumpet of Sedition: Political Theory and the Rise of Capitalism 1509–1688* (London: Pluto Press, 1997), p. 103.

29   Thomas Hobbes, *Behemoth, or The Long Parliament* (1682), ed. Ferdinand Tönnies (Chicago: University of Chicago Press, 1990), p. 2; Hobbes, *Leviathan*, p. 120.

30   Karl Marx, *Capital, Vol. 1* (1867), trans. Ben Fowkes (Harmondsworth: Penguin, 1976), pp. 92, 739; *Capital, Vol. 2*, trans. David Fernbach (Harmondsworth: Penguin, 1978), p. 197; *Capital, Vol. 3*, trans. David Fernbach (Harmondsworth: Penguin, 1981), p. 496.

31 Marx, *Capital, Vol. 1*, pp. 254, 342, 1053–4; *Capital, Vol. 2*, pp. 207; *Capital, Vol. 3*, pp. 397, 403, 958, 963, 969, 1019–20.

32 I.I. Rubin, *Essays on Marx's Theory of Value* (1928), trans. Miloš Samardžija and Fredy Perlman (Montréal: Black Rose Books, 1973), p. 22.

33 The unmentioned backdrop of this argument is of course the possibility of real resistance to corporate power. As contemporary 'anti-capitalist' protest focuses more and more on the power of (global) corporations, work in this area has concentrated on the way corporations collude with states, abuse human rights, create false needs, employ corrupt accounting procedures, and so on. What is barely considered in these debates is the *corporate form* itself. As I aim to show, consideration of this form requires a sense of the importance of the notion of *persona* as the mask the corporation wears on the economic and juridical stage.

34 Marx, *Capital, Vol. 1*, p. 179; *Capital, Vol. 3*, pp. 1019–20.

35 Giorgio Agamben, *Remnants of Auschwitz: The Witness and the Archive*, trans. Daniel Heller-Roazen (New York: Zone Books, 1999), pp. 148–9.

36 *The Digest of Justinian, Vol. I* (482–565), trans. Alan Watson, ed. Theodor Mommsen and Paul Krueger (Philadelphia, PA: University of Pennsylvania Press, 1985); see Skinner, 'Hobbes and the purely artificial person', p. 4.

37 Hobbes, *Leviathan*, p. 112; *De Cive*, II.5.10, p. 170; *De Homine*, XV, pp. 84–5.

38 Geoffrey Kay and James Mott, *Political Order and the Law of Labour* (London: Macmillan, 1982), pp. 2–3, 97; Evgeny B. Pashukanis, *Law and Marxism: A General Theory* (1924), trans. Barbara Einhorn (London: Ink Links, 1978), p. 121.

39 The argument which follows aims to build on that concerning company law in Chapter 5 of *Administering Civil Society: Towards a Theory of State Power* (Basingstoke: Macmillan, 1996).

40 Briefly, Aron Salomon divided his nominal capital of £40,000 into 40,000 shares of £1.00 and gave one share each to his wife, four sons and one daughter. When the company went into liquidation the issue rested on whether Salomon himself was personally liable, given that the company was not joint stock and the other shareholders appeared not to be *'bona fide'*. The Lords decided that such a one-man (or two-man, three-man etc.) company was not an abuse of the 1862 Act.

41 Kay and Mott, *Political Order and the Law of Labour*, p. 9.

42 I am building here on the arguments of Paddy Ireland: 'The triumph of the company legal form 1856–1914', in J. Adams (ed.) *Essays For Clive Schmitthoff* (Abingdon: Professional Books, 1983); 'The rise of the limited liability company', *International Journal of the Sociology of Law*, 12, 1984, pp. 239–60; 'Capitalism without the capitalist: the joint stock company share and the emergence of the modern doctrine of separate corporate personality', *Legal History*, Vol. 17, No. 1, 1996, pp. 40–72; Paddy Ireland, Ian Grigg-Spall and Dave Kelly, 'The conceptual foundations of modern company law', in Peter Fitzpatrick and

Alan Hunt (eds) *Critical Legal Studies* (Oxford: Basil Blackwell, 1987). My disagreement with Ireland concerns his insistence on describing the new company that emerged as an 'object' cleansed of people (e.g. 'capitalism without the capitalist', pp. 40, 46. Elsewhere, in 'Company law and the myth of shareholder ownership', *Modern Law Review*, 62, 1999, pp. 32–57, he describes this as 'depersonification'). The point of course is that as much as it might in many ways be an object, so it is also a *subject* in its own right – an object personified.

43   The shareholder 'has no property in, or right to, any particular asset. He has only the right to have all the assets administered by the directors in accordance with the constitution of the company' (L.J. Cohen, in *Hood-Barrs* v. *I.R.C.* [1946]). Likewise 'in the case of land the owner possesses a tangible asset, whereas a shareholder has no direct share in the assets of the company. He has such rights as the memorandum and articles give him and nothing more' (Lord Potter, in *Short* v. *Treasury Commissioners* [1948]).

44   Does this mean that 'after 1862, any group could become a corporation', as some argue (e.g. Runciman, *Pluralism and the Personality of the State*, p. 249)? Well, yes and no. Yes in the sense that once the necessary documents have been deposited with the Registrar of Companies – the memorandum of association setting out the name, capital and objects of the company, the articles of association setting out the company's constitution, a list of the board of directors and the powers of the shareholders' meeting – an economic association can become a limited company, a legal person in its own right of the sort I have been describing here. No, however, because historically this did not apply to trade unions.

   It is significant that the process by which the legal subjectivity of modern capital was shaped took place at the same time as a similar process concerning the legal nature of trade unions was taking place; a process, in other words, by which the collective subjectivity of labour was being organized. Between 1871 and 1906 the freedom or 'right' to strike developed: through the Trade Union Act (1871), the Conspiracy and Protection of Property Act (1875), the *Taff Vale* decision of 1901 in which a registered union was made liable for damages from its funds for torts committed by those acting on its behalf, and the Trade Disputes Act of 1906 which gave unions legal immunity so long as the 'golden formula' of acting in 'furtherance of a trade dispute' was followed. Through the right to strike the state clearly recognized the collective power of the working class, as many have noted. But in recognizing it the state also sought to shape it in ways amenable to the state and capital. And this shaping concerned the corporate form. Under the 1871 Trade Union Act a system of voluntary registration was established, and in practice most significant trade unions did register for the income tax privileges attached. Yet the simple act of registration did not suffice to give trade unions corporate status in the way that it did for capital. Registration seemed to give trade unions *some kind* of legal personality, but it remained, and remains, unclear *what* kind. The Royal Commission on Trade Disputes (1903) recommended unions be given statutory recognition as legal entities, which the Trades Dispute Act (1906) watered down into the granting of some privileges *qua* corporation; a host of other cases to 1971 left the situation unclear such that prior to 1971 registered unions appear to have had a *degree* of legal personality. The Trade Union and Labour Relations Act (1974) provided that 'a trade union . . . shall not be, or be treated as if it were a body corporate' and yet held that a union could form contracts, own property and sue and be sued 'to the extent and in like manner as if the union were a body corporate'; a similar position has since been laid down in the Trade Union and Labour Relations (Consolidation) Act (1992) (TULRCA). As such the decision by the Law Lords in *Amalgamated Society of Railway Servants* v. *Osborne* (1910) has perhaps not been bettered: recognizing the analogy between registered unions and registered companies but wishing to declare the action of devoting funds for political purposes *ultra vires*, the Lords decided that the unions must be *quasi-corporations*. (In this regard it is worth noting that the TULRCA allows for 'special register bodies' giving unions full corporate status, but for this they have to be concerned with maintaining professional standards and either registered under the Companies Act (1985) or incorporated by charter.)

As quasi-corporations the state gave unions a degree of formal parity with capital. The contemporaneous development of the corporate form for capital and quasi-corporate form for labour meant that collective bargaining became possible. The reason for this development is clear. For the system of wage-labour to be fully operational the state had to constitute a new legal subject capable of *purchasing labour power* as an object on the market whilst simultaneously capable of *owning itself* in law and being able to act as one of the parties to the labour contract: the company. It also had to constitute the organs of labour in a fashion which gave them some means of recognizing other legal subjects and of being recognized as legal subjects themselves: trade unions. Trade unions were thus corporate enough to act as subjects or persons in law. In other words, *trade unions were constituted by the state as the legal subjectivity of the working class*. Although trade unions are not quite persons in the way that corporations are, they are persons *enough* to allow for their recognition by other persons and the law as a whole, just as they are corporate *enough* to allow the attempt at the corporate organization of capital accumulation in the twentieth century. To possess a passport into the state domain they needed enough of a personality to pass border controls. The reasons for this partial fulfilment of legal subjectivity undoubtedly lies in the fact that one is the form for capital, while the other is the form for labour, and the different roles attendant on them. Companies, for example, are expected to collect taxes on behalf of the state and administer national insurance. This also places trade unions in a much weaker position *vis-à-vis* the state. While companies have a legal obligation to administer their affairs according to established legal and administrative practices and the possibility exists of official inspection under the policing powers of the Board of Trade or, in the case of public companies, regulation by the Stock Exchange, such a minimal and highly flexible approach to the organizations of capital stands in stark contrast to the massive legal and administrative intervention in the affairs of trade unions. For a fuller account see *Administering Civil Society*, pp. 140–65.

45 Kay and Mott, *Political Order and the Law of Labour*, pp. 9–10.

46 52 & 53 Vict. Ch. 63 s. 19; *Law Reports*, Vol. XXVI, 1889, p. 336; on the US case see Sanford A. Shane, 'The corporation is a person: the language of a legal fiction', *Tulane Law Review*, 61, 1987, pp. 563–609, p. 590, and Roland Marchand, *Creating the Corporate Soul: The Rise of Public Relations and Corporate Imagery in American Big Business* (Berkeley, CA: University of California Press, 1998), p. 7. It is also the case that they are persons enough to have a nationality, as illustrated by *Continental Tyre and Rubber Co., Ltd* v. *Daimler Co. Ltd* (1915). The case turned on the issue of whether the company was an English subject by virtue of its being incorporated under English law and independent of its directors (who were all German subjects resident in Germany), and its stockholders (all but one of whom were German). The Court of Appeal decided that the corporation was an entity created by statute and thus 'a different person altogether from the subscribers to the memorandum of the shareholders on the register'. In other words, the company did not just have a personality at law, but was in fact an English company and a British subject. The House of Lords, however, decided that the company was 'German in fact although British in form'.

47 Pashukanis, *Law and Marxism*, p. 129.

48 Marx, *Capital, Vol. 1*, p. 165.

49 For a similar point but on the basis of a completely different argument see Slavoj Žižek, *The Ticklish Subject: The Absent Centre of Political Ontology* (London: Verso, 1999), p. 350.

50 Marx, *Capital, Vol. 1*, p. 280; *Capital, Vol. 3*, p. 969.

51 For these and other examples see C.T. Carr, *The General Principles of the Law of Corporations* (Cambridge: Cambridge University Press, 1905), pp. 76–87; Murray A. Pickering, 'The company as a separate legal entity', *Modern Law Review*, Vol. 31, No. 5, 1968, pp. 481–511; David Nicholls, *The Pluralist State* (London: Macmillan, 1975), pp. 64–6.

52 In *H.L. Bolton (Engineering) Co. Ltd* v. *T.J. Graham & Sons. All England Law Reports*, 1956, Vol. 3, p. 630.

53 Cited in Gary Slapper and Steve Tombs, *Corporate Crime* (Harlow: Longman, 1999), p. 31.

54 See Peter A. French, 'The Corporation as a moral person', *American Philosophical Quarterly*, Vol. 16, No. 3, 1979, pp. 207–15, p. 211; *Collective and Corporate Responsibility* (New York: Columbia University Press, 1984), p. xi.

55 See David Taylor, 'Disaster victims furious as corporate killing law stalls', *Evening Standard*, 6 March 2002; George Monbiot, 'Wreckers unite', *Guardian*, 19 February 2002.

56 Frederick Engels, *The Condition of the Working Class in England* (1845) (London: Granada, 1969), p. 126.

57 Celia Wells, *Corporations and Criminal Responsibility* (Oxford: Clarendon Press, 1993), p. 92; Slapper and Tombs, *Corporate Crime*, p. 198.

58 Compare the speed and determination with which the police and prosecution system pursued Gary Hart, the driver of the car which caused the train crash near Selby, Yorkshire, in 2001, with the slowness and lack of determination in pursuing a prosecution against Railtrack for its negligence during the period of the Southall, Ladbroke Grove and Hatfield train crashes.

59 It has now reached the stage where corporations are insisting that, as persons, they should be protected by the Human Rights Act. In September 2000 a quarrying company called Lafarge Redland Aggregates took the Scottish Environment Minister to court on the grounds that, given the delay in the public inquiry into its plan to dig up a mountain, its human rights had been breached (under Article 6 of the European Convention which determines that cases should be heard 'within a reasonable time'). Similarly, firms in the USA have argued that regulating their advertisements or restricting their political donations infringes their human right to free speech – George Monbiot, 'Big business has us bang to rights', *Guardian*, 5 October 2000. Corporations once wanted to present themselves as having 'souls'. Now they have given up political theology for straight politics: they demand rights.

60 Slapper and Tombs, *Corporate Crime*, pp. 106–7.

61 Edmund Burke, 'Speech on the opening of impeachment [of Warren Hastings], 16 February 1788', in *The Writings and Speeches of Edmund Burke, Vol VI*, ed. Paul Langford (Oxford: Clarendon Press, 1991), pp. 316–17.

62 The importance of the 'corporate veil' to contemporary capitalism has been recently reiterated in the Court of Appeal in *Adams* v. *Cape Industries plc.* (1991).

63 See Pickering, 'Company as a separate legal entity'.

64 Gerald E. Frug, 'The city as a legal concept', *Harvard Law Review*, Vol. 93, No. 6, 1980, pp. 1059–154; Max Weber, *Economy and Society: An Outline of Interpretive Sociology*, ed. Guenther Roth and Claus Wittich (Berkeley, CA: University of California Press, 1978), p. 1277.

65 Paul D. Halliday, *Dismembering the Body Politic: Partisan Politics in England's Towns, 1650–1730* (Cambridge: Cambridge University Press, 1998), p. 31.

66 Carl Schmitt, *The Concept of the Political* (1932), trans. George Schwab (Chicago: University of Chicago Press, 1996), p. 44.

66 The four volumes of Gierke's *Das deutsche Genossenschaftsrecht* were published between 1868 and 1913. Sections are available in Otto Gierke, *Political Theories of the Middle Age*, trans. F.W. Maitland (Cambridge: Cambridge University

Press, 1900); *The Development of Political Theory*, trans. Bernard Freyd (London: George Allen & Unwin, 1939); *Natural Law and the Theory of Society 1500 to 1800*, trans. Ernest Barker (Boston, MA: Beacon Press, 1957); *Community in Historical Perspective*, trans. Mary Fisher, ed. Anthony Black (Cambridge: Cambridge University Press, 1990).

68 See, for example, Gierke, *Natural Law*, p. 50; *Community in Historical Perspective*, p. 109.

69 Maitland, 'Introduction' to Gierke, *Political Theories of the Middle Age*, p. xxvi.

70 John Neville Figgis, *Churches in the Modern State* (London: Longmans, Green & Co., 1914), pp. 87–8, 92–3; see also pp. 42, 179, 249–50.

71 Figgis, *Churches in the Modern State*, p. 41.

72 F.W. Maitland, 'Moral personality and legal personality' (1903), in *The Collected Papers of Frederic William Maitland, Vol. III* (Cambridge: Cambridge University Press, 1911), pp. 314–16.

73 Gierke, *Community in Historical Perspective*, pp. 196–214.

74 F.W. Maitland, 'The corporation sole' (1900), in *Collected Papers, Vol. III*, p. 242.

75 Frederick Pollock, *Essays in the Law* (London: Macmillan, 1922), pp. 153–4

76 Barker, 'Introduction' to Gierke, *Natural Law*, pp. lxxi–lxxii, lxxvi. As David Nicholls points out, in their more clear-sighted moments, pluralist writers realised that *all* legal personality (even the legal personality of individuals), is 'artificial' – *Three Varieties of Pluralism* (London: Macmillan, 1974), p. 10.

77 Respectively: Ernest Barker, cited in Julia Stapleton, *Englishness and the Study of Politics: The Social and Political Thought of Ernest Barker* (Cambridge: Cambridge University Press, 1994), p. 142; Max Radin, 'The endless problem of corporate personality', *Columbia Law Review*, 32, 1932, pp. 643–67, p. 662; Morris Raphael Cohen, 'Communal ghosts in political theory' (1919), in *Reason and Nature: The Meaning of Scientific Method* (New York: Free Press, 1953), pp. 386–400.

78 W. Jethro Brown, 'The personality of the corporation and the state', *Law Quarterly Review*, 21, 1905, pp. 365–79, p. 367; Maitland, 'Moral personality and legal personality', p. 309.

79 It would appear that this was first stated categorically by C.J. Holt in a House of Lords debate on corporations in 1690 – Sir William Holdsworth, *A History of English Law, Vol. IX* (1926), (London: Methuen, 1966), p. 65, and Holdsworth, *A History of English Law, Vol. III* (1908) (London: Methuen, 1966), p. 476.

80 David Millon, 'Theories of the Corporation', *Duke Law Journal*, 201, 1990, pp. 201–62, p. 206; Gregory A. Mark, 'The personification of the business corporation in American law', *University of Chicago Law Review*, 54, 1987, pp. 1441–83, p. 1454.

81 *De Homine*, p. 85, emphasis added.

82 Barker, 'Introduction' to Gierke, *Natural Law*, p. lxvii; and see Mark Neocleous, ' "The law does not write fiction": Hegel, corporations, and the British state', in Iain Hampsher-Monk and Jeffrey Stanyer (eds) *Contemporary Political Studies, 1996* (Belfast: Political Studies Association, 1996).

83 On the subordinate and derived powers of cities as corporations, in which the *political* subjugation of the city as a body politic within a wider system of power gradually found expression in the invention of *legal* incorporation, see Engin F. Isin, *Cities Without Citizens: The Modernity of the City as a Corporation* (Montreal: Black Rose Books, 1992); also see Gerald E. Frug, *City Making: Building Communities Without Building Walls* (Princeton, NJ: Princeton University Press, 1999).

84 For example, the Dutch East India Company took over the Banda Islands in 1621, enslaving their inhabitants and executing their leaders, and fought a five-year war in the Moluccas, while the English East India Company took Bengal by force in 1764 and in southern India fought four wars (in 1769, 1780, 1790–2 and 1799) with the rulers of Mysore.

85 Shephard B. Clough, *The Economic Development of Western Civilization* (New York: McGraw-Hill, 1959), p. 153; Maitland, 'Trust and corporation', p. 375.

86 Matthew H. Edney, *Mapping an Empire: The Geographical Construction of British India, 1765–1843* (Chicago: University of Chicago Press, 1997), p. 2.

87 Halliday, *Dismembering the Body Politic*, p. 32.

88 Karl Marx, 'Contribution to the critique of Hegel's philosophy of law' (1843), in Karl Marx and Frederick Engels, *Collected Works, Vol. 3* (London: Lawrence & Wishart, 1975), p. 46.

89 Paul Hirst, *The Pluralist Theory of the State* (London: Routledge, 1989), p. 20.

90 This is the standard claim found in most commentaries. See, for example, Francis Coker, 'The technique of the pluralistic state', *American Political Science Review*, Vol. 15, No. 2, 1921, pp. 186–213; Ellen Deborah Ellis, 'The pluralistic state', *American Political Science Review*, Vol. 14, No. 3, 1920, pp. 393–407; Hirst, *Pluralist Theory of the State*, pp. 25; Cécile Laborde, *Pluralist Thought and the State in Britain and France, 1900–25* (Basingstoke: Macmillan, 2000), p. 55; Henry Mayer Magid, *English Political Pluralism: The Problem of Freedom and Organization* (New York: AMS Press, 1966), pp. 64–5; David Nicholls, *The Pluralist State* (London: Macmillan, 1975), pp. 42–53; Runciman, *Pluralism and the Personality of the State*, p. 257; Andrew Vincent, *Theories of the State* (Oxford: Basil Blackwell, 1987), pp. 200–2. In fact, given the diversity and the fact that most of them changed positions at some point, the best that can really be said is either that they had no 'view' to speak of or that they were deeply ambivalent, as Andrew Vincent notes – 'Can groups be persons?', *Review of Metaphysics*, Vol. 42, No. 168, 1989, pp. 687–715, p. 711.

91 Figgis, *Churches in the Modern State*, p. 79; also pp. 85–7.

92 Ernest Barker, *Political Thought in England 1848 to 1914* (1915), 2nd edn (Oxford: Oxford University Press, 1947), p. 158.

93 Schmitt, *Concept of the Political*, pp. 40–1, 44; 'Ethic of state and pluralist state' (1930), in Chantal Mouffe (ed.) *The Challenge of Carl Schmitt* (London: Verso, 1999), pp. 196, 200.

94 Gierke, *Political Theories of the Middle Age*, pp. 68–71; Joseph Canning, *A History of Medieval Political Thought 300–1450* (London: Routledge, 1996), pp. 172–3.

95 Ernest Barker, 'The "rule of law"', *Political Quarterly*, Vol. 1, No. 2, 1914, pp. 117–40; 'The discredited state', *Political Quarterly*, Vol. 2, No. 1, 1915, pp. 101–21; Geoffrey Sawyer, 'Government as personalized legal entity', in Leicester C. Webb (ed.) *Legal Personality and Political Pluralism* (Victoria: Melbourne University Press, 1958), p. 166.

96 Maitland, 'The crown as corporation' (1901), in *Collected Papers, Vol. III*, p. 268; see also Brown, 'Personality of the corporation and the state', p. 377.

97 Frederick Pollock, *A First Book of Jurisprudence* (New York: Franklin, 1896), p. 113.

98 Harold Laski, 'The sovereignty of the state' (1915), in *Studies in the Problem of Sovereignty* (New Haven, CT: Yale University Press, 1917), p. 4. In 'Morris Cohen's approach to legal philosophy' (*University of Chicago Law Review*, Vol. 15, No. 3, 1948, pp. 575–87), Laski comments that Cohen's attack on 'communal ghosts' made him realize that the idea of the collective as 'person' is merely a metaphor and nothing else. Yet the idea of the will of the state continues through his work. See *Authority in the Modern State* (New Haven, CT: Yale University Press, 1919), p. 67; *A Grammar of Politics* (London: George Allen & Unwin, 1925), pp. 29, 35.

99 R.M. MacIver, *The Modern State* (1926), (Oxford: Oxford University Press, 1964), p. 479.

100 Maitland, 'Moral personality and legal personality', p. 312.

101 Maitland, 'Introduction' to Gierke, *Political Theories of the Middle Age*, p. xlii.

102 Cited in Mark Weller, 'The international response to the dissolution of the socialist federal Republic of Yugoslavia', *American Journal of International Law*, 86, 1992, p. 588. This logic carries over into unions of states, as one writer on international law has noted: 'a treaty of union founds a body that possesses personality, but it is more than merely the technical, "legal" personality of the typical international organization . . . The "personality" formed by union is an original capacity to act akin to that possessed by the states themselves. It is a "real" personality' – Murray Forsyth, *Unions of States: The Theory and Practice of Confederation* (New York: Leicester University Press, 1981), p. 15. And going back to the argument in Chapter 2, the point is that for international relations to exist 'the idea of the state [must be] firmly planted in the "minds" of other states' – Barry Buzan, *People, States and Fear* (Hemel Hempstead: Harvester Wheatsheaf, 1991), p. 78.

103 'The state [therefore] has to be a corporation so long as the corporation wants to be a state' – Marx, 'Contribution to the critique of Hegel's philosophy of law', p. 46.

104 See John Dewey, 'Corporate personality' (1926), in *The Later Works, 1925–1953, Volume Two*, ed. Jo Ann Boydston (Carbondale, IL: Southern Illinois University Press, 1984), p. 38; see also Sheldon Wolin, *Politics and Vision:*

Continuity and Vision in Western Political Thought (Boston, MA: Little, Brown and Company, 1960), p. 417.

105 See, for example, Roger Scruton, *The Meaning of Conservatism* (London: Macmillan, 1984), p. 51; 'Gierke and the corporate person', in *The Philosopher on Dover Beach: Essays* (Manchester: Carcanet Press, 1990).

106 Benito Mussolini and Giovanni Gentile, *The Doctrine of Fascism* (1932), trans. Douglas Parmée, in Adrian Lyttelton (ed.) *Italian Fascisms* (London: Jonathan Cape, 1973), p. 43.

107 Ernest Barker, *Principles of Social and Political Theory* (Oxford: Clarendon Press, 1951), pp. 71, 133. Even Maitland, writing well before the rise of fascism, ends his 'Introduction' to Gierke's *Political Theories* by commenting (p. xliii) that it is easy to overlook the significance of the doctrine of the real nature of groups if we have had no experience of the first 'police states'. As W.Y. Elliott put it in a 1924 commentary on Laski's work: 'in such a [pluralist] community the individual grows less and less, the corporation grows more and more, until one, like the medieval church, tends to absorb all'. For 'medieval church' here one might read 'fascist state'. 'The pragmatic politics of Mr. H.J. Laski', *American Political Science Review*, Vol. 18, No. 2, 1924, pp. 251–75, p. 260.

108 Laski, 'Morris Cohen's approach', pp. 578–9.

109 Barker, 'Introduction' to Gierke, *Natural Law*, p. lxxxv.

110 F.W. Maitland, 'Trust and corporation' (1904), in *Collected Papers, Vol. III*, p. 374.

111 Kung Chuan Hsiao, *Political Pluralism: A Study in Contemporary Political Theory* (London: Kegan Paul, 1927), pp. 137–9.

112 Thomas Pynchon, *Gravity's Rainbow* (London: Vintage, 1995), p. 81.

Chapter 4

1 Christopher W. Morris, *An Essay on the Modern State* (Cambridge: Cambridge University Press, 1998), pp. 1, 36, 46.

2 Frederick Pollock and Frederic William Maitland, *The History of English Law Before the Time of Edward I, Volume I* (1895) (Cambridge: Cambridge University Press, 1968), p. 230.

3 Kurt Burch, *'Property' and the Making of the International System* (Boulder, CO: Lynne Rienner Publishers, 1998), pp. 143–8.

4 Jean Gottman, 'The evolution of the concept of territory', *Social Science Information*, Vol. 14, No. 3/4, 1975, pp. 29–47, p. 29.

5 Lucien Febvre, *'Frontière*: the word and the concept' (1928), in *A New Kind of History: From the Writings of Febvre*, trans. K. Folca (London: Routledge & Kegan Paul, 1973), pp. 208–218.

6 Jens Bartelson, *A Genealogy of Sovereignty* (Cambridge: Cambridge University Press, 1995), p. 98; John Agnew and Stuart Corbridge, *Mastering Space: Hegem-*

ony, Territory and International Political Community (London: Routledge, 1995), p. 85.

7 Donald M. Lowe, *History of Bourgeois Perception* (Brighton: Harvester, 1982), p. 63.

8 And this was genuinely international. For example, Thongchai Winichakul notes that between 1900 and 1915 the traditional Thai words *krung* and *muang* largely disappeared, because they imaged dominion in terms of sacred capitals and visible, discontinuous population centres with no specification as to size, degree or kind of power. At the same time the word *prathet*, which in old usage referred to a piece of the earth's surface without any qualification of size, population or power (so it could thus refer to a region, town, district, even part of a forest), was beginning to refer more and more to the nation as a politically bounded territorial entity. See Thongchai Winichakul, *Siam Mapped: A History of the Geo-body of a Nation* (Chiang Mai: Silkworm Books, 1998), pp. 49, 81.

9 Quentin Skinner, *The Foundations of Modern Political Thought, Volume Two: The Age of Reformation* (Cambridge: Cambridge University Press, 1978), p. 351; Alessandro Pizzorno, 'Politics unbound', in Charles S. Maier (ed.) *Changing Boundaries of the Political: Essays on the Evolving Balance Between the State and Society, Public and Private in Europe* (Cambridge: Cambridge University Press, 1987), p. 32.

10 Henri Lefebvre, *The Production of Space* (1974), trans. Donald Nicholson-Smith (Oxford: Blackwell, 1991), p. 280; Michel Foucault, 'Governmentality' (1978), trans. Pasquale Pasquino, in Graham Burchell, Colin Gordon and Peter Miller (eds) *The Foucault Effect: Studies in Governmentality* (London: Harvester, 1991), p. 87. See also Michel Foucault, 'Questions on geography' (1976), in *Power/Knowledge: Selected Interviews and Other Writings 1972–1977* (Brighton: Harvester, 1980), pp. 68–9. As Gianfranco Poggi puts it, 'the state does not *have* a territory, it *is* a territory' – *The State: Its Nature, Development and Prospects* (Cambridge: Polity Press), p. 22.

11 Michael Hardt and Antonio Negri, *Empire* (Cambridge, MA: Harvard University Press, 2000), p. 167.

12 Garrett Mattingly, *Renaissance Diplomacy* (London: Jonathan Cape, 1955).

13 Thomas Hobbes, *Leviathan* (1651), ed. Richard Tuck (Cambridge: Cambridge University Press, 1991), p. 269.

14 Lefebvre, *Production of Space*, pp. 33, 38–9.

15 For example, Anthony Giddens, *The Nation-State and Violence: Volume Two of A Contemporary Critique of Historical Materialism* (Berkeley, CA: University of California Press, 1985); Michael Mann, *The Sources of Social Power, Vol. II: The Rise of Classes and Nation-states, 1760–1914* (Cambridge: Cambridge University Press, 1993); Charles Tilly, *Coercion, Capital, and European States, AD 990–1992* (Oxford: Blackwell, 1992).

16 Michael J. Shapiro, *Reading the Postmodern Polity: Political Theory as Textual Practice* (Minneapolis, MN: University of Minnesota Press, 1992), p. 5;

Doreen Massey, 'A global sense of place', *Marxism Today*, June 1991, pp. 24–9, p. 28.

17 Anthony D. Smith, *National Identity* (Harmondsworth: Penguin, 1991), p. 9.

18 William E. Connolly, *Identity/Difference: Democratic Negotiations of Political Paradox* (Ithaca, NY: Cornell University Press, 1991), p. 198; *The Ethos of Pluralization* (Minneapolis, MN: University of Minnesota Press, 1995), p. 137; 'Democracy and territoriality', *Millennium*, Vol. 20, No. 3, 1991, pp. 463–84; Morris, *Essay on the Modern State*, p. 238; Edward Said, 'Zionism from the standpoint of its victims', *Social Text*, 1, 1979, pp. 7–58, p. 19.

19 In the context of the politics of Northern Ireland, Allen Feldman notes that the doorstep murder transgresses the space of the home as a sanctuary construct. Conversely, most paramilitaries had a distaste for crossing the threshold in search of their victim (hence 'the doorstep') – Allen Feldman, *Formations of Violence: The Narrative of the Body and Political Terror in Northern Ireland* (Chicago: University of Chicago Press, 1991), p. 71. For the home as eulogized and sacred space supposedly beyond power in Latin America, see Jean Franco, 'Killing priests, nuns, women, children', in Marshall Blonsky (ed.) *On Signs* (Oxford: Blackwell, 1985), pp. 414–20.

20 Lefebvre, *Production of Space*, p. 280.

21 Janice E. Thomson, *Mercenaries, Pirates, and Sovereigns: State-building and Extraterritorial Violence in Early Modern Europe* (Princeton, NJ: Princeton University Press, 1994), pp. 117–18; Tilly, *Coercion, Capital, and European States*, pp. 80–2; Fernand Braudel, *The Mediterranean and the Mediterranean World in the Age of Philip II* (1949), trans. Sian Reynolds (London: HarperCollins, 1992), pp. 624–49.

22 Thomas W. Gallant, 'Brigandage, piracy, capitalism, and state-formation: transnational crime from a historical world-systems perspective', in Josiah McC. Heyman (ed.) *States and Illegal Practices* (Oxford: Berg, 1999), p. 40.

23 See Eric Hobsbawm, *Bandits* (London: Weidenfeld & Nicolson, 1969); *Primitive Rebels: Studies in Archaic Forms of Social Movement in the 19th and 20th Centuries* (Manchester: Manchester University Press, 1971), pp. 13–29. It should also be noted that the Nazis often legitimized the hunting down of Jews on the grounds that the latter were bandits. See Christopher R. Browning, *Ordinary Men: Reserve Police Battalion 101 and the Final Solution in Poland* (London: Penguin, 2001), pp. 148–9.

24 Thomson, *Mercenaries, Pirates, and Sovereigns*, pp. 10, 88.

25 The importance of this practice was reinforced in the 'war on terrorism' of 2001, in which the British Home Office seized passports from British Muslims aiming to travel to fight for the Taliban. See Kamal Ahmed, Anthony Barnett and Martin Bright, 'UK state of emergency', *Observer*, 11 November 2001. Likewise, Sussex University students who in Spring 2002 had travelled to the West Bank to show solidarity with the Palestinians were immediately deprived of their passports on arrival back in the UK.

26 Tilly, *Coercion, Capital, and European States*, p. 54.

27 Perry Anderson, *Lineages of the Absolutist State* (London: New Left Books, 1975), p. 30.

28 Carlo Levi, *Christ Stopped at Eboli* (1947), trans. Frances Frenaye (London: Penguin, 1982), p. 137.

29 Cynthia Weber, *Simulating Sovereignty: Intervention, the State and Symbolic Exchange* (Cambridge: Cambridge University Press, 1995), pp. 4, 27. Conversely, it is also the case that 'few nations bother to imprison people for crimes committed elsewhere, and when they do, as the case of Panama's Mañuel Noriega shows, it is highly controversial. When the Ayatollah Khomeini called for Salman Rushdie's head, it stunned everyone because he was trying to push one nation's death penalty over the line of the nation' – Thomas Richards, *The Imperial Archive: Knowledge and the Fantasy of Empire* (London: Verso, 1993), p. 2.

30 Leo Kuper, *Genocide: Its Political Use in the Twentieth Century* (New Haven, CT: Yale University Press, 1981), pp. 161–85; Omer Bartov, *Mirrors of Destruction: War, Genocide, and Modern Identity* (Oxford: Oxford University Press, 2000), p. 167.

31 Recent research by the Glasgow University Media Group has shown that words such as 'murder', 'atrocity' and 'savage cold-blooded killing' tend to be used to describe Israeli deaths but not Palestinian – Greg Philo, 'Missing in action', *Guardian Education*, 16 April 2002.

32 Bernard Nietschmann, 'The Third World War', *Cultural Survival Quarterly*, Vol 11, No. 3, 1987, pp. 1–16.

33 Connolly, *Identity/Difference*, p. 207.

34 Hobbes, *Leviathan*, p. 491.

35 Charles Tilly, 'War making and state making as organized crime', in Peter B. Evans, Dietrich Rueschmeyer and Theda Skocpol (eds) *Bringing the State Back In* (Cambridge: Cambridge University Press, 1985), p. 171; Frederic C. Lane, 'The economic meaning of war and protection' (1942), in *Venice and History: The Collected Papers of Frederic C. Lane* (Baltimore, MD: Johns Hopkins University Press, 1966), pp. 383–98. For a similar point concerning the relations between states, in which one state 'protects' another and thus renders the other subordinate, see Martha K. Huggins, *Political Policing: The United States and Latin America* (Durham, NC: Duke University Press, 1998), p. 199.

36 Michael Walzer, *Spheres of Justice: A Defence of Pluralism and Equality* (Oxford: Blackwell, 1983), p. 32.

37 G.W.F. Hegel, *Elements of the Philosophy of Right* (1821), trans. H.B. Nisbet (Cambridge: Cambridge University Press, 1991), para. 324A. Hegel's insight here is worth contrasting with the phenomenally silly idea, identified in the Preface, that we have moved into an era of a politics/state/democracy without enemies. This idea, associated with what might be called the sociology of the third way, is indicative of the dead-end into which political sociology is being driven.

38 Carl Schmitt, *The Concept of the Political* (1932), trans. George Schwab (Chicago: University of Chicago Press, 1996), p. 26.

39 Cited in the *Independent*, 12 February 1995.

40 Schmitt, *The Concept of the Political*, p. 27.

41 Jean-Luc Nancy, *The Birth to Presence*, trans. Brian Holmes (Stanford, CA: Stanford University Press, 1993), p. 44; Giorgio Agamben, *Homo Sacer: Sovereign Power and Bare Life*, trans. Daniel Heller-Roazen (Stanford, CA: Stanford University Press, 1998), pp. 29, 109.

42 The comments here follow Rogers Brubaker, *Citizenship and Nationhood in France and Germany* (Cambridge, MA: Harvard University Press, 1992), pp. 25–9.

43 Rogers Brubaker, 'Are immigration control efforts really failing?', in Wayne A. Cornelius, Philip L. Martin and James F. Hollifield (eds) *Controlling Immigration: A Global Perspective* (Stanford, CA: Stanford University Press, 1994), p. 230.

44 Gilles Deleuze and Félix Guattari, *A Thousand Plateaus: Capitalism and Schizophrenia* (1980), trans. Brian Massumi (London: Athlone Press, 1987), p. 23.

45 Nevzat Soguk, *States and Strangers: Refugees and Displacements of Statecraft* (Minneapolis, MN: University of Minnesota Press, 1999), pp. 11, 15. Also see Michael Dillon, 'The scandal of the refugee: some reflections on the "inter" of international relations and continental thought', in David Campbell and Michael J. Shapiro (eds) *Moral Spaces: Rethinking Ethics and World Politics* (Minneapolis, MN: University of Minnesota Press, 1999), pp. 92–124.

46 Arjun Appadurai, 'Sovereignty without territoriality: notes for a postnational geography', in Patricia Yaeger (ed.) *The Geography of Identity* (Ann Arbor, MI: University of Michigan Press, 1996), p. 50.

47 Soguk, *States and Strangers*, pp. 17–30; Liisa H. Malkki, 'Speechless emissaries: refugees, humanitarianism, and dehistoricization', *Cultural Anthropology*, Vol. 11 No. 3, 1996, pp. 377–404.

48 Soguk, *States and Strangers*, pp. 128–31.

49 Brubaker, *Citizenship and Nationhood*, p. 46; Julia Kristeva, *Strangers to Ourselves*, trans. Leon S. Roudiez (New York: Columbia University Press, 1991), pp. 40, 149; *Nations Without Nationalism*, trans. Leon S. Roudiez (New York: Columbia University Press, 1993), pp. 25–6; Gérard Noiriel, *The French Melting Pot: Immigration, Citizenship, and National Identity*, trans. Geoffroy de Laforcade (Minneapolis, MN: University of Minnesota Press, 1996), p. 46.

50 See Jacqueline Stevens, *Reproducing the State* (Princeton, NJ: Princeton University Press, 1999), p. 273.

51 Kristeva, *Strangers to Ourselves*, p. 96.

52 Cited in Noiriel, *French Melting Pot*, p. 52.

53 John Torpey, *The Invention of the Passport: Surveillance, Citizenship and the State* (Cambridge: Cambridge University Press, 2000), pp. 4–20.

54 Noiriel, *French Melting Pot*, p. 59; Torpey, *Invention of the Passport*, p. 9.

55 Bonnie Honig, *Democracy and the Foreigner* (Princeton, NJ: Princeton University Press, 2001), pp. 2–3, 34, 80.

56 Barbara A. Babcock, 'Introduction', in Barbara A. Babcock (ed.) *The Reversible World: Symbolic Inversion in Art and Society* (Ithaca, NY: Cornell University Press, 1978), p. 32.

57 Adolf Hitler, *Mein Kampf* (1925), trans. Ralph Manheim (Boston, MA: Houghton Mifflin, 1943), pp. 150, 302; also pp. 303–5, 623; *The Testament of Adolf Hitler: The Hitler-Bormann Documents, February–April 1945*, trans. Colonel R. Stevens, ed. Francois Genoud (London: Icon Books, 1962), p. 60.

58 Cited in Tim Mason, *Social Policy in the Third Reich: The Working Class and the 'National Community'* (1977), trans. John Broadwin (London: Berg, 1993), p. 97.

59 Cited in Hannah Arendt, *The Origins of Totalitarianism* (San Diego, CA: Harcourt Brace & Co. 1973), p. 269.

60 Arendt, *Origins of Totalitarianism*, pp. 267, 281–2.

61 For an account of the extent of these ideas in Germany prior to the Nazi seizure of power see David T. Murphy, *The Heroic Earth: Geopolitical Thought in Weimar Germany, 1918–1933* (Kent, OH: Kent State University Press, 1997). For an account of some important differences see Mark Bassin, 'Race contra space: the conflict between German *Geopolitik* and national socialism', *Political Geography Quarterly*, Vol. 6, No. 2, 1987, pp. 115–34. For an account of geopolitics as an essentially bourgeois mode of thought see Karl A. Wittfogel, 'Geopolitics, geographical materialism and marxism' (1929), trans. G.L. Ulmen, *Antipode*, 17, 1985, pp. 21–72.

62 Arendt, *Origins of Totalitarianism*, p. 279; see also Bartov, *Mirrors of Destruction*, p. 93.

63 Michael Dillon, 'The sovereign and the stranger', in Jenny Edkins, Nalini Persram and Véronique Pin-Fat (eds) *Sovereignty and Subjectivity* (Boulder, CO: Lynne Rienner, 1999), p. 133.

64 J.B. Harley, 'Text and contexts in the interpretation of early maps', in David Buisseret (ed.) *From Sea Charts to Satellite Images: Interpreting North American History Through Maps* (Chicago: University of Chicago Press, 1990), pp. 3–4.

65 David Buisseret, 'Introduction', in David Buisseret (ed.) *Monarchs, Ministers and Maps: The Emergence of Cartography as a Tool of Government in Early Modern Europe* (Chicago: University of Chicago Press, 1992).

66 Jeremy Black, *Maps and Politics* (London: Reaktion Books, 1997), pp. 1, 12; Matthew Edney, 'Mathematical cosmography and the social ideology of British cartography, 1780–1820', *Imago Mundi*, 46, 1994, pp. 101–12; J.B. Harley, 'Maps, knowledge, and power', in Denis Cosgrove and Stephen Daniels (eds) *The Iconography of Landscape* (Cambridge: Cambridge University Press, 1988), pp. 283–4; Lisa Jardine, *Worldly Goods: A New History of the Renaissance* (London: Macmillan, 1997), pp. 299, 427; Yves Lacoste, 'An illustration of geographical warfare: bombing the dikes on the Red River, North Vietnam', in Richard Peet (ed.) *Radical Geography: Alternative Viewpoints on Contemporary*

Issues (London: Methuen, 1978), pp. 244–5; Mark Monmonier, *How to Lie With Maps* (Chicago: University of Chicago Press, 1996), p. 88.

67 Winichakul, *Siam Mapped*, p. 56.

68 Denis Wood, with John Fels, *The Power of Maps* (New York: Guilford Press, 1992), pp. 17–19; Winichakul, *Siam Mapped*, p. 126; Kennan Ferguson, 'Unmapping and remapping the world: foreign policy as aesthetic practice', in Michael J. Shapiro and Hayward R. Alker (eds) *Challenging Boundaries: Global Flows, Territorial Identities* (Minneapolis, MN: University of Minnesota Press, 1996), p. 177; David Turnbull, 'Cartography and science in early modern Europe: mapping and the construction of knowledge spaces', *Imago Mundi*, 48, 1996, pp. 5–23; Black, *Maps and Politics*, p. 18; Mary W. Helms, *Ulysses' Sail: An Ethnographic Odyssey of Power, Knowledge and Geographical Knowledge* (Princeton, NJ: Princeton University Press, 1988), p. 20.

69 J.B. Harley, 'Rereading the maps of the Columbian encounter', *Annals of the Association of American Geographers*, Vol. 82, No. 3, 1992, pp. 522–42, p. 531.

70 Black, *Maps and Politics*, pp. 19, 137; Matthew H. Edney, *Mapping an Empire: The Geographical Construction of British India, 1765–1843* (Chicago: University of Chicago Press, 1997), pp. 3, 15, 36; Harley, 'Texts and contexts', p. 11; Graham Huggan, 'Decolonizing the map: post-colonialism, post-structuralism and the cartographic connection', *Ariel*, Vol. 20, No. 4, 1989, pp. 115–31; Geoff King, *Mapping Reality: An Exploration of Cultural Geographies* (Basingstoke: Macmillan, 1996), pp. 28–9, 49, 104; Winichakul, *Siam Mapped*, p. 120; Wood, *Power of Maps*, p. 46.

71 Gearóid Ó Tuathail, *Critical Geopolitics: The Politics of Writing Global Space* (London: Routledge, 1996), pp. 2, 109; Timothy W. Luke, 'Discourses of disintegration, texts of transformation: re-reading realism in the new world order', *Alternatives*, 18, 1993, pp. 229–58. See also Kristin Ross, *The Emergence of Social Space: Rimbaud and the Paris Commune* (Basingstoke: Macmillan, 1988), pp. 85–6; Anne Godlewska, 'Napoleon's geographers (1797–1815): imperialists and soldiers of modernity', in Anne Godlewska and Neil Smith (eds) *Geography and Empire* (Oxford: Blackwell, 1994), p. 34.

72 Edward Said, *Culture and Imperialism* (London: Chatto & Windus, 1993), p. 271, emphasis added. Also see *Orientalism: Western Conceptions of the Orient* (London: Penguin, 1991), p. 12.

73 Anderson, *Imagined Communities*, pp. 173, 184.

74 Daniel J. Boorstin, *The Discoverers* (New York: Random House, 1983), pp. 267–71; Chandra Mukerji, *From Graven Images: Patterns of Modern Materialism* (New York: Columbia University Press, 1983), pp. 91–7.

75 'Gone Missing', *New Statesman*, 27 May 1983, p. 5; Monmonier, *How to Lie With Maps*, pp. 117–121; J.B. Harley, 'Silences and secrecy: the hidden agenda of cartography in early modern Europe', *Imago Mundi*, 40, 1988, pp. 57–105; 'Maps, knowledge, and power', pp. 284, 306, 307–8; 'Deconstructing the map', in Trevor J. Barnes and James S. Duncan (eds), *Writing Worlds:*

Discourse, Text and Metaphor in the Representation of Landscape (London: Routledge, 1992).

76 King, *Mapping Reality*, pp. 31, 36; M.J. Blakemore and J.B. Harley, 'Concepts in the history of cartography', *Cartographica*, Vol. 17, No. 4, 1980, pp. 1–120, p. 99.

77 Wood, *Power of Maps*, pp. 22, 70, 105.

78 Black, *Maps and Politics*, pp. 12, 17, 88.

79 Pierre Bourdieu, *Outline of a Theory of Practice*, trans. Richard Nice (Cambridge: Cambridge University Press, 1977), p. 164.

Coda

1 Paul Hirst and Grahame Thompson, *Globalization in Question*, 2nd edn (Cambridge: Polity Press, 1999), pp. 1, 3; Linda Weiss, *The Myth of the Powerless State* (Ithaca, NY: Cornell University Press, 1998), pp. x, 167.

2 Kenichi Ohmae, 'Putting global logic first', *Harvard Business Review*, Vol. 73, No. 1, 1995, pp. 119–25.

3 Kenichi Ohmae, *The Borderless World* (New York: Collins, 1990); Masao Miyoshi, 'A borderless world? From colonialism to transnationalism and the decline of the nation-state', *Critical Inquiry*, 16, 1993, pp. 726–51.

4 Zygmunt Bauman, *Globalization: The Human Consequences* (Cambridge: Polity Press, 1998), pp. 55–76; Matthew Horsman and Andrew Marshall, *After the Nation-State: Citizens, Tribalism and the New World Disorder* (London: HarperCollins, 1994); Jean-Marie Guéhenno, *The End of the Nation-State*, trans. Victoria Elliott (Minneapolis, MN: University of Minnesota Press, 1995).

5 Paul Virilio, *Speed and Politics: An Essay on Dromology* (1977), trans. Mark Polizzotti (New York: Semiotext(e), 1986), p. 133; *The Information Bomb*, trans. Chris Turner (London: Verso, 2000), p. 9; Richard O'Brien, *Global Financial Integration: The End of Geography* (London: Royal Institute of International Affairs/ Pinter Publishers, 1992).

6 For this point from different springboards see Simon Bromley, 'Globalization?', *Radical Philosophy*, 80, 1996, p. 4; Saskia Sassen, *Losing Control? Sovereignty in an Age of Globalization* (New York: Columbia University Press, 1996), pp. 25–8.

7 Leo Panitch, 'The new imperial state', *New Left Review*, 2, 2000, pp. 5–20, p. 15. See also Peter Burnham, 'Globalization: states, markets and class relations', *Historical Materialism*, 1, 1997, pp. 150–60; Jan Aart Scholte, 'Global capitalism and the state', *International Affairs*, Vol. 73, No. 3, 1997, pp. 427–52.

8 Michael Mann, 'Nation-states in Europe and other continents: diversifying, developing, not dying', *Daedalus*, Vol. 122, No. 3, 1993, pp. 115–40; Charles Tilly, *Coercion, Capital, and European States, AD 990–1992* (Oxford: Blackwell, 1992), p. 227.

9 Karl Marx and Frederick Engels, *Manifesto of the Communist Party* (1848), in Karl Marx, *The Revolutions of 1848*, ed. David Fernbach (Harmondsworth: Penguin, 1973), pp. 69, 71.

10 Karl Marx, *Grundrisse*, trans. Martin Nicolaus (London: Allen Lane, in association with *New Left Review*, 1973), pp. 524, 539.

11 Marx and Engels, *Manifesto of the Communist Party*, p. 71.

12 Marx and Engels, *Manifesto of the Communist Party*, p. 72.

13 For the distinction between democratic globalization as a form of opposition to capital and the assertion of the sovereignty of nation-states as a bulwark against global capital see Michael Hardt, 'Today's Bandung?', *New Left Review*, 14, 2002, pp. 112–18. On non-territorial democratization see William E. Connolly, *The Ethos of Pluralization* (Minneapolis, MN: University of Minnesota Press, 1995), p. 135; *Identity/Difference: Democratic Negotiations of Political Paradox* (Ithaca, NY: Cornell University Press, 1991), p. 215; 'Democracy and territoriality', *Millennium*, Vol. 20, No. 3, 1991, pp. 463–84; Arjun Appadurai, 'Sovereignty without territoriality: notes for a postnational geography', in Patricia Yaeger (ed.) *The Geography of Identity* (Ann Arbor, MI: University of Michigan Press, 1996), p. 49.

14 The phrase is from James C. Scott, *Seeing Like a State* (New Haven, CT: Yale University Press, 1998), p. 55.

15 On fascism as reterritorialization see Gilles Deleuze and Félix Guattari, *Anti-Oedipus: Capitalism and Schizophrenia* (1972), trans. Robert Hurley, Mark Seem and Helen R. Lane (London: Athlone Press, 1984), p. 258.

Index

THEORIES OF SOCIAL REMEMBERING

Barbara A. Misztal

- Why does collective memory matter?
- How is social memory generated, maintained and reproduced?
- How do we explain changes in the content and role of collective memory?

Through a synthesis of old and new theories of social remembering, this book provides the first comprehensive overview of the sociology of memory. This rapidly expanding field explores how representations of the past are generated, maintained and reproduced through texts, images, sites, rituals and experiences. The main aim of the book is to show to what extent the investigation of memory challenges sociological understandings of the formation of social identities and conflicts. It illustrates the new status of memory in contemporary societies by examining the complex relationships between memory and commemoration, memory and identity, memory and trauma, and memory and justice.

The book consists of six chapters, with the first three devoted to conceptualising the process of remembering by analyzing memory's function, status and history, as well as by locating the study of memory in a broader field of social science. The second part of the book directly explores and discusses theories and studies of social remembering. After a short conclusion, which argues that study of collective memory is an important part of any examination of contemporary society, the glossary offers a concise and up to date overview of the development of relevant theoretical concepts. The result is an essential text for undergraduate courses in social theory, the sociology of memory and a wider audience in cultural studies, history and politics.

192pp   0 335 20831 2 (Paperback)   0 335 20832 0 (Hardback)